PENGUIN BOOKS
BUTTER CHICKEN IN LUDHIANA

Pankaj Mishra divides his time between Delhi and Simla. He is at present working on his next book.

PANKAJ MISHRA

Butter Chicken in Ludhiana

Travels in Small Town India

PENGUIN BOOKS

PENGUIN BOOKS
Published by the Penguin Group
Penguin Books India Pvt Ltd, 11 Community Centre, Panchsheel Park, New Delhi 110 017,
India
Penguin Group (USA) Inc., 375 Hudson Street, New York, New York 10014, USA
Penguin Group (Canada), 10 Alcorn Avenue, Toronto, Ontario, Canada M4V 3B2 (a
division of Pearson Penguin Canada Inc.)
Penguin Books Ltd, 80 Strand, London WC2R 0RL, England
Penguin Ireland, 25 St Stephen's Green, Dublin 2, Ireland (a division of Penguin Books Ltd)
Penguin Group (Australia), 250 Camberwell Road, Camberwell, Victoria 3124, Australia
(a division of Pearson Australia Group Pty Ltd)
Penguin Group (NZ), cnr Airborne and Rosedale Road, Albany, Auckland 1310, New
Zealand (a division of Pearson New Zealand Ltd)
Penguin Group (South Africa) (Pty) Ltd, 24 Sturdee Avenue, Rosebank, Johannesburg
2196, South Africa

Penguin Books Ltd, Registered Offices: 80 Strand, London WC2R 0RL, England

First published by Penguin Books India 1995

Copyright © Pankaj Mishra 1995

All rights reserved

15 14 13 12

For sale in the Indian Subcontinent only

Typeset in Palatino by Rekha Printers Pvt. Ltd., New Delhi
Printed at Mahalaxmi Printers, New Delhi

Butter Chicken in Ludhiana

Travels in Small Town India

Prologue

'Very senior officer and very honest,' Mr Chugh was saying, now for the fourth time, 'but his wife won't let him be. She wants him to make money. She's mad, I tell you, and she'll drive my brother mad.'

A short, stoutish, balding man in his early fifties, he spoke as though he was an acquaintance. In fact, I had met him barely ten minutes ago on platform No.36, where he was waiting, like me, for the late-night bus to Muzaffarnagar. There, amidst the general wretchedness of Delhi's Inter State Bus Terminal (ISBT)—the thick fog of low-octane diesel smoke, the stench from open, unflushed toilets, the roar of bus engines, the countless cassette-players blaring simultaneously, the slushy floor, the swirling mobs of bewildered travellers, the thuggish touts for private buses, the aggressive child-beggars, the bawling babies, the Hindi porno magazines in their yellow polythene covers—amidst such oppressive disorder, the anxiety-ridden face of Mr Chugh seemed like a mirror-image of my own: a fellow-sufferer, I thought, and immediately felt a bond of empathy between us.

'Do you know anything about this Muzaffarnagar bus?'

He had spoken to me first in English, in a thin, quavering, unnaturally high-pitched voice. Subsequently, he was to speak only in Hindi. But the English then was important. It was the sole means open to Mr Chugh of distinguishing himself from the faceless squalor of his surroundings; and it was a coded overture to another presumed English-speaker, an invitation to privileged distress.

I replied that the bus hadn't arrived and that this was all I knew.

'Have you asked the Roadways office?'

I hadn't. I wasn't even aware of its existence.

'Let's go. Let's see what those buggers are up to.'

His company gave me the strength to walk up two ramps to the UP Roadways office, and enquire about the delayed bus. Then, on being told about its uncertain status, we wandered around the huge waiting-hall on the first floor, trading tales of public-sector ineptitude—no better basis for such impromptu acquaintanceships—before finding a small partitioned-off waiting-room in a corner. There, shielded from the rest of ISBT by its cracked and grimy glass wall through which the dimly-lit waiting-hall appeared subaqueous and the bales of human bodies asprawl on the floor like so much marine detritus under a fan which, miraculously, in the midst of such complete breakdown, still worked, we seated ourselves, and Mr Chugh got started on topics only a severely undermined traveller would take up.

An intense excitement animated his sweat-drenched face; his voice cackled with nervous energy; he was in a hurry to confide in me as much as he could. And, less than fifteen minutes after we had met, I was taken on a whirlwind tour of Mr Chugh's life.

I learnt, for instance, that he lived in Muzaffarnagar; that he was returning from Jaipur where his brother lived with his mad wife; that he himself had been a doctor in Toronto. But—and here the story turned strange—he was not paid his salary for ten years. So, he came back to India and started working as a consultant to an engineering firm. But he was disappointed by India. His wife was like his mad sister-in-law; she wanted him to make money. He was now thinking of going back to Toronto. They were now willing to pay his salary.

At any other time, Mr Chugh's story would have seemed slightly garbled, hiding some unpleasant reality (for instance, the bit about his withheld salary: was it because of some wrongdoing on his part?). In its present setting, however, emerging as though from the disorderly world around us, it appeared plausible. And the mood was infectious. Mr Chugh asked me no questions about myself; but twice I had had to stop myself from blurting out a few family secrets of my own.

Soon, Mr Chugh began to repeat himself: not just the themes, but also the exact sentences he had used earlier. It looked as if he was working himself into a state. The thought that he might any moment go completely berserk crossed my mind. It was disturbing: sitting next to him, staring into his thick-jowled, ruddy-cheeked face, and slowly realizing that such delirium could be less aberrant than what a sweltering May night at ISBT might make it seem, that it might have its sources in the peculiar circumstances of Mr Chugh's life.

But he was, at worst, a harmless bore, and I could, I found out, easily turn away from him even as he raved on, and let my attention wander around the small enclosure we were in.

There were two other people in the waiting-room. They were a plump English couple in their mid-thirties— mentally christened Heather and James by me—whom I had overheard quarreling two hours ago as I walked behind them into ISBT.

'Why *couldn't* you *settle* with him *beforehand*?' Heather was demanding to know.

'Well, why couldn't *you*?' James retorted in just as sibilant a voice. 'No one asked you to just stand around like some decoration while I deal with auto-rickshaw drivers.'

'Oh, *shut up!*'

'And, why get so fucking uptight over a few rups?'

They were, I gathered from their enquiries, making the English pilgrimage to Simla. Few English tourists in my knowledge ever failed to make it there. Whenever asked about this, they would seem embarrassed, as if caught airing some illiberal belief.

'I don't know,' they would first say, and then add: 'I suppose it's because it has such *English* associations.'

This was partly true. Simla was usually the last destination in the over-ambitious itineraries of English tourists, the place where, after weeks and weeks of the alienating strangeness of India, they could at last relax, find some comforting familiarity in such weak simulations of England as Simla offered.

For Heather and James at least, Simla was coming at the end of several weeks of arduous travel. Like many other people who have been on the road for too long, they had let themselves go. Their fluorescent backpacks had in places turned black with grime; James had let his beard grow beyond a stubble and into an ugly bristly growth; he wore the kind of printed trousers that should ideally not be seen outside circuses; Heather fared little better with her unwashed shaggy-dog hair and very short shorts from which jutted out a pair of pallid, cylindrical, visibly-veined thighs.

Their sullenness, palpable even to the casual observer, was of people who have been travelling together for far too long and whose flagging relationship only some external event or thing could now restore. Already, some of the acrimony I had witnessed looked defused by the awfulness of what they had encountered inside ISBT. A fuller reconciliation would have to wait till Simla where, at an open-air restaurant on the Ridge I knew from the many idle afternoons spent there, they would meet and talk with other similarly-jaded English tourists.

Beginning with banal enquiries, the conversation would expand; soon it would have no other subject than the ordeal that travelling in India had been for them. Tales of distress would come pouring out from all sides. At first solemn, the mood would gradually lighten till high comedy was being made out of the peculiar horrors of this or that hotel, anecdotes sharpened for the retelling back home. Then as the afternoon progressed, the estranged couples would start speaking to each other in much the same friendly way they were speaking to others; and by evening past disagreements would have been forgotten, several reconciliations effected, within the new happy community of shared woe.

Thinking of all this, I had almost forgotten Mr Chugh. He had stopped speaking some time ago and was now fast asleep. His head lolled around on his chest; at times, it drooped alarmingly to my side, as if seeking some resting point there. Hurriedly, I got up and put my backpack on my chair so that Mr Chugh, when he reached the crucial point in his sideways quest, could find something there to arrest his fall, and walked down to the platform to ask about the bus.

There was still no news about it. I was told to wait another hour.

I came back to find the seats adjacent to mine occupied and the waiting-room whirring with a new energy. The three newcomers were in their early twenties. They were carrying large plastic sacks of what looked like children's clothing to me, and had the loud exuberance of people who had pulled off a nice deal for themselves during the day and for whom the night was the wide arena to celebrate it in.

Most likely, they were shopkeepers returning from a day-trip to the wholesale market at Sadar Bazaar and now going home to one of the many small towns around Delhi:

Rampur, Bulandshahr, Gajraula. (Fearful places in my imagination, especially Gajraula where, four years ago, several nuns had been raped inside a convent.)

It seemed so, and from not just the plastic bundles; but the uniform hairstyles—no sideburns and oily little curlicues arranged on the nape; and the clothes—both shirt and trousers strictly polyester, even in May; and the shoes—their brand-name spelt Nikki instead of Nike.

And, of course, the language. Heather and James—both of whom were dozing by now—had caught their eye, especially Heather's thighs which, for no other reasons than aesthetic, she should have concealed, and which now attracted the kind of lewdly malevolent remarks like:

'*Jaangh dekh bandariya ki, bhenchod*, Look at that monkey's thighs, sisterfucker.'

'*Pure makhkhan hai, bhonsdiwali*, Pure butter, that cunt.'

The night proved to be very long. Unable to doze off like the rest, I spent my time pacing the waiting-hall and periodically walking down to check on the bus. Mr Chugh kept sleeping all this time, his head firmly anchored to my backpack, until when he mysteriously disappeared during one of my trips down, lured away, it seemed possible, by some private-bus tout. Feeling slightly ashamed, but determined to do so nevertheless, I checked my backpack for missing items. Very quickly, I reassured myself and settled down to wait, it turned out, for a few more hours. For, when finally the delayed bus arrived, it was discovered to have a faulty engine. It went back to the garage and came back two hours later—still unwashed, the pale vomited morsels from last time still clinging to its outer walls—only when everything had long ceased to matter, after the mind and senses had abdicated and the poisonous air, the grime, the noise, the stench, the progressively obscene conversation around me had become part of an unreal world one would soon be leaving behind, hopefully, for ever.

But I had hoped too early, for it was in Muzaffarnagar a few days later that the idea first came to me of travelling around the small towns and cities of India.

I had gone there as my friend's representative to an engagement ceremony. A number of subsidiary events were attached to it, and they were a crowded four days. But despite the occasion, they weren't particularly gregarious. Apart from my friend, I knew no one there; and in any case I would have found little to say to the young men wearing silk Hawaiian shirts, diamonds rings and pseudo-Italian shoes, who gossiped about the dowries paid and received by this or that personage, boasted about the bribes they had given to municipal officials and sales-tax inspectors, and spoke with awe and reverence of a certain police inspector who had personally killed seven Muslims in a communal riot some months ago.

They were, truth be told, an unsettling four days. I did not know the people whose hospitality I received in such generous measure. In fact, they repulsed me slightly. But their hospitality flattered me and obliged me to show gratitude. And I found I could not do so with complete sincerity. There was too much to see and take note of; and often, seeing more than I should have, I felt like an impostor, abusing the reflexively warm welcome extended to me.

And it wasn't just the casually observed young men with their gold chains worn over sacred threads that claimed one's attention. There was much more. I searched for, but failed to find, a single good bookshop or garden or public park worth its name in the entire city. In place of a newspaper, there was a shoddily-printed tabloid reporting on outlandish, probably fictitious, crimes. Then, there were the houses I visited, the houses painted a screaming pink, with bathroom tiles set in living-rooms, the houses with their throne-sized dining chairs, huge black or brown leather sofas, massive chandeliers, tall glass-shelves crammed with gaudy trinkets, and over-sized paintings of dramatic sunsets and angelic children with tears in their eyes on the walls. Even the food I ate at these homes was like the standardized fare served in restaurants with pretentious names like 'Tawa', 'Angithi', and 'Tandoor': oily, spicy, overcooked and, as I found out again and again, indigestible.

Small, scattered details, meaningless in themselves. It was only when they were seen together that a coherent picture emerged.

For instance, the house I stayed at: it was in a large middle-class colony, typical of the thousands of such hodgepodge agglomerations of buildings that exist in cities all over India. The roads within the colony were all unpaved, and were most certainly unusable during the monsoons. Wild grass and weeds grew unchecked everywhere. At the back of every house lay gigantic mounds of garbage. Water spurted noisily from a leaking pipe, and into a small drain someone had very cleverly directed to his garden.

It wasn't for lack of money that things were as they were: the houses belonged to extremely prosperous people. There were cars parked in front of every house; on the roofs were a surprising number of satellite dishes. The houses themselves were in a peculiar medley of expensive styles, ranging from bewilderingly eclectic wedding-cake fantasies to heat-inviting glass-and-concrete insipidities—symbols in their wasteful incongruity of what Veblen, writing of another newly-emergent class almost a hundred years ago, termed 'predatory prowess'.

No, it wasn't for lack of money that such appalling civic conditions were allowed to prevail. If anything, the blame lay with the sudden plenitude of money: far from fostering any notions of civic responsibility, it had encouraged in its beneficiaries only a kind of aggressive individualism. The colony didn't matter as long as one could obtain, through bribing, through one's predatory prowess, illegal water, power, and telephone connections for one's house. Certainly, houses were castles here and 'Each to his own castle' seemed to be the operative motto, even as the garbage mounds grew higher, the wild grass lapped the high boundary-walls, and one's customized Maruti 1000 frequently got stuck in the wet mud when the rains came.

Such proclamations of personal independence and self-sufficiency took several collective forms. The most obvious ones. were duplication and imitation. In the bazaars of Muzaffarnagar, I found several shops selling the kind of imitation Nike sneakers I had seen on the two young shopkeepers at ISBT. Indeed, the imitation industry seemed in an advanced stage: the bazaars offered almost every famous brand-name: Wranglers' jeans, Jurassic Park T-shirts, Chanel and Dior perfumes, Casio watches.

Elsewhere, I found a 'fast-food' restaurant where a pizza was grated Amul cheese on sliced white bread, and a vegetable burger comprised of a *tikki* slapped between two fruit-buns. The restaurant, however, was crowded; duplication, however inept, was paying off. For instance, the muzak at this restaurant, which was of India's biggest non-film musician: a Rap singer from Lucknow who, by deftly replacing social comment with cretinous chatter, had turned himself into a millionaire. Significantly, his most successful album was entitled *Main bhi Madonna*, roughly translated as 'Me too Madonna'.

Main bhi, 'Me too':· all the pathos of small-town aspiration could seem to lie in these two words.

But then, to see only the pathos was to miss the ambition, the very real hankerings that simmered beneath the often comic surfaces. The wedding-cake houses, the 'fast-food' restaurant, the Rap singer, the cheap perfumes:

there *was* something profoundly pathetic about all of them. Nevertheless, taken together, they spoke of an untroubled confidence, the growing ability of places like Muzaffarnagar to deal with the larger world on its own terms.

Fuelling this confidence, as I discovered in Muzaffarnagar, was the wealth of the new provincial middle-classes. 'India's modest middle-class,' V.S. Naipaul had once sneeringly commented, 'as yet with no common traditions or rooted strength, still only with the vulnerability of the middle-classes of all very poor countries. In the poverty of India, their ambition was great, but their expectations were very small.'

Twenty-four years later, this was only partly true. Modest wasn't a word one could use any longer in connection with the middle classes; neither in numbers nor in ambition nor in expectations could they be called that. Indeed, as I saw later, the appropriation of brand-names alone could not satisy them; they aimed at nothing less than the creation of a whole new pan-Indian culture.

The advent of cable TV was for these new classes another step on the road to full cultural emancipation— from, in this case, the state-owned Doordarshan whose genteel shibboleths had long monopolized the airwaves. In Muzaffarnagar this time, I discovered a new aesthetic on display on formerly staid TV screens, and nowhere more so than on ZEE TV, established by a *beedi*-smoking former flour-mill owner from Haryana, where in absurder parodies of absurd American shows, paunchy, ribald adults plastered each other's faces with cake, and acne-ravaged pubescents pontificated in a bastardized kind of Hindi on dating and extra-marital sex, and cheesecake starlets mouthed solemn inanities about The Meaning of Love, Life, even, at times, the Cosmos.

In music, a new kind of lyric had arisen, which sought to probe into the contents of a blouse. Although the liberal metropolitan press denounced it as vulgar and obscene, its immense popularity in the provinces only proved that an audience had been created there, whose taste songwriters could underestimate only at immense profit to themselves.

Its political assertiveness, however, could only be underestimated at immense risk to everyone. The clearest example of this came when the Babri Masjid was demolished. The movement leading up to the event—the biggest of its kind since Independence—had received its most active support from middle-class populations in small towns and cities; it now turned out that a majority in the demolition-squad also came from provincial backgrounds.

History was made that day, but not by metropolitan India which was relegated to the level of captive bystanders, released afterwards to deal with the repurcussions of the event through either post-facto analysis or communal rioting. Provincial India had upstaged it, and in doing so had only given a small demonstration of its potential.

For, apart from demolishing the Babri Masjid and so peremptorily revising the national agenda, it was also, in much less conspicuous ways, bringing forth a new kind of sensibility: one that could combine in itself a taste for strident politics, violent films, ostentatious architecture, lewd music, rumour-mongering newspapers and overcooked food.

Indeed, as I discovered in Muzaffarpur, such aesthetic and political tendencies were now well institutionalized. From all accounts, Indian small towns and cities had shed their earlier sleepy, half-apologetic air, and were pervaded instead, at least in the wealthier quarters, by a new aggressiveness.

The vulnerability, however, had remained, the vulnerability of the middle-classes of all very poor countries, and the pitiable thing was never more evident than in the high walls topped with jagged glass and barbed wires that surrounded the posh houses, in the armed private guards providing protection to those who could afford it against the world that began just outside the middle-class colonies—the world of stunted shacks and naked-brick, box-shaped houses standing cheek to jowl alongside open gutters and around algae-covered, malaria-breeding ponds, of unpaved roads choked with rubble and building materials, of inexplicable piles of rusting machinery everywhere, of soot-encrusted auto-repair shops, of slushy dung-splotched alleys, of misspelt signboards in English (five 'Mens' tailors, three 'Ladis' tailors), of traffic hold-ups at every little crossing with one newly-acquired Maruti trying to get ahead of another newly-acquired Maruti, of tiny glass cubicles for STD-ISD-PCO calls, of hideously-painted posters for Italian porn films (*Love Crazy Love, Love in Venice*) stuck on every available space—the world which was the other side of places like Muzaffarnagar, and which at times made one wonder if much of urban India wasn't simply a horrible mistake.

The squalor, however, was part of the new prosperity; the two things went together in India. In any case, as I realized in talking to people in Muzaffarnagar, the former wasn't much noticed; it was wealth that mattered, the wealth that in recent years had given small towns and cities their high visibility in all sectors of Indian life.

It wasn't uniformly spread across India; there were many places where it hadn't reached at all. Muzaffarnagar was a beneficiary of the Green revolution; Murshidabad, on the other hand, was a victim of all-round neglect. Kottayam was different in another way, while Jehanabad was another story altogether, and so indeed was every other place one thought of.

Plainly, there was no one conclusion to be drawn about these places; the evidence was far too inconsistent and contradictory. At best, one could hope to trace the contours of a nascent sensibility, of the kind the combination of money and leisure has traditionally created. By the same token, one could also hope to bring to light the facts and realities that so conspicuous a phenomenon inevitably obscures.

My own plan, as it developed over the months following my visit to Muzaffarnagar, was to travel through at least twenty towns and cities across India, so as to get a fairly representative cross-sample, with no fixed agenda except what was created for me in specific circumstances.

The opportunity came after I finished some long-pending academic tasks, when a long stretch of winter suddenly lay empty before me. Swiftly, I drew up a list of places I thought I should visit. Gradually, however, over the next few weeks, and after much mulling and many alterations, I arrived at a suitable itinerary. Then, finally one day, the financial worries, the logistical concerns were behind me, and I was ready to leave.

I began from Simla. I had spent the past summer there, shielded from the tourists in a small village where the most conspicuous activity during the day was the light changing from the white glare of the afternoon to the soft blues and greens of late evening. A lone Maruti van sometimes hurtled down the narrow dusty road and disgorged a party of overdressed tourists—the men in three-piece suits, the women in shimmering salwar-kurtas, the kids in screaming fluorescents—at a viewing point from which could be seen the entire valley in its gorgeous verdancy, as well as the snow-capped mountains in the distance. The tourists would stand and stare perplexedly for a few seconds, and then they would be in a hurry to leave, to flee the oppressive silence and solitude, and go back to Simla wherein beckoned the Mall's colourful bustle, the Beautiful People from Chandigarh—the petulant Punjabi beauties and their strapping young squires—the video-game parlours, the shops blaring out the hits of the summer, the hotels with their nightly cable offerings of new Hindi movies.

Understandably, I waited for the summer to pass.

Towards the end of October, I went to Simla and found it cleansed of tourists, and restored to its permanent residents. Winter was moving in; it was chilly in the shade; and all along the Mall there were now huddled groups of office-workers soaking up the sun's warmth, clutching tepid glasses of tea while the video-game parlours remained silent and uniformed waiters struck melancholy poses in front of empty restaurants.

I strolled down to the bus-stand to enquire about buses to Mandi, five hours away to the north. I was directed to a bus which, even as I asked, was going to Mandi, and which I decided to inspect before taking it the following day.

Travelling in Himachali buses had never been less than an ordeal for me: they were generally filthy, invariably over-crowded. But there were no comparable alternatives; and too often in the past, I had taken the painfully expensive taxis only to find that I had entrusted my life to a reckless young lout, the ink on whose driving licence was not yet dry, but who clearly believed himself, as the wind blew back his long hair on the narrow winding bumpy roads, one with the immortal gods.

A taxi to Mandi, however, was unaffordable, if not unwise. There remained the buses of which the best example, a superfast service, stood before me, and as I looked it over, I felt my heart sink. Five hours of being bounced around in this ramshackle vehicle, hemmed in from all sides by people and luggage, didn't seem an agreeable prospect, or, for that matter, an auspicious beginning to the arduous travels ahead.

So I went back to the ridge, and bought a ticket on the daily 'luxury coach' to Manali. The service was run by the state-run tourist department; it was expensive enough to make one expect it would live upto its name.

The ticket bought, I checked into the YMCA for the night—somewhat nervously, as two friends who had stayed there recently had come away with some mysterious skin infection. But the place in my own experience had been reasonably clean; it was certainly a lot quieter than other hotels in the same price-range, and had, with its large gloomy rooms and eccentric servants, far more character.

The company at dinner comprised largely of a party of Finnish missionaries who flashed warm Christian smiles at everyone as they walked in. There were two young British couples whom I overheard discussing Boy George with a strange passion. There was an American couple in their mid-forties who ignored everyone else, slouched over a distant table, talking subduedly between themselves.

Later, however, they came over to join the after-dinner group of coffee-drinkers as they sat around the TV set, listening to two plumpish Italian girls narrate their tales of woe in heavily-accented but accurate English.

The girls had been cheated right and left ever since they arrived in India, apart from being sexually harassed. Most recently, they had paid Rs 1000—more than double the usual rate—to come to Simla from Kalka. If that was not enough, the taxi-driver had on the way made some improper suggestions.

'We hate India,' one of the girls declared. 'I don't know why people in Italy praise India so much. It is the worst country I have been to.'

The other girl said, 'I think the entire country needs very urgent sex-therapy. Sex is all Indians ever think of. It is an obsession.'

The Britons laughed uneasily at this; the Finnish looked eager to blame it all on the heathens' lack of faith; the Americans, ever sensitive to issues of both sexual harassment and cultural relativity, looked very anxious.

I was the only Indian in the group, and I had only been half-listening, trying to concentrate on the Hindi news on television, read this evening, as seemingly on all others, by the cadaverous Salma Sultan. Now as the narration gathered intensity, I felt a few glances in my direction—not hostile, merely curious, as if to see what I made of all this.

I didn't make much under the circumstances. I had heard too many of these stories. Later on my travels, I would encounter far more disturbing ones, and they would force me to reconsider my own attitudes of indifference. At the time, I turned defensive and thought: Well, travelling in India may have its hazards for woman tourists, but are they really more than those faced by tourists all over the world? Indeed, it was possible that a brown-skinned Indian tourist in Milan would have a sadder story to tell. Or an African tourist in Southern Louisiana.

But this much was clear even then: people talked of a new world, the Global Village, and how the world had become a smaller place. But, one didn't have to travel too far in it to realize it was still a very big place, and that the old barriers were still in place. Modern tourism had done away with the inconveniences of the past; only rarely— and often voluntarily—did a tourist encounter ferocious tigers, poisonous snakes, and murderous bandits on his way. But, it had not done away with, and often had merely exacerbated, the xenophobia, racism and sexism of the old world.

None of this in any case would have consoled the two Italian girls. So that rather than attempt a redressal of sorts—which in the circumstances could have degenerated into a pointless effort to demonstrate that while Indians do think of sex, only a few can afford to think of it to the exclusion of everything else, and that those few are probably comparable in number to their Italian counterparts—rather than take this churlish line, I got up and walked back to my room, leaving behind a sudden silence, and dreamt, later in bed, of waking up horribly disfigured by some mysterious skin infection.

The bus for Manali was due to depart at 8 a.m. But the

time came and went and it did not appear. The minutes passed agonizingly slow after that. Half an hour later, there was still no sign of the bus.

It was a motley crowd that waited for the bus this morning: honeymooning couples, resolutely self-absorbed, their links with the outside world tenuous at best; foreign trekkers in fluorescent anoraks and mud-encrusted Timberlands, seemingly resigned by now to Indian delays; and large families, with children and white-haired parental figures, admirably game for a nine-hour-long journey that could wear out much younger people.

Increased prosperity had made for increased mobility, and there were several people—the elderly passengers among them—of whom it was safe to say that a few years ago they would have not ventured out of their native towns except for reasons of the greatest urgency.

They still, however, travelled in the old way, with jute baskets full of *mathri*, *daalmoth* and *achar*, thermoses, water-kegs and holdalls stuffed full with mattresses and quilts—all recalling a time when one left home perhaps once in two-three years, and always with as many of its portable comforts as could be possibly crammed into a railway compartment.

It was, however, difficult to see how they could be crammed into a bus; and the assorted pieces of luggage, looking oddly vulnerable and exposed piled up alongside the road, were causing anxiety in certain quarters. Certainly, the tall, big-boned, quite beautiful woman standing next to me, tightly holding on to her young son's hand, travelling light with sleek VIP Skybags, and presently surveying with contempt those who weren't, was very worried about them.

She had already mentioned the possibility to her husband that her own luggage may not be accommodated in the bus.

'People are so *stuppid*!' she had added fiercely, in

Punjabi-accented English, 'Going to Manali with holdall and all! So *stuppid!*'

The husband, a portly, balding, harried-looking man, had not replied, but instead, with the instant receptivity borne of long years of henpecking, turned to look despairingly at the pile of luggage.

Now, as she silently fretted and slackened her leash, her son strayed over to the group of children in the families with the much-resented jute baskets and holdalls. Her husband saw him, looked for one moment as if he would stop him, and then said nothing. In any case, it didn't take her too long to discover he was gone.

She saw where he was, and distaste appeared on her face. It was though in a marvellously controlled and melodious voice that she sang out: 'Avinash beta, come here! Come and tie your shoelaces!'

Avinash beta promptly came over. His mother said nothing, but retook her son's hand and crushed it in her own, making him wince. I checked to see if his shoelaces were undone. They weren't. The bit about tying them up was clearly a coded command from mother to son.

On my other side stood Mr Rai with his wife. Mr Rai was a doctor in Patna, Bihar: 'GP, General Practitioner,' he informed me. This was his first visit to Simla. He had found it 'very dirty', and coming from a resident of Patna, the observation appeared especially damning.

Like every other Bihari I'd met, Mr Rai too revelled in his home-state's reputation for unmatched venality, and was an avid raconteur of the many believe-it-or-not stories emanating from it. Briskly, he told me a few. One of them went like this:

A prominent doctor in Patna had his car stolen from him at gunpoint. The doctor immediately reported this to a high-ranking police officer who also happened to be his friend. But the police officer pleaded helplessness. Only one person in the entire state, a very powerful

minister, could help the doctor, he said. Accordingly, the
doctor took an appointment with this powerful minister
and went to see him on the scheduled day. The minister
gave him a very sympathetic hearing. '*Aap jaise prestigious
doctor ko bhi nahin chhoda!* They didn't even spare a
prestigious doctor like you!' he exclaimed. '*Kaisa luccha
log hai,* Such sordid people they are!' Afterwards, he
escorted the doctor out to the front yard where several
cars were lined up in a row and asked him if his own
was amongst them. Sure enough, it was. Slightly
bewildered, the doctor was beginning to express his
profound gratitude when the minister stopped him. He
said, '*Ab aisa hai, doctor sahib, kuch compromise-vompromise
kar lijiye,* Now look here, doctor sahib, the best solution
would be a compromise.'

The doctor didn't understand. Neither did I. Mr Rai
explained. It was the minister's own men who had stolen
the car; the minister's job was to negotiate a good ransom
for it.

The ransom in this case came to Rs 1.5 lakh. Why so
much? I asked. After all, with a few thousand rupees
thrown in, one could buy a new car with that sum.

Mr Rai was waiting for this cue; it was time now for
his punch-line. Because, he blurted out between loud
chortles, if the doctor hadn't coughed up the required
amount, his car would have been stolen again—and then
again and again with the ransom going up each time.

The bus finally arrived at nine-thirty. No apologies or
explanations were, of course, forthcoming from anyone.
We were lucky to get what we did: a passably clean bus
with push-back seats. Hurriedly, we loaded our luggage
on the roof, and settled ourselves in our seats. Five minutes
later, we were off.

Three minutes later, we came to a complete halt. The driver switched off the engine, jumped out of the cockpit, strolled over to the back of the bus and squatted in front of the rear tyres, peering dimly at the underside.

He came back again, and disengaged the gears. The bus rolled silently down the road for some time, and then stopped before what looked like an open-air garage for tourism department buses.

It was clear something was wrong; but we were not to be told until we demanded to know. The driver and attendant joined their mates on the ground, and stood around laughing and joking. A couple of mechanics slid underneath the bus, and began to loudly hammer something.

This went on for another thirty minutes or so; the driver's circle steadily expanded as more people came and gathered around the bus. The laughter grew louder. A general purposelessness hung heavy in the atmosphere.

The trekkers got off the bus and tried to guess what had gone wrong. The honeymooners stayed inside; so did I, going through a pile of newspapers I had bought while waiting for the bus.

Meanwhile, a section of the passengers was growing increasingly restive at the delay. It was, not surprisingly, the Bengalis. Droves of them came up to Simla during Puja holidays; they were now going to Kulu for the Dussehra Mela. Certainly, they were by far the most intrepid travellers in India. I had seen them, young and old, men and women alike, trudging up the steep path to Gangotri. I had arrived once, after a long exhausting trek, at Har-ki-Doon to find them already ensconced there. They were on the beach at Dwarka; Kanyakumari was full of them; the forest in Kanha echoed with their exuberant melodious voices. Wherever you went in India, you found Bengalis. Someone I knew had even stumbled across them in remote Burma.

One of the more conspicuous complainers was a Mr Banerji whom I had overheard introduce himself to a fellow-Bengali on the bus as an engineer from Burdwan. Kneeling on his chair, he described his various ordeals to a sympathetic audience of Bengalis. Apparently, he'd had problems every inch of the way, with reservation clerks, taxi drivers, hotel touts, hotel receptionists, restaurant staff, tourism department officials, and just about everyone else.

His struggles had left him exhausted, he said. But now, speaking about them, I thought, seemed to revive him a little, infuse him with some energy. Enough at any rate for him to propose to fellow-Bengali males that they should go together in a delegation to find out more about their present troubles.

The others agreed, and from where I sat, I saw Mr Banerji, four-five men in his wake, approach the attendant—a scrawny young man in denim jacket and jeans—and ask him what was wrong with the bus.

The attendant was chatting with someone when Mr Banerji asked him, and he did not even turn towards him as he replied—in a voice full of that casual arrogance that Hindi-speakers to the north of Delhi commonly have:

'*Brake kamzor hai, aur kya?*, The brakes are weak, what else?'

I felt a buzz of agitation pass through the Bengalis behind Mr Banerji.

Mr Banerji said, in a firmer tone: 'How so? Why weren't they checked before?'

'*Mujhe kya maloom*, How do I know?' spat out the attendant.

The rudeness sparked off something in Mr Banerji; and all the frustrations of the past few days exploded in an outburst of much power and force—even more impressive for being entirely in Hindi.

'*Kya matlab, brake kamzor hai*, What do you mean the

brakes are weak!' he shouted. *'Tum shala hamari jaan se khel raha hai. Hilly road par bina brake check kare kaise chal sakta hai. Tumhara report karoonga. Tum shab shala suspend hoga.* You are playing with our lives. How can you travel on hilly roads without checking the brakes? I'll report you all! I'll have you all suspended!'

Here Mr Banerji's Hindi ran out, and he switched to English. But he kept up the tone, and his gestures continued to be as vehement as before, attracting now a fair deal of attention from other passengers, the idlers standing around the bus, the driver, the attendant.

It was left to Mr Banerji's companions to calm him down. But he had made his point. The passengers were now more aggressive than before, and suddenly full of loud complaints. The driver and attendant looked subdued: they had apparently taken seriously Mr Banerji's threat to report them.

Things began to move at a faster pace. All attempts to repair the brakes were abandoned. Mr Banerji, who by his zeal and initiative had elected himself our group's leader, went with the driver to call the Tourism office and ask for another bus.

It arrived, promptly enough, just fifteen minutes later. We hastily unloaded and loaded our luggage. Only when I was in my seat did I realize that the bus had not been washed since its last trip: a faint smell of vomit hung in the air; the curtains were encrusted with dried mucus from countless nose-wipings in the past; the floor was littered with peanut shells and empty Frooti packs.

I hadn't even started and already it seemed like a very long trip.

The road to Mandi snakes down from behind Summer Hill and the Himachal University campus, and descends all the way to Bilaspur. To the east are visible the white tops, tinted golden in the sun, of mountain ranges in the tribal area of Kinnaur—whose opening up to tourists has led recently to a spate of thefts from its fabled temples. Looking back, one is able to see for miles on end the imposing Scottish Baronial edifice of the Indian Institute for Advanced Studies—formerly the Viceregal Lodge, the one building of clean determinate origin in a city where architectural miscegenation is rampant.

From a distance, especially when approaching it from the plains, Simla has the appearance of a desperately poor Latin American slum: a ragged jumble of tin and timber on a steep hill-side. The vision clarifies as one gets closer; and though the crumminess never quite disappears, what catches, and indeed consoles, the eye are the old buildings scattered here and there in the chaos: Gorton Castle to the left, the Gothic spires of Christ Church directly above, the post-office elegantly askew behind new and ugly— the two words invariably go together when speaking of modern Indian architecture—constructions.

Bemusingly eclectic, a mishmash of styles from Gothic to Tudor to Swiss-chalet, they prompted the severe classicist Edwin Lutyens to say: 'If one was told the monkeys had built it all, one could only say, "What wonderful monkeys—they must be shot in case they do it again!"'

Human beings presumably, and not monkeys, had built the new buildings of Himachal University. The design offered some clues: monkeys would not have let drab geometry ride roughshod over convenience and harmony the way it does in these bleak, climatically inappropriate godowns; they would not have wanted to spend the long damp winters of Simla within their cement walls.

Offering as though an immediate contrast, just a few kilometres out of Simla were buildings created by a different kind of human beings—by native builders, a fast-dwindling species, who, using local craftsmen and materials, had immemorially built houses in tune with the landscape, whose simple unpretentious styles had created elegance in the midst of extreme poverty.

Ironically, once patronized by the rich and powerful, they were now employed only by those who couldn't afford the modern style—as was in evidence on this road to Mandi. Houses with slate roofs and timber walls kept appearing on both sides; neat and compact they looked, set between wheat fields, shaded by sal trees, their courtyards glowing a brilliant orange from the corn-cobs left out to dry.

The assembly elections for Himachal Pradesh were due next month. Open jeeps full of fierce-looking campaigners, loudspeakers blaring some incoherent spiel, zoomed past us on the narrow road. Hung between trees, Congress and BJP flags made of thin, transparent polythene fluttered weakly in the breeze. Electoral advertisements had taken up every inch of available space, obscuring road signs, kilometre markers, and were even daubed waveringly on cows and sheep.

Fresh from his triumph in Simla, Mr Banerji became increasingly vocal as the journey progressed. He sat directly in front of me, and so in order to converse with me had to twist his torso. It must have been a very inconvenient physical posture. But if he was in pain, it did not show; success animated his features, heightened the excitement in his voice.

What set him off was my revelation that I had studied at Jawaharlal Nehru University (JNU) in New Delhi.

He asked me no other questions; his curiosity about me was fully satisfied. He knew me now: I was a fellow-traveller in a great ideological movement.

Mr Banerji himself hadn't been to JNU; but several of his friends had. Rapidly, he recounted a series of names, none of which I had—or could have—heard.

These friends had been activists of the CPI(M)-affiliated Student Federation of India (SFI) in the mid-seventies. Mr Banerji himself, he eagerly revealed, had been a bit of an activist in his college days in Calcutta—but, he was eager to make clear, of *AISF*, the *CPI*-affiliated student's organization.

It was clear that such fine ideological distinctions still mattered to him a great deal, for when I informed him that the SFI no longer held power in JNU's student union, and that it had conceded its place to the CPI(M-L)-affiliated AISA, he snorted and said:

'All anarchists, these CPI(M-L) people! A disgrace to communist parties!'

He asked me about the CPI(M-L)'s performance in Bihar.

I told him the little I knew, which was that it had done quite well recently.

He listened with an unhappy, doubtful expression on his face. He brightened up as I tempered my account with some negative prognostications; then, interrupting me, launched himself into a withering analysis of the CPI(M-L)'s weaknesses.

Luckily, after some time Mr Banerji found his posture too painful to maintain. He turned his back, and, finally, fell silent.

But not for long. What aroused his excitable nature now was the song *Choli Ke Peechhe Kya Hai*—the number one hit of the season, whose adolescent lewdness had provoked a tiresome number of articles in the press as well as a lawsuit in Delhi. There was no getting away from it anywhere; it was one of the inevitable hardships of travel in India this year. The attendant had a special liking for it, and had played it four times already on the audio system of the bus. Busy discussing communist politics with me, Mr Banerji had not even noticed. Now he did, and was appalled.

'Yes, yes, attendant?!! Attention please!' he abruptly got up from his seat, and started gesturing vehemently to the attendant in the glass-enclosed cockpit.

The attendant saw him, but took his own time coming over to where Mr Banerji stood, holding tight to the seat in front, fairly incensed by now.

'*Kya hua*, What happened?' he asked with the usual insolent tone in his voice.

'*Yeh obscene music band karo*, Stop this obscene music,' ordered Mr Banerji.

The attendant merely stared, a little surprised by Mr Banerji's passion.

'Did you hear me? Stop this music at once,' Mr Banerji repeated, and then turning towards the rest of the passengers, added: 'Please do not mind, ladies and gentlemen, but if we do not say something, this obscenity will go on. We must protest against such kinds of music, otherwise there will be no end to it.'

Then, turning again to the attendant, he said in a louder voice: '*Suna nahin tumne? Band karo music*, Can't you hear me? Stop the music!'

The attendant, still slightly taken aback, mumbled something about government rules. What he in effect said, ludicrous as it may sound, was that the government had provided the bus with an audio-system, and that he was supposed to keep the music going till the bus reached Manali.

But Mr Banerji hadn't understood him, and he was still trying to figure it out, when opposition came from an unexpected quarter.

It was one of the honeymooners. Barely a word had been heard from them so far in the journey. Uniformly attired—the men in newly-tailored suits, the women in flashy sequined salwar-kurtas—they had sat, their arms around each other, inaudibly talking and giggling all through the way.

During a brief stop for tea, the men had gone out to fetch eatables for their wives. I had noticed one of them in particular: a tall, hefty, impossibly broad-shouldered man. I had heard him talk to the attendant. They appeared to be well-acquainted with each other. Or, it may have been just the cosy intimacy created by their use of Punjabi.

He had the—in other circumstances, rather amusing—masculine over-assertiveness of newly-married men. You saw them in the restaurants of Simla, Mussoorie and Nainital, being needlessly aggressive with the waiter. Then, as the waiter went back with fresh instructions, you saw the smug self-satisfaction descend on their faces, you saw their wives' expressions change from slight uncertainty to plain adoration, and you knew an important point had just been scored.

All masculine self-absorption, this honeymooner had lashed out at a small dog who had gone too close to him as he stood by the roadside, urinating. The dog had caught the full force of the kick on his mouth, and had limped away, howling with pain. Then, this act of casual cruelty instantly forgotten, the honeymooner had come back, smiling, to take his seat beside his wife.

It was he who now stood up, and said:

'Boss.'

Mr Banerji, intent on having his way with the attendant, didn't even hear him, until he repeated in a much louder tone:

'Boss.'

Eager for support from somewhere, Mr Banerji turned back to look at him.

'Boss,' said the honeymooner, 'what is your objection? We are enjoying the music. Why are you stopping it?'

Mr Banerji looked uncomprehending for a moment. Then it dawned on him what the man was saying. He looked again at the honeymooner, who was at least six inches taller than him; and, abruptly, the fight went out of Mr Banerji. He looked absolutely crushed.

And both his syntax and vocabulary deserted him as he weakly protested: 'But it is very *bad* song.'

The honeymooner was unmoved. 'Bad for you, not bad for me,' he said, and then added, 'It is personal taste. You don't-like it. I like it.'

The tone brooked no argument; and Mr Banerji, going by the helplessness writ large on his face, did not fail to sense its steely firmness. He knew that he had encountered a will stronger than his, and that he would have to back down.

Emboldened by the honeymooner's stance, the attendant added:

Yeh luxury bus hai. Music to chalega. Nahin chahiye to ordinary mein chalo, This is a luxury bus. The music will go on. If you don't want to hear it, travel by ordinary bus.'

The battle was lost. The attendant turned and made his way back to the cockpit, slamming the door behind him with unexpected force. The honeymooner was already in his seat. Mr Banerji grudgingly lowered himself into his, muttering something inaudible in Bengali to his wife. I repeatedly caught the words 'vulgar' and 'obscene' and 'degraded culture'. After that, I heard no more from him for the rest of the journey.

However unsuccessful Mr Banerji's present struggle against obscenity was, he would have been gratified to know that it was in line with his party's position on the issue. Travelling through Bengal months later, long after *Choli Ke Peechhe* had been supplanted on the charts, I came across a news-story in a local paper. It reported the extreme anger within the Left-Front Government over an official function of sorts in Cooch Behar where senior police officers were alleged to have danced in full public view to the notorious song. 'Vulgar', 'obscene', 'degraded culture' were some of the terms used to characterize their behaviour. Strict action was being contemplated.

2

At Mandi I checked into a guest-house close to the bus-stand. The first person I queried about a hotel after the bus dropped me off took me there, and then waited to receive his commission as I filled in the register. He was in his late teens, scruffily dressed in a jersey made of sackcloth and torn polyester pants. The room-rent was Rs 50. How much was his cut? I wondered. Did he regularly hang around the bus-stand waiting for clients?

I caught up with him later. It was dusk, and there were no lights on the road. I tried to make out his face in the fading light, but failed. He, in turn, was surprised by my questions.

He had made five rupees out of me. Yes, that was his occupation. How much did he earn in a day? It depended: sometimes nothing at all, sometimes twenty-five to thirty rupees, and could he go now please, there was a bus coming in from Chandigarh.

Part of the hotel looked new, part old. Like most buildings in small towns, it had been built in a haphazard way: a room built here, a room built there, later a room built on the roof, and so on. My room was in the newer part. The door looked freshly-painted, but it was too big for the frame, and didn't close at all.

The manager—a short balding thickset man in his early

forties—assured me my things were safe, and that I didn't really need the door at all.

I toyed with the idea of asking for a discount on the room-rent. Instead, I asked for a pillow and two blankets.

The manager was taken aback, but recovered enough to say that there was an extra charge for them: ten rupees for each blanket; three for the pillow.

But your room has no door, I said.

The manager looked offended. Of course, his room had a door. What was that over there?

But the door doesn't close, I said.

It didn't matter, he replied. My things were safe.

We stared at each other for a few seconds, and then I picked up my bag, and made as if to leave. I was only pretending, of course: it would have required real coercion to get back the fifty rupees advance I had already paid him.

But the manager seemed to relent. He said he'd give me a special student discount on the blankets—five rupees instead of ten—and charge nothing for the pillow.

This was agreeable enough. I didn't, in any case, relish the prospect of going out to search for another hotel. There was no guarantee that it would have proper doors.

So I stayed.

There was barely enough space in the room for a double bed and a dust-laden table. But there was a small black-and-white television set which the manager's helper turned on the moment he entered the room. A cross-country skiing match was in progress; a high-pitched hysterical voice filled the tiny room: *'AND NOW YOU SEE KIRSTEN MILLER SURGING AHEAD FROM THE RIGHT !!!!'*

So as to not hurt his feelings, I waited until he had deposited the blankets and left, and then switched off the television.

There were tiny curly strands of hair sticking to the

pillow I had been provided. On the bedsheet, there was towards the middle an Australia-shaped cream-coloured stain. None of these things could bear much speculation. I told myself: I have to spend at most two nights here. If things get worse, I can always leave.

Later, I dined at HPTDC's Tourist Lodge, situated on a ridge directly above the bus-stand.

There was no one in the large cavernous hall when I went in. The receptionist saw me walk in, and looked as if he was going to tell me that the restaurant was closed. Barely a minute later, the music started: old film songs, mercifully, from the fifties, sung by new voices. This was a good sign, I thought: my presence had been acknowledged. Soon, hopefully, there would be a waiter at my table, and I would finally eat something after nine hours.

But then minutes passed and no one came. I would hear steps outside, and feel my expectations rise. Then they would fade away and I would go back to gazing at the twinkling lights of Mandi below me.

Another twenty minutes passed before the waiter came. Before that there was the noisy arrival of two car-loads of government officers' families. First, the children appeared, racing each other into the lobby, yelling at the top of their voices, their shoes making a hideous squeaky sound against the polished floor; then their proud mothers, pictures of queenly arrogance in their silk sarees, their Pashmina shawls, their blithe kitty-party chatter; then their minions holding picnic baskets and thermoses; and finally, the soft-bellied safari-suited officers themselves, striding confidently into the lobby, supremely assured in their assumption—here, in this small government-run hotel—of authority.

From where I sat, I saw the receptionist leap to his feet. He was then obscured from view: he may have been prostrate on the floor. The family filed into the restaurant, one by one. Soon, the place was buzzing with activity. The manager appeared; waiters materialized out of nowhere, and hovered around the new arrivals. At last, I was noticed, sitting by myself in a remote corner, and a waiter was sent to my table.

I was woken up early the next morning by the manager's helper shouting *'chai'*, going around loudly knocking on doors. Mine he simply pushed and came in, holding a glass of tea in his hands. Apparently, this morning cup of tea was on the house because when I indicated I didn't want any, he brightly declared: *'Free hai*. It's on the house.'

It wasn't for free, of course. Its probable price was far less than what I had just paid: being rudely woken up in the morning. But I didn't tell him that. There would have been no point. I simply took the glass from him, and then with the same resigned feeling watched him switch on the television set.

The tea was repellently syrupy. I left most of it on top of the television set, took my money out from my bag, and went walking through the streets of Mandi.

Even by Himachali standards, Mandi is an exceptionally small place. The entire town is spread over two steep hillsides separated by the river Beas; the slightest tremor, one feels, would send it crashing down into the river. A rickety bridge connects the old part of the town to the new. Narrow cobbled lanes meander off the main road and into dense concentrations of houses and shops. Most houses are new, with that incomplete, unfinished look to them: iron girders jutting out, bricks stacked on rooftops.

Once the capital of a large state, Mandi dates back to the early sixteenth century. Its importance primarily lay in its location at the crossroads of two important routes to

Kangra and Kulu valleys. Things haven't changed much since then. Mandi remains an important transit-point, and little else. The shops lining the main road cater to passing tourists in much the same way they once did to passing travellers. By itself it offers nothing. I had heard much about its temples; but they seemed this morning inferior versions of those in the Kangra valley, architecturally and sculpturally undistinguished, almost bland.

The remarkable thing about them was that they still stood. The successive waves of invasions from the West that destroyed much of North India's temples left miraculously untouched the temples of the hill states, with the result that they have now the largest concentration of pre-Muslim temples anywhere in North India.

The hill-states were too insignificant; none of them promised the fabled booty of Somnath. The invaders' interests lay elsewhere, in Delhi, the Gangetic Plains, and Bengal from whose Sen dynasty most of Mandi's rulers came as refugees for the next 450 years of its existence.

Once ensconced here, they let themselves slip out of history—in sharp contrast to the restive rulers of the hill-states to the north, who frequently warred with each other and the Moghuls. For centuries, nothing happened in Mandi. Apart from a minor tiff here and there, the town slept through the most tumultuous period in Indian history.

Isolation breeds timidity—a creditable virtue, but not to all. William Moorcroft, travelling through these parts in 1820 on his way to Bukhara, met the king of Mandi and declared him an immature, cowardly person whose father, for his sake, had banned the firing of guns in his territory.

Moorcroft found this pathetic, but then how could he have understood, belonging as he did to a race of explorers and colonizers, the benefits of quietism, of opting out from the pointless upheavals of history, of living in a stupor of non-achievement, of simply staying put *at home*?

At eight in the morning, the loudspeakers came alive, and life in Mandi ceased to be tolerable. There were at least four of them on each electric pole in the main bazàar, each broadcasting a different message, all of them individually and collectively incoherent. But, once again, the message didn't matter; the medium did. It was essential to have a loudspeaker on the pole, to register one's presence, to have a share in the cacophony.

A small podium had been erected at the end of a sidestreet. A giant lotus made with marigolds adorned the backdrop. Electricians busily went around setting up mikes and amplifiers. Grave with self-importance, a few young men wearing khadi kurta-pyjamas held huddled confabulations in a corner.

When I came back fifteen minutes later, after a walk through the bazaar, speeches were being made, but by local politicians. This was to warm-up the audience before the star speaker arrived—who knew how many hours later—tired and hoarse after many speeches elsewhere, and unwilling to say more than a few words. This was also a chance for budding politicians to practice their public-speaking skills.

A small crowd had gathered in front of the podium; I joined them.

A few minutes later I left them to stand a good distance away from the speakers. Most of these young and passionate speakers had mistaken shouting for good oratory. *RAM MANDIR.....KAR SEVA....ROYALTY... DEVELOPMENT....* were some of the words I caught; the rest remained massively incomprehensible.

But my eyes were kept engaged by the people on the podium. Two of them looked old, in their sixties, with that jaded, satiated look to them—drooping postures, eyes cast downward—that marked them off as have-beens: former MLAs in all probability, who had had their time, and knew it wasn't going to come back. All they could aspire to be now was MLA-makers, prospect-boosters, podium-fillers.

The younger set, on the other hand, was conspicuous by its feverish energy, its foxy alertness. Eagerly, their eyes scanned the audience, seeking a familiar face, an encouraging response, even as they pretended to be attentively listening to their colleagues' speeches.

I was particularly struck by a ruddy-complexioned, good-looking fellow wearing a khadi woollen jacket over eyeraising blue stonewashed jeans. His hair was long and styled in the way made popular by Sanjay Dutt: no sideburns, a rat's tail curled up on the neck. He wore a tiny earring in his left ear—though that was probably attributable to local custom. And as he stretched back to consult a colleague, the beginnings of a paunch became visible.

He had already spoken, and was now busy looking over the crowd in front, flashing quick smiles at those he knew, sometimes bowing his head respectfully in the over-sincere manner of politicians.

He saw me looking at him. I had my notebook out; he saw that, and thought I was a journalist. The next time I looked up, he was smiling at me. I nodded back.

Soon he was beside me.

Are you a journalist? he wanted to know.

It seemed better to let him think I was. I nodded again.

'What do you do?' 'Are you a journalist?': I was to grow weary of answering the same questions wherever I went in the coming months. At times, I would experiment. I would tell people I was a student. But that, I quickly found out, was to invite immediate condescension, even, at times, dismissal. For, to be a student was to be a mere spectator in a world of movers and shakers. 'Writer' fared no better. It provoked as much suspicion and pity as a confession of alcoholism. 'Journalist', with its connotations of power, alone made a favourable impression, though again 'freelance' cut no ice, institutional affiliation was what they wanted to know.

So that when he asked me, '*Kaun se paper se*? From which newspaper?' I quickly lied and said, '*Newspaper nahin, agency se*, No newspaper, from an agency.'

He didn't probe any further; he seemed satisfied with that.

'Pleased to meet you,' he said unexpectedly in English, and extended a hand. 'My name is Rajesh Trehan.'

His handshake was firm, with an extra squeeze towards the end.

I congratulated him on his speech. His face grew flushed; he looked overwhelmed.

Having thus established myself, I asked him a few questions. Was he from Mandi? What work did he do? Why was he supporting this candidate?

He looked happy, even flattered, to answer my questions. Yes, he was from Mandi; he was into real estate.

Here in Mandi? I asked

No. He had a hotel in Manali. He owned land in Sundernagar, but brokered purchase deals all over the state. A lot of people from Punjab wanted to buy land here; he helped them in that.

That sounded very dubious to me. It is difficult for outsiders to buy property in Himachal Pradesh.

I told him that, and he smiled. There were ways, he said, still smiling, to get round that.

Meanwhile, as we talked, other people on the podium had become interested in me. I still had my notebook out, and the fact that I was talking to one of their compatriots marked me out as a journalist. Soon, I realized, there would be more people around me, and it would become harder to maintain my lie.

I asked Mr Trehan if there was any restaurant nearby where I could get something to eat.

His face went blank for a moment. My question

had caught him off guard; he had been thinking of other things.

'Restaurant?' He thought for a while, still slightly confused, and then said, a trifle apologetically: '*Restaurant kahan yahan? Mandi chhoti jagah hai, Bhaisahab*, No restaurants here, Mandi is a small place, Bhaisahab.'

I had wrongly phrased my query. He had been thinking of a large, gloomily-lit place that gave butter chicken the pride of place on its menu. I wanted a small *chai*-shop—some place I could nibble some buttered toast, and talk in relative privacy.

I clarified that to him now. He looked relieved. Sure, there was a *chai*-shop just around the corner.

As we walked there, he asked me if I was going to Manali.

No, not on this trip, I replied.

'Next time you go there,' he said, 'you should stay at my hotel. Be my guest. There's a great restaurant there.'

Coming from someone I had met barely a few minutes ago, the offer was suspiciously generous. But there was no doubting why it had been made: because he thought I was a journalist, and therefore a potential source of free publicity for himself and his hotel.

We seated ourselves in a *chai*-shop not far from the election meeting. The owner, holding a pan of steaming tea, bowed reverently as we came in. Other people in the shop looked up, and seemed to suddenly stiffen.

These small attentions perked him up. He began talking as soon as we sat down. I asked a few questions, but he didn't need much prompting.

He told me before starting that he wasn't going to give me any of the politician's usual spiel. He said he considered me too intelligent for that.

He paused a little after saying that, as though waiting for me to thank him for this quick and flattering insight into my mind, before moving on to say that he was going to be very sincere with me.

But what that meant, he didn't really know. He had been a politician and a businessman for far too long; and, frequently, while speaking to me, he would lapse into election-time inanities, before recovering to speak the by now hopelessly compromised truth.

He had big plans for the region. No, that was not right. He had big plans for himself. His greatest ambition was to build in Mandi a tourist resort: with swimming pool, sauna, pony-riding facilities, tennis, conference hall, and satellite TV.

But, it would also, he quickly added, help the people of Mandi. Other people would follow him; Mandi, teeming with tourist resorts, would be transformed. The people would change. They were much too simple and naïve, too lazy and unambitious at present; they lacked initiative; they lacked drive. Had I been to Manali recently? Did I know how the place had been transformed? It was no longer a poor, backward jungle. Everywhere you looked, you now found hotels and restaurants.

It was one of the reasons he said he was supporting the BJP. It was easier to get hotel-plans approved by them. He had a contact in the last government who had helped him set up his hotel in Manali.

But, no, that wasn't why he was supporting them. He believed in the BJP's ideology. He believed in *Hindutva*. He believed only swadeshi could save the Indian economy from being bartered away to foreign powers who were jealous of India's cultural heritage, and so wanted to enslave India.

Did he, I asked him, have any political ambitions?

His face clouded: sincerity, truthfulness, dissimulation, idealism, frank opportunism—what was it going to be?

He began by saying that if the party needs him...but

soon discarded it as an embarrassingly transparent falsehood, and fell silent.

I waited. He was thinking hard.

The reply, when it came, was as truthful as he could manage. He was a businessman, and businessmen needed politicians. In the past, they financed them, and then asked for favours in return. It was an unequal relationship: the politician didn't always fulfil his part of the contract. Now, there was nothing to stop businessmen from becoming politicians themselves. They, after all, had the money, the resources.

But—and here he made his token bow to idealism—it was also true that younger people were needed in politics. The earlier generation had proved corrupt, and it was for the younger generation to set an example for the rest of the country. And the BJP was one party which was encouraging young people. Did I notice that Advaniji has only young people as his advisers? He didn't hope to rise that far, of course. But he wanted to make his humble contribution all the same.

There was a superficial polish about him that he could not have possibly acquired in Mandi. It spoke of an acquaintance with the larger world, of regular visits to Chandigarh and Delhi. Despite his small-town background, he was typical of the new kind of businessmen you increasingly met on your travels: people created by the recent liberalization of the economy, by the wholesale marketing of India.

Unabashed in their self-love, in their frantic hankering for wealth, fame, status, they were an adman's fantasy come true—the up-market crowd, finally!—in their Arrow shirts, their Woodland shoes, their Park Avenue trousers, their VIP briefcases. It was they who picked up cheap

Indian reprints and translations of Dale Carnegie's *How to Win Friends and Influence People* and Norman Vincent Peale's *The Power of Positive Thinking* from amidst the sex and letter-writing manuals at railway bookstalls, and keenly perused them on trains—making you wonder what magical formulas of successful self-boosterism, if any, these post-Depression Gurus of Middle America, now hopelessly passé in their homelands, taught their Indian disciples.

Mr Trehan certainly had learnt his lessons well. As I left, he asked me, with that utter naïveté peculiar to very shrewd people, if I would write about him.

Definitely, I said.

(And I have—though, admittedly, not in the way he would have liked.)

Could I send him a clipping at this address? he asked, producing a handsome, gilt-edged visiting card.

Definitely, I said again.

(But I can't, for obvious reasons.)

Was there anything else? He seemed to be turning something over in his mind.

Finally, he said: 'Don't forget my offer for Manali. Be my guest. Anytime you want!'

There was a twinkle in his eyes as he said this. He shook my hand, again with that extra warm squeeze towards the end that perhaps Dale Carnegie thought should seal a new, mutually beneficial relationship.

I left him and walked back towards where the town ends and the road to Kulu begins its steep climb.

Soon, the houses were past me. The noise from the loudspeakers faded away, and the roar of the river below became audible at last. I passed a small encampment of Gaddis, local shepherds from the Kangra valley. Their nomadism brings to mind the Gujars; but there the resemblance ends. These short, colourfully dressed, benign-looking shepherds present in fact quite a contrast to the tall, aquiline-nosed, fierce-looking Gujars. They were presently on their way home to Kangra after a long summer in the pastures of Lahaul and Spiti. In less than five months' time, they would be ready to leave their home again.

Winters in the valley, summers in the high passes: I wondered how long they had been following this routine.

But surely the more important question was how long would it be allowed to continue. I had been reading about an outrageous government scheme to 'resettle' the Gujars; it brought to mind the various, inevitably genocidal attempts in Europe to resettle the Gypsies.

Civilization, however, is on the move; and as E.M. Cioran remarks, nothing more characterizes the civilized man than the zeal to impose his discontents on those so far exempt from them. The two worlds—the town behind me with its half-built houses and satellite dishes, its go-getting politicians and entrepreneurs, a microcosm of the corrupt ruthless turbulent world elsewhere, and, here, on its margins, as it were, the world of these shepherds still adhering to a centuries-old lifestyle, embodying an old forgotten idea of content—these two worlds looked increasingly incompatible. And, however much you wished the weaker one to endure, it didn't seem long before it cracked, before the brute forces of change overran these last unprotected outposts of a simpler—and dare one say *happier?*—world.

3

For the journey back to Simla, I took the superfast service and did not regret it. The bus started early in the morning; there were few passengers; the roads were clear; we reached Simla in less than four hours.

After two days there, I was on the road again, this time to Ambala. I took a bus to Kalka. Sitting on a back seat, I spent the entire journey in a state of fearful anticipation, watching the young women in front vomit out of the window one after the other, and taking evasive action when they did so.

From Kalka, I took the Himalayan Queen to Ambala. With me in the air-conditioned chair car was a party of parliamentarians from Kazakhastan. It's not everyday that one encounters such exotic visitors, and I wouldn't have known about their identity if the two inebriate Indians who accompanied them hadn't told me.

The Indians worked for a pharmaceutical company that was to be paid five crores of rupees for supplying some kind of technical know-how to the Kazakhis. There was nothing to it, they quickly assured me. No actual work was required. They merely needed to 'talk sweet'; the Kazakhis simply needed to be kept happy.

And that seemed a fairly easy task. The Kazakhis had already been softened after a free holiday in Simla. The Indians now opened in alarmingly quick succession three bottles of Johnny Walker Black Label, and talked sweet.

Some excerpts:

Indian: 'Dear Comrades, what are the values of commerce?' (Pause. The Kazhaki side looks baffled.)

Indian: 'What are the values of commerce? They are nothing. Human values are more important.'

Kazakhi: 'Yes! Human values are more important!'

Indian: 'Let us make a pledge to help each other in development work all our lives.'

Kazakhi: 'Yes. Let's work for the development of both India and Kazakhastan.'

Indian: 'Sir, we in India have great respect for your country. We think it is very democratic, we think it is more democratic than America.'

Kazakhi: 'Thank you. The Kazakhi intelligentsia has great respect for India. We think it is a great country.'

Indian: 'Sir, we in India have great respect for the Kazakhi intelligentsia. We think it is very intelligent.'

Someone from the Kazakhi side: 'Let's clap.'

(Loud clapping and incomprehensible sounds from the Kazhaki side.)

Indian: 'Three cheers for Indian-Kazakhi friendship! Hip, hip....'

(The other Indian joins in with a weak 'Hooray'. The Kazakhis look baffled again.)

Kazakhi (seizing the initiative): 'That calls for another toast!'

The Indians stand up with an enthusiastic cry of 'Yes!' and shake hands all around for the tenth time.)

I sat next to an absurdly precocious ten-year-old boy reading a comic-book edition of Moby Dick. Curious to know how this Great American Existential Epic had been turned into kiddie-fodder, I borrowed the book for a while. This broke the ice as it were, and for the rest of the journey I was repeatedly queried on white pigeons, sparrows, and various other obsessions of his.

The boy had four pet pigeons in Simla. 'I had six,' he said, 'but two were recently killed by an eagle.'

I was beginning to commiserate when he said: 'And then a very bad thing happened.'

I waited.

'The two pigeons killed had just given birth. And now the baby pigeon doesn't know who he is. He is going through an identity crisis.'

A man holding up a cardboard placard with my name spelt boldly—and inaccurately—on it was one of the first surprises awaiting me at Ambala railway station.

As far as I knew, my visit was entirely incognito. True, I had a contact in town I was to call upon sometime during my stay here. He was a businessman: a wealthy man, an experienced man. My acquaintance in Delhi, who had given me his name, had suggested him as a useful reference. Apparently, Mr Sharma had spent all his life in Ambala. He knew the town inside-out. But how did he know I was coming?

A mystery. And it wasn't about to be cleared up by the man sent to meet me. All he knew was that Mr Sharma was waiting for me at his house. This puzzled me further. Was I supposed to stay at his house?

I had been looking for hotel signs inside the old-fashioned railway station, hoping to find a place sufficiently close to the town. After my last experience, I was determined to get a reasonably decent hotel, and was prepared to spend the rest of the evening going from one place to another until I found it.

But, Mr Sharma now appeared to settle the issue for me. The offer was too tempting to refuse. There was no time to waste; the driver stood ready, holding open the Maruti van's back-door for me. Banishing all doubts from my mind, I climbed in.

It was clear in a matter of minutes that I had made a mistake. The driver was a maniac, who took the corners like a Grand Prix rallyist, and removed both hands from the steering-wheel on straight stretches. Admittedly, the roads were broad and mostly empty, but one could never discount the unseen person or animal suddenly darting in front of us. Things weren't improved by the oncoming military trucks whose drivers imagined themselves rushing emergency supplies to the Wagah border, and winning chestsful of medals afterwards. I braced myself, remembering the notorious incompetence of military drivers, everytime the trucks whizzed past. The absurd thought briefly crossed my mind that I was about to be killed, and that getting me into the car was an elaborate ruse to have me murdered. But it seemed a troublesome way of going about it. The driver himself wouldn't have survived a crash. Sending him to receive me was a small flaw in Mr Sharma's hospitality; I was to count myself lucky if it didn't turn out to be a fatal flaw.

Mr Sharma was indeed, as the driver said, waiting for me. Or, he may have been waiting for someone else. It was certain, however, from the way he lay there slumped on the divan, as if dumped there by a crane, that he had been waiting for a long time, and that he was presently incapable of doing anything else.

My friend had placed him somewhere in his fifties; but he looked at least seventy with his flock of white hair—

so luxuriant that it looked suspiciously like a wig—his haggard, deeply-lined face, his habit of squinting hard at you as he spoke with a voice that seemed to emanate from a loudspeaker in a deep cavern.

'*Aaiye Mishraji, aaiye. Kahan se aarahen hain*? Come in, Mishraji, come in. Where are you coming from?' he said as the driver ushered me into the living room.

Still recovering from the car-ride, and already wondering what I had let myself into, this confused me further. I thought he knew where I was coming from. How else could he have sent the car to the station? And what was this 'Mishraji' business?

I began to say I was coming from Simla when he interrupted me with: 'Oh Yes. You are coming from Simla. Lovely place. I have a house there. Have you gone to Summer Hill?'

I began to say I had when he again interrupted me: 'Very nice house. Bud I can't go there. Too much business, too much work here in Ambala. My children sometimes go there,' he said, and then without turning his face and while still looking at me bellowed out loud: '*KAVITA! AMMA SE KAHO MISHRAJI AAGAYE HAIN!* Kavita! Tell Amma Mishraji is here!'

I heard a brief patter of slippers on the floor, and then there was silence again. The message was being inaudibly conveyed.

I managed to ask Mr Sharma, who looked slightly winded after his loud shout, how he came to know about me.

'Khanna told me,' he said, meaning my acquaintance in Delhi. 'He said you were coming here for some book-vook, and wanted a place to stay....'

That was only partly true. I did want a place a stay, but on no occasion had I discussed my living arrangements with Mr Khanna.

Mr Sharma was saying: '....So I thod thad instead of staying ad some dirty hotel you should stay with us. You are a student; I am a businessman bud I have great regard for studious people.'

He paused to take a deep breath, and then added: 'And after all, if Brahmins don't help each other what is going to happen to us...'

Then as he continued in Hindi, his voice aquired a new intensity: '*Aajkal to behenchod scheduled caste backward caste ka raj hai, Brahman saale scheduled caste ho gaye hain*, Today it is the sisterfucking scheduled castes and backward castes who have power, it is the Brahmins who have become a scheduled caste...'

A servant appeared, holding glasses of water and cups of tea. Mr Sharma promptly fell silent. The servant was presumably from one of the castes he was excoriating.

Then, as soon as he left, Mr Sharma was off again.

'Now Brahmins should be agitating for special quotas. We should claim minority status...' Mid-sentence, he abruptly roared again: 'DHANIYA!'

The servant who had just left came scurrying back in.

'*Yeh joothe glass nahin dikhte tujhko*? Can't you see these dirty glasses?' Mr Sharma demanded to know.

Dhaniya jerked his head sideways and produced on his face an expression of abject apology. Then, muttering inaudibly, he picked up the glasses and slunk off.

Mr Sharma continued: 'Have you heard this: this new leader of scheduled caste people, what's his name?...Kanshi Ram, starts every function by asking Brahmins to ged out. Now, who is scheduled caste here? We should appeal to the UN and ask them to protect our human rights...'

At this last sentence even Mr Sharma felt he had stumbled across the bounds of plausibility. His voice weakened; he looked intently at me for support; he asked: 'Don't you think so?'

I made some small noises about how deeply disturbing it all was before being interrupted again.

'People have forgotten,' Mr Sharma said, in a softer, more melancholy, tone, 'people have forgotten how Brahmins made this country so great. *Gandhi chhodo, woh to baniya tha*, Leave aside Gandhi—he was a Baniya. But think of other people. Pandit Nehru, G.B. Pant, Deen Dayal Upadhyaya, Dr Radhakrishnan, C. Rajagopalachari, E.M.S. Namboodripad...'

The list went on. The remarkable thing about it was the coexistence in it of people from diametrically opposite sides of the political spectrum: Namboodripad, a communist and a lapsed Brahmin, was there along with Upadhyaya, a right-wing Hindu ideologue. Plainly, Mr Sharma had not let petty ideological differences interfere with his pride in his Brahminness.

Soon, he was down to listing cricket players: Gavaskar, Vengsarkar, Shastri, Tendulkar...

Then came film stars. Vyjayantimala, Hema Malini....

Presently, Mrs Sharma appeared in the living room. For someone in at least her late forties, she looked remarkably well-preserved. Indeed, seen beside her Mr Sharma looked much older.

Her cheeks were a bright red. No amount of staying at home could give her that colour; it had to be rouge, liberally applied. There was mascara on her eyes. Her hair was drawn back in a tight sixties-style bun. And she wore an elegant chiffon saree which would have done credit to a much slimmer figure than hers. It was a pampered look, all in all, one that spoke of chauffeur-driven cars, of long languorous afternoons spent playing gin rummy and watching Pakistani soap-operas, arranging marriages and matching horoscopes.

Her first words to me were: '*Arre beta, chai nahin lee tumne*, Arre beta, you didn't have any tea?'

A plainly incredulous Mr Sharma spoke out: '*Arre! Sookhi chai pilaogi?!!* Would you give him just tea?!!'

'It's coming, it's coming,' Mrs Sharma responded in English, with a cool, almost melodious, accent.

As if on cue, Dhaniya arrived with a plateful of wonderfully aromatic paneer pakoras. Mrs Sharma poured out the tea, served the pakoras. We drank; we ate. Still as immovable as ever on the low-slung divan, Mr Sharma fell into a deep brooding silence and left Mrs Sharma to do most of the talking.

She quizzed me for the next half-hour about myself, my immediate family, my extended family. I replied as patiently as I could, slightly distracted by the picture on a side-table next to her, a picture taken in Mussoorie, of a young woman wearing cut-off jeans and a large straw hat.

Other people came in—a couple of business associates of Mr Sharma, and a handsome young man in his early twenties. We were introduced. His name was Dharam Kumar. He interested me. I gathered from Mrs Sharma that he was a nephew of Mr Sharma, recently arrived from his ancestral town, Rampur, in Western UP. Since there were no job prospects in his hometown, he had come to work for one of Mr Sharma's businesses. During the few minutes he spent in the Sharmas' company, he looked distinctly awkward and uneasy, and I had hoped to find out more about him.

But first I wanted to find out the reasons behind Mr Sharma's profuse hospitality. I had been given a large guest-room, furnished in the most expensive—and needless to say, hideous—style with silk bedspreads and curtains, bulbous suede sofas, wall-to-wall carpet, colour TV and a small fridge—quite like a 'honeymoon suite' I had once seen in a new hotel in Mussoorie.

Then, the dinner that evening was a very large and elaborate affair; it certainly wasn't what anyone ate every

day. I was undoubtedly the guest of honour at the table—
if such things are determined by the number of questions
one is asked while eating one's food.

Mr Sharma's younger daughter, Neha, was the first to
enter the dining room, giggling over something, followed
by another girl, whose name was Roli and who, Mrs
Sharma whisperingly informed me, was a friend of Neha
from Delhi in addition to being—and here a bit of awe
entered her voice—the daughter of a very rich and very
famous industrialist. Both stared at me blankly as they
took their seats at the dining-table, and then continued
scrutinizing my face with the same unblinking gaze.

Neha, Roli....How does one describe them? There is a
sameness about spoilt upper-middle-class maidenhood that
frustrates conventional description. Words fail one utterly.
Indeed, words seem an offence against a thing so
heartbreakingly simple. One has to fall back upon
enumerating the eclectic furniture of their minds and souls.
Not a satisfactory solution by any means, but naming
individually the ingredients is what one will eventually
do, faced with the onerous task of describing two tubs of
Processed Amul Cheese.

So, here goes: Nancy Drew, MTV, Barbara Cartland,
Mills & Boon, Cliff Richard, *Santa Barbara*, Agatha Christie,
Stardust, Shah Rukh Khan, *The Bold & The Beautiful*, Sanjay
Dutt, *Femina*, Pooja Bhatt, *Khubsoorat*, Milind Soman,
Sushmita Sen, Tom Cruise, Richard Gere, Julia Roberts,
Sharon Stone, Bryan Adams, Michael Bolton, Danny
McGill...

Mr Sharma's eldest daughter, Kavita, was the next to
enter the dining room, wearing jeans and a light-grey
pullover, a look of frank appraisal on her oval face as I
stood up and Mrs Sharma introduced me incorrectly as a
writer writing a book on Ambala.

It was her photo I had seen in the living room.
But it wasn't easy to tell. The photo had misled; it was

possible it had been worked over in the developing room—
as photographers do for marriageable, but unattractive,
young women. Certainly, Kavita had the withered jaded
sulkiness of women who have been made to wait far too
long for marriage. Her hair, in defiance of current trends,
was long and straight. She wore no make-up except some
barely discernible white lipstick.

Like Neha and Roli before her, she continued to look
unsmilingly at me well after she sat down, and their
collective gaze was beginning to make me feel very
awkward. Luckily, Mr Sharma, who had somehow
managed to lift himself up from the living-room divan
and into the dining room, chose that moment to say:

'*Ab to suna hai ki kitaab-vitaab likhne mein bhi bahut paisa
hai*, I have heard there's a lot of money to be made in
writing books.'

Before I could say something, Mrs Sharma spoke up:
'Yes, Mrs Bindra was saying today, she must have heard
this from her son, Amarjit, he's very fond of reading and
all, she was telling how this writer...what's his name?...
became a *crorepati* with just one book...'

'Vikram Seth?' Kavita prompted.

'Yes...yes...some Seth,' Mrs Sharma added.

'It's a bad book,' declared Kavita.

The words were out of my mouth before I realized it.
'Have you read it?' I asked.

'No,' she replied slightly awkwardly, 'I haven't read
it, I just heard it was bad.'

I almost asked: 'From whom?' But it would have
meant taking the matter too far.

There was only one person left to come, and that
was Dharam Kumar who now appeared in the dining
room, still as nervous as the first time I had seen
him.

It was his thick mop of hair that now caught my eye.
The hair was simply too long. It was arranged in a style—

overlapping the ears, parted almost down the middle—popularized by Amitabh Bachchan in the late seventies and which, though still sported by him in the few pictures of him I saw here and there, was now clearly dated. It made Dharam Kumar resemble those young, paan-chewing rakes swaggering around the main streets of the small towns one passed through in a thick cloud of dust on your way to a bigger destination, instinctively pitying the place for its hopeless backwardness, its stagnant air, its dejected appearance, its dilapidated cinemas showing last year's flops.

Neha went over to the TV set in the corner and switched it on. Our evening's entertainment was to be *The Bold and the Beautiful*, which was about to begin when Dharam Kumar came in. He stood uncertainly for some time after everyone took their usual seats; and then slid into the chair facing mine.

Immediately, Neha spoke up:

'Not here. Not here. You'll block the TV.'

He stood up abruptly and knocked his knees against one of the table legs.

The assorted steel bowls and tureens and jugs and glasses and plates trembled for a second; their glinting reflections in each other's polished surfaces shifted, and then were still again.

Mrs Sharma remained frozen for more than a second in her position, dipping a ladle into one of the bowls. Nothing was spilt: I quickly ascertained that and then turned to Dharam Kumar who stood there half-bent, pain and embarrassment alternating wildly on his face.

'Are you hurt?' I asked.

'No, no...just a little...injury,' he mumbled.

Mrs Sharma said: 'Come and sit beside me, Dharam.'

Neha and Kavita gaped with open mouths as he half-hobbled, half-walked across to Mrs Sharma's side. I saw something flicker in Kavita's eyes: a sudden interest, a quickening of womanly curiosity, prompted as though by a new awareness of the handsomeness of the man before her.

It disappeared the next moment, the smug crevices reappeared around her mouth as Dharam Kumar eased himself into his chair and, simultaneously, the first scene of that evening's entertainment began on the blazing television set in the corner.

The omnivorousness of the sexual instinct: it was the high-powered engine which dragged the lumbering plot of *The Bold & The Beautiful* from day to day, week after week. Today was no different. Ridge has been furtively having sex with his sister-in-law, Caroline. Her husband comes to know of it, shoots Ridge in a fit of rage, and then promptly loses all memory of the incident. Meanwhile, Ridge's fiancée, Brooke, has got wind of his relationship with Caroline: this, the story until today in one of the infinite sub-plots of that much-loved—by India's English-knowing sophisticates—of soaps.

Mrs Sharma scooped out a ladleful of aromatic dal and poured it into the bowl on my plate, her gold bangles clanking, as she repeatedly jerked the ladle free of all possibility of spillage and then dipped it again into the steaming bowl. As she brought it up over the bowl again, I spoke out: '*Bas, bas*, Enough, enough.'

Mrs Sharma smiled, very much at this moment the proud patron of my gastronomic pleasures, and said:

'Why *bas*? You are a growing boy. You should eat a lot.'

I do not remember what I said, but I did see Neha turn her head back from Ridge's depravities to exchange a brief grin with Kavita.

Mr Sharma—who did not seem to have much interest in degenerate Los Angeles plutocrats—asked me:

'*Aapko apni kitaab ke liye kitna paisa mila hai*, How much money have you got for your book?'

I espied Kavita looking at me from the corner of her eye. She looked sceptical. Her expression said: How much money after all can somebody writing a book on Ambala make?

I said: 'That depends on how many copies the book sells.'

'No,' Mr Sharma said, 'thad is the royalty. How much advance did you get?'

It was clear Mr Sharma knew much more than he let on about the book trade.

I told him.

Mr Sharma's face fell. He looked absolutely crushed. I saw plain pity on Kavita's face. Dharam Kumar, who had been listening to our conversation in the absence of anything better to do, looked slightly confused. Only Mrs Sharma kept her countenance intact and managed to ask: 'How did this... what's his name?... Vikram Sethi earn so much money?'

Luckily, *The Bold and the Beautiful* chose just this moment to dissolve into its signature tune, oddly interposed always after the first five unheralded minutes; and there now appeared on the screen in swift succession shots of an overflowing decolletage adorned with a diamond necklace, bare thighs emerging out of a high-cut swimsuit, busy-looking executives set against skyscrapers, fashion models posing as extravagantly theatrical mummies—all this meant to extinguish any doubts, if existing, about *The Bold and the Beautiful* as the truest portrait of the world's maddeningly infinite and unattainable sexiness. Presently, offering a less-charged titillation, some familiar locally-made ads for soft-drinks came on—trendily-dressed teenagers prancing around in wet clothes—and all eyes turned to me in expectation of my answer.

'Well,' I said, 'he's a big writer, it's a big book.'

Mr Sharma, overcoming his disappointment at last,

asked me: 'How much number of books you write before earning thad much money?'

It would have been too much of a task to explain that it was not a matter of numbers but...

So I said: 'At least ten books.'

Mr Sharma seemed to ponder this.

He began, *'Chalo, maan liya aapne ek saal mein ek kitaab likhi*, Let's assume you write one book every year...' and then stopped to ponder a little more.

I waited.

'Bud see!' he cried. 'One book every year. Thad means after ten years, you'll be a *crorepati!'*

He looked pleased with his calculations. 'Very good!' he chirped. 'Thad is better than doing business. Very good! Very good!'

Looking slightly pleased herself, Mrs Sharma asked: 'How many books there are on Ambala?'

This was the moment to make it clear I was not writing a whole book on Ambala. But I let it pass, and said: 'Not many. Have you heard of Kipling?'

I saw Kavita at the far end of the table nod her head vigorously in assent. Mrs Sharma looked like she was remembering hard: her schooldays, probably...a snake...a mongoose...Rikki Tikki...Tavi?

In *The Bold and the Beautiful*, Brooke had reached a kind of temporary reconciliation with Ridge. In other words, this was where the script-writer had chosen to insert the sex scene for the day. The tension was building up; both Ridge and Brooke were edging closer to each other. A couple of whispers, and then they were in each other's arms with Ridge saying:

'I want you now, Brooke.'

A moist-eyed Brooke replied: 'You can have me, Ridge,' and crushed her lips against Ridge's.

I was looking at Neha who had gone perfectly still. Only her eyes widened slightly in expectation;

her mouth was open, her throat presumably dry, her face strangely effulgent with the erotic curiosity of virginal adolescence.

Mrs Sharma finally gave up and asked: 'No. Who's he?'

I told her. I had been reading Angus Wilson's *The Strange Ride of Rudyard Kipling*. The book was still fresh in my mind. And so I told Mrs Sharma about *Kim*; I told her about the *Jungle Books*; I told her about *Plain Tales from the Hills*; and I took my time telling her.

There was only one way to forestall further questioning, and that was to keep talking yourself. Mrs Sharma looked a bit unsettled by this sudden outpouring of perfectly useless information. Kavita nodded her head a few times during my account. It was when I was about to go into the details of Kipling's troubled sojourn in America that Mr Sharma, who had been strangely quiet until now, finally interrupted me, saying:

'*Yeh saale Angrezon ne Hindustan ke upar kitaben likhkar khoob paisa kamaya*, These bloody Englishmen made a lot of money out of writing books on India.'

Mr Sharma, Mrs Sharma, Kavita were still looking at me; another avalanche of queries seemed headed my way. In desperation, I turned to Dharam Kumar, and asked:

'Which school did you go to in Meerut?'

It wasn't a purely idle question. I knew Meerut slightly; I had plans to go there soon; and then I wanted to know more about Dharam Kumar.

The limelight turned on him. Dharam Kumar blinked, swallowed, and cleared his throat in rapid succession. I saw Neha and Kavita exchange scornful looks that said: 'Oh there he goes again, the stupid yokel from Meerut.'

It was becoming rapidly clear to me that Dharam Kumar was an unwanted member of the Sharma family, cast in the role of a poor parasite on his rich relatives. Kavita and Neha in particular had an intense dislike for their cousin. His rustic gawkiness shamed and embarrassed them in front of friends like the ineffably glamourous Roli. It was imperative to separate themselves from him, to disentangle their identities from his; and one of the ways was to pour scorn and contempt on him.

Aware of their hostile scrutiny, he balked at first, almost ashamed to reply to my question—which I now regretted asking. Neha, meanwhile, got up with a great flourish, said 'Excuse Me' in her most haughty convent-school manner, and left the table. Roli followed suit.

Their departure seemed to give Dharam Kumar the courage he had been lacking. He waited until they had disappeared, and then replied in a curiously sibilant tone: 'St. Joseph's Cross School.'

St. Joseph's Cross School?

Even the name sounded dubious. I couldn't recall a school with that name in Meerut. It was probably very recent, cleverly exploitative of the Indian regard, not entirely misplaced, for Christian schools and English-medium education. Scores of such schools, more than half of them fraudulent, had come up all over small-town India, some with incomplete buildings that frequently collapsed and left in their stead a turbid dust of recriminations and denials hanging over buried bodies.

What was the school like? Brief images flashed before my mind's eye: some primly devout nuns leading an all-school choir of secretly mocking heathen teachers and students in prayer every morning on an unpaved open courtyard in front of a rectangular naked-brick building. Shabbily-dressed, grossly-underpaid teachers slumped on wicker armchairs in a staff room darkened by gloom and resentment. A gaggle of noisily rebellious students, the sons of middle-level shopkeepers, sure of their paternal inheritance, and so, indifferent to continuously falling marks and the not infrequent canings in the principal's office for using a Hindi swear-word.

I began to wonder where Dharam Kumar had figured in all this. But I had been thinking too long, and not doing enough talking. Mr Sharma and Mrs Sharma used the opportunity to assail me with a fresh set of questions, this time about my career plans.

I explained as best as I could that I had none at the moment. They weren't satisfied: I was too old to be not thinking about the future, they said. Surely, I must have thought of something to do.

I invented a few probable careers: writing, journalism, advertising....Finally, I made the time-honoured excuse of having to use the bathroom urgently. Dinner was already over. Mrs Sharma deputed Dharam Kumar to show me the nearest bathroom.

I had got up from my chair and was moving towards the corridor where Dharam Kumar stood when I first heard Neha's voice. She was saying something while still in her room and it was too unclear for me to hear. And then I saw her come out into the corridor and towards where I, and Dharam Kumar a few paces ahead, were standing, her face distorted with anger, hysterically shouting:

'WHO HAS BEEN USING MY CAMAY SOAP?!! DOES ANYONE IN THIS HOUSE CARE THAT I BUY IT FROM MY POCKET MONEY?!! DOES ANYONE CARE?!!'

I heard Mrs Sharma say in her oddly melodious singsong:

'Neha, stop shouting.'

This only aggravated her more.

'Stop shouting! Stop shouting!' she mimicked. 'Do you people care at all about me?!! Do you ever think about my needs?!!'

For a dreadful second I thought I had mistakenly used Neha's bathroom and washed a few skins off her precious Camay soap. But then I saw Dharam Kumar's face turn pale; and in that appalling moment of his guilt, I knew I was safe.

Also, it was at him that Neha was staring with wildly inflamed eyes, her entire torso heaving with the large deep breaths she took. Despite the rage that bloated her features, she looked curiously expectant, as if before a sneeze, waiting perhaps for that encouraging prod—some further provocation from Dharam Kumar—which would make her expel the rest of her bile.

This went on for a painful eternity before Mrs Sharma bustled in from the dining room to where Neha stood and putting her arm around her started whispering something in her ear.

I stole a glimpse at Dharam Kumar. He stood there immobilized, aware of his guilt, but too fearful to say anything.

It was only after Mrs Sharma had led Neha away to her bedroom to pacify her there in seclusion, that he said:

'*Mujhe maafi maangni chaiye Neha didi se. Mein aaj raaste mein saabun kharidna bhool gaya tha*, I should ask Neha didi to forgive me. I forgot to buy soap today on my way back from the office.'

'*Kyon bhool gaya tha re*? Why did you forget?' barked Mr Sharma. '*Jaanta hai kitna mahnga saabun hai yeh*, Do you know how expensive this soap is?'

I left Ambala the next morning much to the surprise and dismay of the Sharmas. Mr Sharma said he had arranged a day-long car trip through the town for me. Mrs Sharma said she was planning to take the entire family out for dinner at Ambala's best restaurant. Kavita said nothing, but seemed to suggest she wouldn't have minded discussing Kipling with me over tea.

I lied and said I had to reach Delhi before 3 p.m. in order to send an important document abroad.

Mr Sharma promptly offered to send it from Ambala, but I was ready for that. Oh no, the document is in Delhi, I lied again.

Finally, after many more cajolings, the Sharmas let go. They looked almost angry in their disappointment as I left; and, while being driven to the railway station by the same lunatic speedster who had received me, I had this time a much stronger suspicion that getting me into the car with him was an elaborate ruse to have me murdered. There was certainly a good reason this time.

Or perhaps, I thought at the station, Mr Sharma had merely instructed him to terrify me to the point of derangement.

Whatever it was, Mr Sharma, I was to learn later from Mr Khanna in Delhi, had ample cause to be displeased with me. According to what Mr Khanna said, from the moment he came to know about me, he had seen in me a prospective husband for his daughter, Kavita. With that intent, he had mercilessly stalked Mr Khanna while I was in Simla, plying him on the phone with queries about my family he was in no way equipped to answer. Mr Khanna had tried to warn me, but was unable to reach me in Simla.

Suddenly, I had a logical explanation for Mr Sharma's over-generous hospitality, the car at the station, the plush guest-room, the multi-course dinner. Suddenly, it all became clear to me with the result that I began to feel much better about leaving Ambala as abruptly as I did. I had been feeling somewhat guilty about that. Now I knew I was right to follow my instinct that night, the very urgent impulse that came over me after dinner, the impulse to leave as soon as possible, to put behind me the unpleasantness I had witnessed. I had got out in time, and no amount of self-congratulation seemed enough for that.

It was in the same celebratory mood that weeks later I clipped out a magazine advertisement heralding Camay soap's imminent arrival in India, and sent it to Neha. Now that the silly thing is here, and available at a much cheaper price than before, one hopes she is more tolerant about other people using it. It is possible, of course, unfortunate as that may sound, that Dharam Kumar now buys his own bar of Camay soap.

4

Back in Delhi, a series of disappointments awaited me. There was nothing new about this, of course; it's just that I wasn't well-prepared this time.

Boredom had finally overtaken me towards the end of my stay in Simla. The view of the snow-capped mountains had long ceased to enchant; the autumnal chill now kept me indoors for most of the day; the days came to have a leaden air about them. Furthermore, I came to see myself cruelly isolated from everything, and nothing more so than what in my restless deprivation I saw as the perpetual excitement of big-city life, the never-ending heady round of new books, films, concerts and seminars.

Desperate for stimulation, I turned into a fervent peruser of Hindi newspapers published from Chandigarh and Simla, which carry not news but speeches and pictures of local political thugs, film gossip and articles on acne, masturbation (very unhealthy, of course), and the propriety of girls wearing jeans (how *dare* they?). Then, I began to go almost everyday to the nearby Hotel Gables to watch, over expensive meals, the asinine serials on STAR PLUS. Soon, I was down to watching ZEE TV, and, given more time, would no doubt have degenerated further.

Not surprisingly, after all this, Delhi became an improbably glamorous place in my imagination.

Deflation followed swiftly therafter. The cold had made the smog over the city even denser. The homicidal Redline buses did not look sated even after a summer-long murder spree. Autorickshaw drivers still tried to cheat you everytime you travelled with them. Shopkeepers snapped at you without any provocation at all. Elsewhere too, people were generally as rude and discourteous as before.

As for the much-awaited cultural replenishment, the films were new all right, but they were barely watchable: either current European 'arty' cinema where people sit around analyzing, with painful earnestness, their paltry 'relationships' in between energetic bouts of sex, or, Hollywood confections where one has as demoralizing company the swinging young dudes and dudettes of Delhi, the Julia Roberts- and Tom Cruise-clones—if not the lone furtive-looking porn-addict lured in by a titillating poster. The concerts were unsatisfyingly brief, tailored down to Yuppie requirements; they ended as soon as they began—presumably to allow the double-income couples to go home and cook Maggi noodles for their hungry children. The seminars were as boring as I did not remember them to be in Simla. The only interesting new book was a three-volume reprint of Marquis De Sade's seminal writings which, since I wasn't currently in the mood for sadomasochism, I left for some happier occasion in the future.

The romance quickly palled; I became eager to leave Delhi. An opportunity came when two friends who were going on a ten-day long tour of Rajasthan asked me if I wanted to join them. I happily accepted the invitation.

We left Delhi early one cold morning. The roads were empty, but visibility was poor: the fog was so thick that you could not see anything beyond ten metres or so. It lay close to the ground in dense thickets; then, as if wounded, it agitatedly danced around the car as the headlights attempted to cut a swathe through it.

Traffic built up steadily after Gurgaon—mostly long-distance trucks, with Gujarat and Punjab number plates. Overloaded and precariously balanced, they nevertheless drove fast and recklessly, overtaking each other at sharp bends, with complete contempt for oncoming vehicles. Most of these trucks had no lights at either the back or front, and loomed up frighteningly out of the fog, like gigantic, brightly-coloured *rakshasas*, ready to decimate us and our tiny vehicle if we didn't immediately swerve left—and into a ditch.

All the way to Jaipur, there were piles of brutally mangled wreckage alongside the road. The frequency with which the sight occurred was terrifying. Beyond all repair now, and good only for scrap metal, the overturned vehicles sprawled at odd angles to each other. It wasn't always easy to visualize how such and such accident had happened. Recklessness alone wasn't a sufficient explanation; and one wondered if at some critical moment the drivers had succumbed to a fierce death-wish, that after days and days of driving, the relentless monotony had finally got to them, and in a moment of extreme disgust with their lives, they had finally ended them.

Whatever the causes, the wreckages taught some sobering lessons in safe-driving. But it didn't look as if they were being learnt by anyone. Some of the accidents looked more recent than others. They were the ones where the blood-stains had not been washed as yet, on the road were large patches left by leaking oil, where the goods in the back had not been carted off, and where a police jeep stood at the site of the accident. Often, there were corpses, covered from head to toe in white sheets; and, squatting on the ground beside them, grieving friends and relatives whose faces betrayed neither rage nor regret at such human rashness and idiocy as had caused the death of their loved ones, but a helpless resignation—of the kind one usually sees in pictures of victims of natural disasters. Like them, it was fate they looked to be blaming, rather than negligent driving.

Jaipur, where we stopped to see the City Palace, held few happy memories for me. I had first gone there as a child and was suitably awed, as unformed minds are likely to be, by the city's exotic aura, its fairyland-like pinkness as well as its geometric order: it was possibly the most well-planned of all old cities in India.

It remained unvisited by me for the next fifteen years during which it turned into a so-called 'boom-town'. My last visit here had occurred a year ago. I had come with a friend, hoping to show him some of the things that had impressed me as a child.

To my shock, I recognized nothing from that first time. Jaipur was now only a larger version of the slummy little towns littered across the map of India. Once again, in a way I was beginning to see as distinctly Indian, prosperity had not enhanced, but lowered, living standards in general. Increased traffic had strangulated the city's once spacious avenues; the pavements had been taken over by assorted stalls and *thelas*; the air was acrid with exhaust-smoke from diesel tempos, lorries, cars, scooters; and, marooned in this chaos, the rickshaw-pullers seemed to be drawing attention to their uncertain fate by creating a tremendous din with their bells.

The ugliness was not confined to new constructions; as I discovered now, it had made inroads into the oldest and grandest part of the city. At the City Palace, built in the early eighteenth century, there were shabby-looking kiosks with galvanized iron roofs inside the main courtyard. Worse, inside an even more exclusive courtyard, facing the palace where the present Maharaja lived, on top of the eighteenth-century pavilion of exquisite beauty, there was a gigantic satellite dish-antenna.

Jaipur was full of disappointments; but there was something deeply offensive about the galvanized-iron roofs and the dish-antenna—particularly the latter, positioned as it was bang in the middle of the courtyard, its metal grating glinting dully in the sun and disfiguring everything in the vicinity.

These symbols of India's shabby borrowed modernity weren't what one expected to see, walking into an eighteenth century palace, one's expectations fuelled by countless photographs and books. And the heightened sense of disappointment that had accompanied our present stay in Jaipur now intensified into fantasies of action.

We thought we should complain to someone, bring these aesthetic crimes to some higher authority's notice. In retrospect, it looks like a naïve resolve: more often than not, higher authorites themselves are the hidden perpetrators and colluders behind such crimes. And in any case, complaints of this sort are token gestures at best.

Nevertheless, full as we were of righteous indignation, we decided to exercise what we felt was a citizen's right. We abandoned our tour of the palace and walked back to the building where, we had been told, the local 'high authority', some sort of musuem director, had his office.

At first we were told by a uniformed peon that Director Sahib was very busy, and could not possibly see us.

We insisted. The peon went back and returned with the news that the director would see us, but only for a few minutes, and after some time.

We strolled around to the old library behind the office and chatted there with some old retainers of the Maharaja. They had served the previous Maharaja and spoke of him with much fondness. We asked them about the dish-antenna, and they shook their heads sadly. Things had gone down rapidly in the last ten years, they said. Had I looked at the shops in the courtyard? The previous Maharaja would never have allowed them within the palace. It was all very depressing, but what could one do?

The director finally called us in, warning us again through his peon that he had very little time to spare. His office was a huge room decorated with old exhibition posters. The director himself was a plump man in his early forties who sat behind a large table with a smug expression on his face that broadly said: 'I know everyone who matters. Who the hell are *you*?' On his table were several framed pictures of the director with Rajiv Gandhi and other clean-cut Yuppie-types who had ruled India from the mid to late eighties.

My friend, a well-travelled man, did most of the talking. He had, he said, visited many wonderful monuments around the world. A good number of them were well looked-after; many were simply abandoned to the elements, and had some grandeur as ruins. But never had he seen a building as old and marvellously intact as the City Palace so flagrantly defaced by its present caretakers. Could he imagine, he asked the director, the scandal if one day a dish-antenna were to appear in plain view atop Windsor Castle or the palace of Versailles?

As my friend spoke, the director's expression changed to one that said: 'I know everyone who matters. And you are clearly a nobody.' He was getting impatient. To his credit, he didn't interrupt my friend and heard him out before producing what he thought was a trump card.

Did we know? he asked menacingly, did we know that the part of the palace we were talking about belongs to the Maharaja? Did we know that it is an act of benevolence on his part to let the common public see it?

As for the dish-antenna, it was his as well; he could put it anywhere he liked in his private residence. Really, what the hell were we *talking* about?

But, we knew all that already. Ownership wasn't the point; no one was contesting the Maharaja's right to watch *Saanp Seedi* and *Choppy & the Princess*. It was a matter of taste. Surely, the dish-antenna could have been positioned out of sight. It was also a matter of money: the Maharajah was charging people to see his palace. The least he could do was not put up any obvious eyesores.

The director's expression changed again. Now it said: 'I know everyone who matters. And I know who has sent you here.' Suddenly becoming very angry, he said we were wasting his time, and that we were agent provocateurs sent by Gayatri Devi to make trouble for the Maharajah. (The Maharajah and Gayatri Devi have been involved in a long and bitter legal battle over property.)

This was absurd, and we told him so. But the director had heard all he wanted. He said he had urgent business to attend to; we had taken enough of his time.

He pressed a bell; a peon instantly appeared with some files in hand; the director made a great show of busying himself with them. It was a signal for us to leave. In any case, there was no point in staying. We had registered our complaint; it had been duly tossed aside. There was nothing more to be said.

At Pushkar, there was some trouble finding the tourist bungalow where we had confirmed bookings. Pushkar is a tiny town clustered round a lake, with no roads but winding alleys that a car cannot negotiate. We kept driving through the outskirts and ended up on the far end of the lake where touts besieged us, and all sorts of 'guides' began volunteering unsolicited information in the expectation of being paid at the end. None of them would give us any directions. Finally, we had to drive back unaided to the road from Ajmer to get to the tourist bungalow.

The name was a misnomer; it wasn't a bungalow at all, but a modern seventies-style building tacked onto an old palace. It was run by the Rajasthan Tourist Development Corporation, and an example of how far the state's unlimited material resources could be stretched. It stood on a huge tract of land beside the lake which few private entrepreneurs would have been able to afford. The rooms were large and airy; there was a garden, a restaurant, a conference hall.

As in a lot of state-run hotels, the initial planning was done right. Then, on the day it opened, things began to go steadily downhill, and never looked up. Apathy and neglect were visible everywhere. The place was overstaffed; waiters and bell-boys hung around the lobby looking underworked; but things still moved in a sluggish, indifferent manner. It took ages to enter our names into the register. I was shown into a room that had no light; curly fluffs of dust lay all over the floor; there wasn't even a solitary mug in the bathroom.

The town itself entirely belied my expectations. My memories were of the colourful sweet-smelling squalor of a pilgrim town, a mini-Hardwar, with shops selling flowers, coconuts, conch-shells, framed calendar-art pictures of divinities, and barfis for *prasad*; people coming back from a dip in the holy waters with their freshly-worn dhotis and sarees hitched up; loudspeakers blaring devotional songs; pariah dogs licking food off squashed leaf plates on the road.

All of that was now gone or confined to a small part of Pushkar. The narrow alleys were still there, but they resembled not those of Hardwar or Benares, but of Thamel,

Kathmandu. There were multi-cuisine restaurants with menus displayed on small boards outside in German, Italian, French, but not English. Shops sold 'Western-style' Rajasthani skirts and jackets, beady necklaces, camera film, and cassettes. Signs tacked to walls pointed to a 'German' bakery. Travel agencies advertised camel and horse rides, and 'pushback' deluxe coaches to Jodhpur and Udaipur. In place of crude loudspeakers tied to electric poles, there were sophisticated stereo systems blasting your eardrums with Nirvana and Bon Jovi.

Then, there were the touts. 'Hotel, hotel, you want? Room with attached bath? I take you.' Then, after figuring out that the hotel deal is off, it was: 'Rajasthani clothes you want? Jacket, skirt, T-shirt, shorts, cap, I take you, reasonable price.' At the next corner, it was: 'You want film? Kodak? Original film, not duplicate.' The travel tout asked: 'You want camel safari, horse safari? Very good arrangement. Please come.' Soon, you were too tired to keep saying no. You put a stern expression on your face; you walked faster; you didn't look them in the face. But they were still with you. 'Hash, hash, fresh Manali hash', went the sibilant whisper now, 'you *want*?' It was a strain simply walking through those alleys.

Happily, like Thamel, there were also well-stocked second-hand bookstores—no touts for these, understandably. They provided a useful indicator of the decline in reading tastes among tourists. The new arrivals were mostly trash: sex, money, glamour, power, *The Secret Life of Jackie O, I'll Take Manhattan*, that sort of thing. The good things were to be found among the dusty, tattered-looking rows. There, I found a paperback edition of John Bayley's only novel. On the same shelf was, surprisingly, V.S. Pritchett's *Dead Man Leading*. That these two grand old men of English letters should be represented here spoke in Pushkar's favour, when nothing else did. Unfortunately, unlike Thamel, the books were not reasonably priced. Both were quoted at Rs 200 each. I decided to indefinitely postpone my reading of both Bayley and Pritchett.

We went looking for the 'German bakery' later and found it not far from the tourist bungalow, overlooking the lake. As the name suggested, there were a lot of Germans present, their get-up improbably 'ethnic'—one woman wore a nose-ring so large it threatened to disfigure her nose for ever; another had anklets the size of fetters; another, an effeminate-looking man, had plaited his shoulder-length hair into the kind of thick braids that made him look a cross between Bo Derek and a Naga sadhu. They sat facing the lake, possibly in meditation: it was hard to tell. One found them in similar poses everywhere. Americans liked nothing better than a game of frisbee; the British went looking for impossibly remote forts and palaces; the Italians spent their time shopping for precious stones and gems; but, the Germans never seemed to go anywhere or do anything. They did not even talk much among themselves. They preferred to stare at empty spaces, and they kept at it for hours on end. Still and silent, with a glazed look on their faces, they looked like people waiting for a revelation from above. Some looked as if they have been waiting for a very long time, and they were the ones known to often go berserk, tearing up their clothes in a frenzy, assaulting passers-by, and generally making a nuisance of themselves.

The bakery lived upto its name by producing apple strudel and carrot cakes as good as any I've had elsewhere. Also, the servings were very generous, so that one could eat a slice of cake and feel sated for hours. The coffee was disappointingly weak, made in the North Indian way, with excessive milk and sugar.

Behind us sat two American girls discussing Krishna.

'I mean, he's a fun-Gaad...it's like...you can relate to him very easily, you know?'

'Whendju get interested in him?'

'I dunno...I dunno...it sorta just happened, you know?...it's like these things are fated to happen, youknowwhatImean?'

'Yeah. I am just beginning to get into some of that stuff myself and, really, it's...it's kinda mindbaaggling, some of this Hindu mythology...there's just so much of it...'

'Oh, it's *incredible*! You know, I keep telling my family...that if they could even look at some of that stuff, I mean...they would understand why I wanna get away from all that Christianity shit.'

'Are your parents kinda...devout Christians?'

'*Devout*?!! Born and raised in North Carolina? You better believe it.'

'I know what you mean. I have an aunt whose cousin married a man from North Carolina...'

'Really, where's he from?'

'Do you know Greensboro?'

'O yeah? I have a cousin who used to live there....'

Here the conversation degenerated into an exchange of inane geographical information.

After a late dinner at a nearby restaurant, I went for a walk through the bazaar. Most of the shops had downed their shutters. Music blared out of the few restaurants that were still open. It was hard to see how anyone could sleep in the vicinity until everything had closed for the night.

I fell in with two friends, Mahesh and Rajkumar, who owned a guest house in Pushkar. I was standing on one of the ghats, dark and deserted at this time, admiring the rather pretty reflection of white-washed houses in the still waters of the lake, when they approached me. We were the only people on the ghat. I couldn't at first hear what they said, and took them to be homosexuals—I had been solicited before by them in uncannily similar circumstances. But they only wanted to know if I was a tourist and, if yes, which hotel I was staying in.

I told them. We talked for a while. Their guest-house had just opened a couple of months back. Business was slack at the moment, and not only because there hadn't been any advertising. In this kind of business, it took some time before a name established itself in tourist consciousness. It was important to get foreigners talking about your hotel; nothing counted so much as word-of-mouth publicity.

They mentioned a 'big tourist guide' foreigners always carried with them and how important it was to get favourably mentioned in it. I deduced they were talking about the *Lonely Planet*. I tried to minimize its importance by pointing out that a large number of non-English-speaking tourists did not refer to it at all. They countered by telling me about a hotelier in Paharganj, Delhi they had met recently. A man from England had stayed with him some years ago. He took good care of him, attended to all his needs. When he left, he identified himself as a researcher for the *Lonely Planet*. The next edition carried the hotel's name and address. Business has trebled since then; the hotelier needs no advertising or publicity of any kind; he is assured of customers all through the year; he is now a rich man.

Both Mahesh and Rajkumar were from Ajmer where their fathers owned small businesses. They had passed out together from school. Mahesh had then stopped studying further. He'd always had a difficult time of it; it seemed pointless to go on struggling in the same way through college. Rajkumar had gone on to take a BA degree, and then had futilely applied for a few jobs with the government. He had even sat for the Provincial Civil Services exam once.

Sab bekar mein, It was all a waste, he told me. To get into government service you needed powerful godfathers, and failing that, money to bribe your way through.

Unlike upper-caste youth who readily blame their failures on the large reserved quotas for backward and scheduled castes, Rajkumar didn't mention them at all; I assumed he was one of their targeted potential beneficiaries.

His voice grew passionate as he gave me examples of how this worked. He had friends who had manoeuvred themselves into jobs in this way.

It all sounded true; there were similar stories to be heard all over India. But things hadn't deteriorated to the extent people believed they had. In all the closed systems of patronage and bribery they described, there was always a tiny aperture talent could still squeeze through.

I asked Rajkumar about his academic record: ambition such as his wasn't always matched by ability. Most of the aspirants for government jobs were so hopelessly inept that their frantic striving could not but be simply pointless.

Rajkumar appeared abashed by my question; it wasn't what he had expected. His voice changed into a lower register as he replied.

It was what I had suspected: he had a second-class degree from a third-class university.

Mahesh, who was silent until now, asked me if I would care for some hot milk. I really didn't; it was close to bed-time; but I wanted to talk more with the two of them, and so said yes.

We had been standing in the dark all this time. Now, as we moved out into a neon-lit street, I saw them for the first time. Both were of almost equal height, wore identical clothes (faded denim jeans and jackets and puffy white sneakers) and hairstyles (long hair falling diagonally across low foreheads) and had on their clean-cut faces the eager earnestness of new entrepreneurs.

I talked to Rajkumar on the way. I feared I had embarrassed him with my questions about his academic performance, and wanted to make amends. I asked him how he came to be interested in the hotel business.

He seemed happy to reply; setting up the hotel was for him a proud achievement which he wanted other people to acknowledge.

It was after his unsuccessful attempts at government service that he turned his mind to business. Somebody told him about the generous subsidies given by the government to hoteliers. Pushkar was then opening up to foreign tourists; it seemed the right place for a hotel.

So, he asked Mahesh, who was then doing odd jobs for a marble-export firm, if he would be interested in being his partner. Mahesh agreed, but could not risk leaving his present position until the hotel looked like a certain reality. So it was Rajkumar who had done the spadework, had run around government offices organizing the loan, acquiring land in Pushkar. Mahesh had joined him at a later stage; together they had supervised the construction of the hotel.

We reached a sweet-shop where Mahesh ordered three glasses of hot milk. Most sweet-shops one sees now have altered beyond recognition. They were once a regular institution in every North Indian town, offering a social space more democratic and diverse than any other comparable place. People from all castes and classes gathered here. A single Hindi newspaper separated into its component parts was passed around. Entire mornings were whiled away in discussing some contemporary event or topic.

The sweet-shops now sported a slick up-market look. Very rarely did one find a corpulent *halwai* seated in front of a huge round *kadhai* full of simmering hot milk. The shops now had glass doors, wide shelves, Formica counters, moulded plastic chairs, with the *halwai* relegated to some invisible place in the back-room.

Fortunately the place we went to was a hold-over from the past. The rolls of fat on the *halwai* looked well-preserved, and even at this late hour there were small groups of people standing around, drinking milk, eating *imarti* and *rabdi*. It looked a place where, as in the past, local gossip was still retailed, current events fervently discussed, reputations made and unmade.

We were joined there by a young man named Dilip. He wore exactly the same clothes and shoes as Mahesh and Rajkumar except that his jacket was fancier, of the kind worn by skinny Bombay film-actors to make their torsos appear wider than they actually are. He paid no attention to me and began loudly telling Rajkumar about a Swedish tourist who had lost her passport.

Apparently, the police had refused to register her complaint since they thought she had sold her passport. She had to call the Swedish embassy for help; they asked her to come to Delhi to receive a new passport.

Dilip appeared to know the tourist well. Or, it may have been the proprietorial way in which he spoke of her. His speech, which he rattled off at great speed, was littered with obscenities; nearly every sentence was prefaced and concluded by *behanchod*. There was something faintly condescending too about his manner with Rajkumar; he had the conceited glibness of those recently blessed with more success than they ever dreamed of.

After he left, I asked Rajkumar about him. Apparently, Dilip too owned a guest-house, but had been in business slightly longer than Mahesh and Rajkumar. His father owned hotels in both Jaipur and Ajmer, but Dilip preferred to stay in Pushkar. He was popular with the tourists; they trusted him enough to often ask him to arrange some *ganja* for them.

I wondered if Dilip had made it to the *Lonely Planet*. I imagined the book patronizing him with something like:

'The hotel is run by a marvellous character called Dilip. He is a great mine of information and always ready to go out of his way to please you. And, unlike most Indians, he always delivers what he promises.'

I asked Mahesh about the kind of tourists that came to Pushkar. He had some problems understanding my question; he clearly wasn't used to making large generalizations about people. Rajkumar replied in his stead.

A lot of tourists were Indian, but they came mostly to bathe on festival days. He himself didn't allow any Indians into his guest-house.

Why? I asked, slightly irked by the peremptory way in which Rajkumar declared this.

Rajkumar searched hard for a reply, then said the Indian tourists were all pilgrims who had filthy habits and thought of hotels as dharamshalas where they could do anything they pleased.

I didn't look convinced, so he added that Indians spread dirty laundry all over the place and foreign tourists who came after them complained they had urinated over the toilet seat, and spilled water all over the bathroom. Then, Indians dirtied the towels and linen in the rooms, and haggled over every little thing.

I was struck by the way Rajkumar used the word 'Indians'. It made him appear a visiting commentator on social habits from a foreign country—a modern-day Alberuni or Bishop Heber. In any other circumstances, his critical distance from his countrymen would have been remarkable; now, it was not without pathos. It was inconceivable that before he built his hotel he knew the ways of western-style toilets, that he did not himself seek bargain prices when he travelled out of Pushkar. His foreign guests had 'modernized' him, and in the process had made him a man curiously at odds with his immediate environment, a man out of step with his own culture.

5

We briefly stopped at Ajmer the next morning in order to visit the Chisti *dargah*. I didn't go in; the scene outside the *dargah* was far more interesting. Kitsch was what was on display there, the lower-middle-class Muslim penchant for gaudy colours finding full release in the blue draperies over the gateway, the Islamic green of Janata Dal's election banners, in tiny kiosks selling screaming-pink *chunnis* and purple shawls with yellow tassels, blue velvet-lined stands for the Quran, glass bangles, and salwar-kameez suits bedizened with tinsel.

The place blazed and crackled with colour; the glare was blinding for the first few minutes; and, it took some optic adjustments to see the skinny young urchins coercing unsuspecting visitors into buying prayer-caps, warning them of dire consequences if they went inside with their heads uncovered. Actually, one didn't need a prayer-cap; a handkerchief on one's head sufficed. But before the poor visitors could realize that, the extortionists were upon them, aggressively hawking their wares, muttering their vague threats.

Business was flourishing in other ways too. A couple of long-haired criminalish young men in Pathan suits strode up to incoming visitors, and ordered them to take off their footwear. Already undermined by the prayer-cap hawkers, the visitors had no choice but to instantly comply, whereupon the young men in one swift swooping motion picked up the shoes and slippers and deposited them under a rickety bench kept adjacent to the stairs.

There were no competitors; this was a cornered market—even for beggars. I had heard of something similar at Mahalaxmi temple in Bombay where beggars paid a regular percentage of their earnings to a mafia in exchange for keeping out rivals from outside and keeping the field uncluttered.

I had heard; but now was the first time I saw the system at work, as when a diminutive beggar, knowingly or unknowingly, intruded upon a reserved space and was soundly thrashed by one of the young men minding the footwear.

He was evidently a man of consequence here. Tall, broad-shouldered and surly-looking, he wore a green Janata Dal bandanna around his head and a baggy Pathan suit. No one stepped in to interfere as he repeatedly slapped the beggar, snatched off his fez cap, threw it on the ground, and kicked it—unsuccessfully, as it turned out, his foot missing the cap by a few inches and describing an airy arc over it.

This infuriated him even further, and now he aimed his kick at a surer target: the beggar's abdomen. His victim, who had soundlessly received his blows until then, howled with pain at this. Encouraged, the man kicked him again, this time on his bony buttocks.

The scene began to draw attention. People stopped to stare; I saw, in a party of French tourists that had just arrived, a silver-haired man steady his Camcorder and prepare to shoot.

Then, abruptly, a couple of mysterious situation-controllers emerged from somewhere, smiling indulgently, and restrained the young man; they appeared to be commiserating with him as they led him away. The beggar limped off and quickly disappeared down a long crowded alley. I saw the French tourist aim his Camcorder's snout at him, and then suddenly lower it as the beggar moved out of range. He looked both excited and disappointed. Excited at what he had managed to capture; disappointed at what he hadn't. The tourists began to move again; the prayer-cap hawkers returned to business with renewed frenzy; shoes and slippers were energetically pounced upon and whisked away. As abruptly as it had begun, the scene ended.

We drove south from Ajmer through an empty flat landscape. The real desert was still miles away; but the land was uncropped; there were camel-scrubs beside the road; and the trees wore the stunted skeletal look of the desert.

There was little traffic except for huge overloaded trucks on their way to Ahmedabad, and on this deserted road, and in this featureless landscape, every other kind of vehicle was an event. There were overcrowded tempos with passengers bulging out of the doors, clinging to windows, sitting cross-legged on roofs, staring blankly all the time at passing cars. An Ambassador with Haryana Government number plates shot past us at what looked like an impossible speed for an Ambassador. A long convoy of Army jeeps overtook us by the simple stratagem of blocking our way while they poured onto the highway from a side road. A cane-wielding Captain stood in front of a jeep positioned sideways across the road, and imperiously gestured all vehicles to a stop. We trailed behind the convoy for quite some time, all our honked pleadings falling on deaf ears, before we were allowed to overtake them. Sitting stiffly in the back of open jeeps, holding their automatic rifles, the army men eyed us warily as we went past.

Tiny settlements cluttered the horizon, came closer, and were revealed to be patches of ragtag buildings arrayed along the road. A couple of motor-repair shops, a few shops selling sticky red and yellow sweets, a dhaba, a well, men sunk in sagging string cots, faded election posters on walls, broken dusty paths between buildings, grain-merchants poring over their low-slung desks, tidy rows of children at an open-air school, pools of black, foetid water, a billboard for either Charminar or Red & White cigarettes, a hopeful lift-seeker—and then we would be in empty country again, miles and miles of scarcely a building or person.

Sometime in the afternoon, we left the highway and came on to a narrow road. For much of the way the road had kept well away from the Aravalli hills. But their rock-strewn treeless slopes never went out of sight, and now, suddenly, they were before us. The road began its slow ascent, twisting and turning in tortuous loops; the trucks lost their flamboyant highway speeds and groaned as they negotiated the steep inclines.

The scrubland gradually gave way to wooded hills. Thickly leafed trees shaded the road here; filtered through their dense cover, the sun beams caught the swirling dust in our wake, and illuminated every particle. This was sheep and goat country; we ran into some large herds, surprising both animals and masters. Then the hills were behind us, and we emerged on to a flat and straight stretch of road. There were mustard fields on either side. A few buildings appeared in the far distance, old ramparts and gateways. Soon, we would be at our destination, and able to bathe, eat, relax. For the first time since we started from Pushkar, I had a pleasant sense of well-being.

Ghanerao, an old frontier outpost of the kingdom of Mewar, is now a village, no bigger than a medium-sized *mohalla* in a small town. Surrounded by a dense cluster of old and new houses, and approached through a bewildering network of narrow alleys, it has an old haveli which its hereditary owners have converted into a hotel, and where we were to spend two days. The haveli—called, with typical exaggeration, the Ghanerao Royal Castle—is large and airy, with stables, carved balconies and open courtyards.

Our host was Mr Tomar, a swarthy, slender, pleasant-looking man in his fifties, dressed informally in T-shirt and jeans, with a very suave manner.

Very quickly, over welcoming cups of tea (for which, I discovered later, we were charged), he assured us that he was unlike other haveli-hotel owners in that he was indifferent to money-making. He had enough for a comfortable existence. But he had been bequeathed the haveli; he felt responsible towards it; he felt he owed something to his great ancestors.

What happened in his case—and no doubt, countless others—was that he had increasingly found his own resources too inadequate to maintain the haveli. In other words, he had literally been coerced into opening it to tourists. It was either that or watching a beautiful house fall into ruin. It was apparently with a heavy heart that Mr Tomar had made his choice.

But he was careful about his guests; not just anyone could stay at his haveli. He wasn't, for instance, having any 'neo-rich' types at his house—No, sir. Rapidly, he reeled out the names and titles of his distinguished guests. It sounded like the *Almanach de Gotha*. Former and present High Commissioners and Ambassadors, members of the British aristocracy, Dukes and Duchesses, Viscounts and Viscountesses, Lords and Ladies—Mr Tomar knew them all. They had stayed at his haveli and greatly enjoyed his hospitality; they had left singing his praises; they had promised to be back.

Mr Tomar spoke of them with a casual intimacy that hinted at relationships deeper than those that usually exist between hotel managers and guests. He spoke too of other important people in his exclusive clientele—senior ministers, captains of industry, world-class sportsmen, award-winning filmmakers—but made it seem as if he was especially chummy with the English upper classes. He came back to them repeatedly, throwing out a name and then asking us if we knew the person. Then, without waiting for our response, he would take another name, and so on.

Finally, he asked a minion hovering in the background to fetch the visitor's book; and then sat smiling, an untouched cup of tea in his hand, as we turned the well-thumbed pages, looking at each name very closely, and waiting for a bell to ring somewhere.

No bells rang; there was not a name we could recognize. It may have been that Mr Tomar's Dukes and Duchesses and Lords and Ladies travelled under assumed names, and that the woman with the California address was the alternative-fur-heiress, but it didn't seem much likely.

I said, handing back the visitor's book, and meeting Mr Tomar's expectant smile, 'You seem to know an amazing number of English aristocrats.'

'Oh, yes,' he instantly responded. 'You see, for us, it's a small world.'

The haveli's most distinguished visitor so far, Mr Tomar informed us, had been the great chronicler of Rajput history, James Tod. Mr Tomar had an autographed portrait to prove it—not that we doubted, or wanted proof of, anything he was saying.

'I'll show you the portrait before you leave,' he said.

In the meantime, his cup of tea turning cold in his hand, he led us through a Tod-assisted, dizzying tour of Rajput genealogies, underlining insistently the great political and strategic significance of Ghanerao, illuminating his various connections with ruling families all over Rajasthan.

Towards the end of his exhaustive survey, he repeated: 'You see, for us, it's a small world.'

Just then, striking a serious blow to his claims to prestige and exclusivity, arrived a family of Marwari Yuppies from Bombay. Corpulence was their family motif, along with tight multi-coloured T-shirts stretched over globular paunches. Gold and diamond rings flashed on all their hands; together, the women—a mother and daughter pair—wore enough jewellery to open a shop with. The males—two teenaged boys and their father— compensated for their lack of nose-rings and earrings by wearing thick, ankle-length, fluorescent-striped Force 10 sneakers.

Perhaps they *did* own a jewellery shop, perhaps several, perhaps even Ghanerao Royal Castle, judging by the way Mr Tomar, abruptly abandoning us, leapt to attention. The cup of tea was still in his hand, and it was only now, as the Marwari man held out his hand to shake, that Mr Tomar noticed it.

He busied himself with them; we were finally shown to our suite. It had a spartan appearance which came from not having such regular items as chairs and tables. In their place, there was a thin mattress and a single bolster on the balcony. The bathroom was similarly bare, with just a solitary plastic bucket and mug. There was no power; we had been assured it would come soon. But when it did, the bulbs' feeble glow was just enough to see one's hand in the gloomy claustrophobic dark.

It was clear that, following other haveli-hotel owners, Mr Tomar too had put to clever and profitable use the Rajput ideal of austerity—an admirable notion which, however, in its present context amounted to no more than a ruse to maximize profits to the highest extent possible while minimizing investments to an extent never thought possible by any hotelier in the world. Plainly put, it was a cover for miserliness, for a failure—inexcusable, given the wincingly high tariffs—to provide basic facilities like hot water, proper lighting, and beds which didn't sag like hammocks and, after a sleepless night, left one with an aching back for most of the next day.

Dinner that night was equally frugal: dry potatoes, a yellowish liquid which presumably was 'dal', lukewarm chapatis, rice—all this for Rs 150 per head.

We ate in a large, dimly-lit dining-hall, attended by a couple of submissive-looking servants; with its mounted trophies, stuffed animal heads and framed photos of Mr Tomar's ancestors, it was a place sombre with memories. The only anachronism was a bookshelf full of sex-and-murder novels. At adjacent tables sat a stout, middle-aged English couple, both of whom I had seen arrive early in the evening, clutching heavy British editions of *A Suitable Boy*; a German couple who were planning with Mr Tomar in painstaking detail their trip to Kumbhalgarh Fort the next day; and, a party of Dutch tourists who had been there for some time, and who were arguing in raised agitated voices—probably about whether dinner tonight was as awful or not as lunch this afternoon.

The Marwaris were absent; so was the Indian-American family that had arrived some time back, filling the silent empty courtyard behind us with their twangy American accents and voluminous suitcases.

Mr Tomar moved from table to table. I intermittently heard him speaking to the German couple. He pointed at the framed photos on the walls, and spoke about James Tod's autograph; about his ancestors; about how impossible it was to maintain the haveli with his limited resources; about the tragic compromise he had to make in converting part of his haveli into a hotel; about his determination to not open his haveli to all and sundry. In between, he said at least three-four times: 'You see, for us, it's a small world.'

He then sat with the English couple and pointing to the framed photos on the wall, told them about Colonel Tod's autograph; about his ancestors; about how impossible it was to maintain the haveli with his limited resources; about the tragic compromise he had to make in converting part of the haveli into a hotel; about his determination to not open it to all and sundry; and, about how for him it was a small world.

He joined us at the fag end of our dinner, smiling his suave smile, and solicitous for our welfare. He asked us if we had any problems with our rooms; then, without waiting for us to reply, said that he was thinking of installing cordless telephones in every room so that his guests wouldn't have to come down to the main hall everytime they wanted something.

My friend said, his tongue firmly in his cheek: 'But, this wouldn't be the same place if you bring in such modern appliances, would it?'

Mr Tomar brightened up at that: 'No, of course not. You are very right. You see I really want to give people the original experience. They can get their luxuries in any five-star hotel. But where would they get the experience of living in a haveli like this?'

He then pointed towards the photos on the walls, and after some brief preliminary remarks about his ancestors, told us about Colonel Tod's autograph; about his ancestors; about how impossible it was to maintain the haveli with his limited resources; about the tragic compromise he had to make....

Halfway through his spiel, Mr Tomar was interrupted.

It was the teenaged boy from the Indian-American family that had arrived some time ago.

'Excuse me,' he said, 'may I have a boddle of Bissleri wadder?'

A nonplussed Mr Tomar looked at us first, and then, at him.

'Sorry,' he said, shaking his head in apology, 'I didn't hear you.'

The boy repeated: 'May I have a boddle of Bissleri wadder?'

Mr Tomar heard him attentively; then lunged at the only word he could guess at.

'Oh, *Bisleri!*' he cried, 'Yes, of *course!* How many bottles?'

Later at night, sitting out on the balcony, I saw Mr Tomar in his annoyingly well-lit house. He had given us the impression that part of the haveli was still occupied by him; but that was apparently not true. His house was not in the main building at all, but in a relatively very new and small annexe. Mr Tomar's compromises did seem truly tragic.

He sat all alone on the verandah, intermittently puffing a pipe, his lips otherwise set in a tight clinch, staring straight ahead with a look of demonic concentration on his face.

I was struck by that look. It wasn't of the person we had met earlier in the day, and then later at dinner: naïvely boastful, socially ambitious, ready to please, a simple man, in short. He had retreated from that self and into what could only be a difficult solitude. People that gregarious are hard to imagine alone, or credit with a complex inner life, so complete is their dependence on other people. But that look on Mr Tomar's face now hinted at other things:

at self-awareness, the knowledge of his diminished worth, his daily abasement in front of sundry daytrippers, things, which in these circumstances, could not but be a source of pain.

We went the next morning to visit the fort at Kumbhalgarh. Mr Tomar arranged—at a prohibitive price—for the jeep that took us. He sent along his son, a tall thick-set man in jeans, and a servant armed with a lathi—ostensibly to defend us against bears and crocodiles, which, Mr Tomar assured us, were abundant around Ghanerao.

We went down and up deep shaded ravines, and emerged atop a flat sun-lit plateau. Pyramid-shaped haystacks and low-slung mud villages lined the road; cows with horns as elaborately curved as Rajput moustaches looked up from their grazing to see us go past.

A chilly wind blew in through the open jeep, but Mr Tomar's son, wearing just a thin cotton shirt, seemed immune to it. That he was known, even feared, in this area became apparent when roadside passersby instantly shrank at his sight and raised their right hand in reflexive salute.

Mr Tomar's son, taking these attentions as his normal due, acknowledged them with a curt nod.

A deep gorge; a dam; an artificial lake; and, suddenly, after an abrupt bend in the road, there was the fort above us, its walls sinuously stretching as far as the eye could see in either direction. We passed under the massive gates, and then came up a steep ramp to the inner periphery.

A local guide wearing dark blue polyester pants and a white tericot shirt attached himself to us as we walked up the thick ramparts, and began relating the various acts of bravery and chivalry performed in the cause of defending the fort. In addition, he informed us that American astronauts had reported seeing the fort's walls from outer space.

I was about to challenge this, but then stopped. The guide was young, thin and nervous; his English, surprisingly unaccented and precise. Pride and uncertainty flickered alternately on his thickly moustached face; he spoke with the unassailable confidence that a college-education in the midst of general illiteracy gives one. He clearly believed what he had been told by someone about the astronauts. The knowledge gave an extra-terrestrial significance to the fort; it helped him reconcile himself to the drudgery and desolation of his life in Kumbhalgarh—mostly spent waiting, it seemed, for the odd tourist to turn up. It seemed unfair to deprive him of that.

I examined the visitor's book on the walk up to Badal Mahal. The adjectival overkill was overwhelming. 'Romantic', 'brilliant', 'extraordinary', 'the most beautiful place on earth', 'I have fallen in love with this fort', etc.

And, indeed, the views of the surrounding plains from Badal Mahal were breathtaking. But after my breath had been taken enough times, I went back early by jeep, leaving my friends to battle it out against bears and crocodiles on their trek through thick jungles to Ghanerao.

The jeep was driven this time by one of Mr Tomar's servants, a surly, uncommunicative young man with a tiny gold earring in his left ear, who stopped repeatedly to take on and drop off paying passengers. Since we were already being charged for the ride, this seemed a way for the driver to make some extra income on the sly. He first tried to make it seem he was taking on people out of charity, going to the back of the jeep where I could not see him to receive his fares. Later, when it became too apparent, he dropped the pretence and instead tried to appease me by offering me a cup of tea. I gently refused the offer. He insisted. I refused again; and then sat back for the rest of the drive wondering what local custom I had contravened when the driver, looking enraged by my refusal, addressed no further words to me, and drove back fast and furiously to Ghanerao.

We left Ghanerao the next day. Mr Tomar looked relieved to see us go as our departure left him free to prepare for the arrival that morning of a large seventy-member party of Swiss tourists. He had told us, a bit shamefacedly, about them the previous evening. It was another blow to his claims to exclusivity. And it was clear now that despite all his assertions to the contrary, Mr Tomar hankered after the tourist business.

A further confirmation came just before we left. He asked me casually, as we stood waiting for my friend's car, what I did for a living. I told him I wrote for newspapers. He immediately perked up, and said: 'I hope you'll write good things about Ghanerao, and give it some publicity. We badly need it.'

This clashed with almost everything he had said before about the haveli. But Mr Tomar was beyond simple contradiction. He meant everything he said: feudal pride made him want to protect his haveli from being swamped by tourists; financial exigencies made him want to attract more tourists to his haveli. Both desires existed in equal measure; both were equally legitimate.

We drove south over a bumpy narrow road to Ranakpur. A few miles out of Ghanerao we ran into Mr Tomar's Swiss guests. They were travelling in a bright red wide-bodied bus which wouldn't have looked out-of-place in Montreux, but which, parked right in the middle of a rural *sabji mandi* in Rajasthan, looked like an emanation from outer space. The impression was reinforced by the pink-skinned, yellow-haired tourists who were out in full force, gingerly picking their way through cow dung and slush, glaringly incongruous in this setting. They had the barely restrained eagerness of people who have finally chanced upon the real thing. And indeed, they had. The broken road, the wandering cows, the open gutter, the low ramshackle shops, the ground littered with garbage, the pressing crowd, the dust—this *was* the real India, poor, filthy, backward; and, cameras and camcorders pressed to their faces, the tourists were making the most of it.

At Ranakpur, inside the sprawling temple compound, there was parked a whole fleet of air-conditioned video buses with Gujarat number plates. The Adinatha temple ranks high on the list of Jain reverences, and the visitors were mostly wealthy Jains. But it wasn't easily apparent from the stickers on the buses. These exhorted one to be a proud Hindu: *Garv se kaho ham Hindu hain*. There were pictures of the proposed Ram temple at Ayodhya, and of Ram himself, as imagined by the Vishwa Hindu Parishad (VHP), fierce-looking and appallingly muscle-bound, resembling no one more than Rambo in a *dhoti*.

I had read previously about the Jain support for the pro-temple movement. It had seemed a contradiction, not as blatant as the anti-idolatory Arya Samaj's support for the temple, yet, from all that one knew about Jainism as a decisive break from mainstream Hinduism, very strange indeed. But then, so were, for a religion and adherents supposedly so ascetical, the air-conditioned video buses, and even more so the sensually replete temple, its finely detailed ceilings, its elaborately sculpted pillars, no two of which, the guide repeatedly emphasized, are alike.

After a tour of the temples, I chatted with a teenaged boy who had come on one of the buses with his family.

He wore a printed Hawaiian shirt and purple stonewashed jeans; his hair was short, perhaps in deference to his parents' wishes, but cut stylishly. He was from Rajkot, and had the bold over-assertive manner of small-town *jeunesse dorée*. I could see him hurtling down Rajkot's broadest street in his Maruti 1000. I could see him eating ice-cream with his cronies at the local parlour, and ogling young housewives. I could see him surreptitiously watching porn films at his house, and discussing them fervently at school the next day.

He was poring over a stack of video tapes in the driver's cabin when I approached him. He was looking for *Khalnayak* to screen on the way back to Rajkot. He had seen it two times already; he was planning to see it a few times more. No, he didn't much care for *Choli Ke Peechhe Kya Hai*. He was more taken with Sanjay Dutt.

Why? I asked.

He thought briefly, and then said: 'He's got a good body...he can play all roles, he can become a villain, he can become a hero.'

I asked him if he aspired to have a body like Sanjay Dutt's. He did. In fact, he had already started working on it; he went to the gym regularly and worked out with light weights.

I asked him if he had visited Mahatma Gandhi's home in Rajkot.

But he didn't even know it existed. He said it was in Porbander.

I said Porbander was where Gandhi was born; Rajkot was where his family had a house.

But he insisted I was wrong, so I asked him about the VHP stickers on the buses. He said they were put there by his family. He couldn't understand my next question, or, why someone should feel so puzzled to find pro-temple sentiments among Jains.

I had to resort to a catechism-like questioning to make

myself clear.

'Are you a Hindu?' I asked.

'No.'

'Are you a Jain?'

'Yes.'

'Do you worship Ram at your home?'

'No.'

'So, why do you want a temple in Ayodhya?'

He thought hard for some time, and then said: 'Because we are Hindus.'

'But you just said you were not a Hindu?'

'No, I didn't say that. All Jains are Hindus.'

'In what way?'

He again thought hard, and then said: 'Because both Jains and Hindus go to temples...'

He paused, still thinking hard.

I waited.

'....And both are vegetarians...'

'This is not true,' I said, 'a lot of Hindus eat meat.'

'But they are not real Hindus.'

We seemed to be getting nowhere, so I asked him if he had liked the Adinatha temple.

But he was still thinking about my question, and now he said: 'I'll tell you why Hindus and Jains are one. Because they have the same enemy.' *Ek hi dushman*, he said, dramatically, as if announcing a forthcoming Hindi film.

'*Kaun*, Who?' I asked even though I knew.

'The Mohammeddans. *Woh saale jab tak saaf nahin ho jaate, Hindu aur Jain ek rahenge*, Until they are finished off, Hindus and Jains will remain one.'

I said the Mohammedans were too numerous to be 'finished off' in that way.

He said they would be exterminated one by one. *Chun chun ke maarenge*—another line taken from Hindi films.

But it wasn't just teenage posturing. He was echoing

a sentiment more popular and widespread than one thought. He had probably heard it uttered by someone in his family, or, in his circle of friends. Like them, he was oblivious to the morality of his desires and actions. Even logistics didn't concern him; he actually believed it possible to kill a hundred million Muslims. He was well on his way to becoming one of the new 'liberated' people you increasingly met in the most inapposite of contexts. You met them at your homes, they were friends of the family, they were, at times, your own relatives. You had known them for a long time, they formed the familiar backdrop to your life, and now, suddenly, you realized with a shock that you had never really known them. They were people who had transcended both good and evil because they never knew them, and who had translated the notion of *laissez faire.* into both economic and social terms——banal, middle-class producers-consumers who wore Hawaiian shirts and stonewashed jeans, regularly visited temples, abhorred meat, and concealed murder in their hearts.

6

Travelling through Rajasthan was proving a more tiring business than I had expected. That I had a book to write meant a state of total alertness on my part. But, on these long drives through empty desertscapes, through the monotonous squalor of passing settlements, the eye was gradually losing its power to discern, the mind was becoming an unsettling blank.

In similar circumstances in the past, reading had always restored concentration. But now I found myself too exhausted every night to read. What I needed was a rest; and Udaipur, the city which alone appeared to measure up to guidebook hyperbole, was the most suitable place to have it in.

I stayed at the Shikarbadi hotel, a few kilometres out of town, in a pleasant setting of green lawns, a deer park, a stud farm, peacocks, wild boars and monkeys. This was supposedly the peak season, but there were few other guests around; and, undistracted, one could while away whole afternoons sitting under a neem tree, alternately reading Iris Murdoch and dozing.

A few days of such stillness and solitude, and then I was ready to go out again.

I went around the tourist sights—the City Palace, Jagdish temple, Saheliyon-ki-bari. I went for a cruise around Lake Pichola. I ate an overcooked, greasy, and hideously expensive meal at the Lake Palace Hotel, overlooking a fish pond lit by a tacky string of white lights one finds in rural marriages, and surrounded by a large noisy group of American exchange students in ill-fitting saris.

I did all that, I looked around, I talked to people, and still my notebook remained, apart from some disconnected trivia, accusingly blank.

It wasn't my fault, I thought. Udaipur had settled into a kind of touristy blandness which turned all observation into guidebook fodder.

There were conference facilities at every big hotel. Festivals, conferences, seminars: the place seemed an ideal setting for them. Some weeks ago, there had been an international film festival for children. I had watched the closing ceremony on Doordarshan one empty afternoon in Simla. The camera was still when I first switched on the television set; people were waiting for the chief guest to arrive. Commentators mouthed inanities about the 'cool evening,' 'august gathering,' 'honourable chief guest,' 'prestigious foreign delegates'; then, fell inexplicably silent for minutes on end.

Half an hour later, during which time I finished two newspapers, they were still waiting, and the closing ceremony now resembled an independence-day function of a local primary school with its neat rows of uniformed children waiting to burst into song, its restless adults obsequiously lined alongside a red carpet to receive the honourable chief guest, its frenetic behind-the-scenes activity, its hectic aimlessness and profound irrelevance.

The chief guest finally arrived to the sound of trumpets in the invisible background, a corpulent self-important figure in white starched khadi. The adults bowed and scraped as he went past them to his red-satin-upholstered throne on the podium. The amphitheatre was soon resounding with his praise, delivered in true Rajput bardic style by a turbanned, impressively moustached man with a red carnation in his buttonhole.

Then, as the prestigious foreign delegates looked on resentfully, the chief guest was called upon to speak. Waddling towards the mike, he unrolled an ominously thick wad of pages, and proceeded to bore everyone stiffer with a long, rambling speech.

It was a scene of pure futility, and, in its mix of sycophancy with bumbling inefficiency, typically of the small town. Watching it, I had felt encouraged; Udaipur promised much. Now, I felt deceived. A city of visitors, it appeared to have no inner life of its own; it waxed and waned with the tourist season and one could imagine it completely deserted during high summer, the scorching *loo* blowing unencumbered through its empty palaces and streets.

But I didn't leave empty-handed. On my penultimate day in Udaipur, I went to the railway station to buy some magazines from the bookstall there. On my way back, I stopped at a nearby tea-shack, and met Munna.

He was sitting next to me on the rickety bench, all the insecurity of his state concentrated in the way he sat crouched over his glass of tea, gripping it with both hands, looking down at his slightly ripped canvas shoes. He was wearing a tight flower-patterned tericot shirt a few sizes too small; his white trousers had turned black with grime in several places. Beside him on the bench was a vinyl bag on which the maker's label said: 'Made in USA'. His complexion was dark, not the sun-induced swarthiness of Rajasthanis, but the more elemental colour found in Eastern and Southern India. From both appearance and manner, he looked an outsider, someone remotely familiar, someone I could place, from my experience of these places, in Bihar or Eastern UP.

I was eager to talk to him, but he looked too far gone into his shell. He had probably been like this for many days now, noticing nothing of his new surroundings, fear and nervousness relentlessly preying on him.

I thought up a few first lines, then opted for the most direct approach. Leaning forward, I softly asked him if he was from UP.

He looked up awkwardly from his glass of tea at me. Uncertainly, his eyes lingered on my face for a few seconds, travelled down to take in my clothes, before coming up full of certain knowledge.

I knew well that appraising look; it was constantly directed at me in the days I had spent in the Hindi heartland, by people curious to know both my caste and class at first glance. They were important in even the most casual kind of social interaction; only when they were duly ascertained could a conversation really begin.

Assured by what he saw on my face and clothes, he slowly nodded, a ghost of a smile hovering on his thick lips.

Which part of UP? I asked.

Ghazipur district, he said, his smile slowly broadening.

So I was right: Eastern UP it was.

He wanted to know if I too was from Ghazipur.

His question had the eager enthusiasm of people who, lonely and distraught in an alien country, attach themselves to anyone they consider their compatriot. I could have given him the purest pleasure by saying I was from Ghazipur; and, in these circumstances, he would have believed me, despite his instinctive knowledge of who was and who wasn't a native of Ghazipur.

But that would have meant lying to him. What I now said was closer to the truth.

I said, 'No, I am from Allahabad,' trying to make Allahabad sound like Ghazipur.

He still looked pleased. Allahabad wasn't too far from Ghazipur after all.

He spoke freely to me for the next one hour. Most people clammed up at the sight of my notebook. But it did not affect him at all. He did not even ask me why I wanted to jot down everything, and, patiently, he repeated things I missed the first time.

His name was Munna Yadav, and he lived in a small Yadav village some twenty kilometres out of Ghazipur town. His father was a farmer; so were his elder brothers. He was the youngest of six children. He had dropped out of the village school after the fifth standard.

When I asked why, he first said it was because he didn't like studying much. Later, he added it was also because the teachers at school had a grudge against his father, and took their revenge by brutally beating him. They hit him on his hands till they bled.

And he spread his hands before me, as if to display some still-surviving scars. I looked, but I could not see any at all.

The beatings broke his heart, he said. Then one day he took his books and threw them into the river; he never went back to school after that.

He had then tried to help his father and brothers in their work. Not long after, he realized that the land they had wasn't enough to provide for all of them. There weren't too many means of livelihood where he lived; he knew he had to get out of there.

He had an elder sister who lived in Jalandhar, Punjab, and who now invited him to live with her until he found a job.

I asked him about this sister. It seemed to me extraordinary that someone from so insular and backward a place as a small village in Ghazipur district could have gone all the way to Jalandhar in distant Punjab.

He explained that his sister was married to a migrant labourer from Ghazipur, who had saved enough money working in Punjab to buy some land for himself near Jalandhar. He had been doing very well since then; he had recently built a proper house for himself. The cost came to a full two lakh of rupees. Munna repeated the figure.

When had this happened? I wanted to know. When did his sister marry? But Munna wasn't good with precise dates. All he could say was: eight-nine years ago.

So, all through the bloodiest years of the separatist movement in Punjab, Munna's sister and her husband had been slowly working their way up. Migrant labourers from UP and Bihar, I could remember, had been favourite targets for militants; they were usually massacred in droves; and it was when the government paid out its lowest compensation. Munna's sister and her husband had lived through all that. And, they had not only survived, they had flourished.

Munna went to Jalandhar, but found it difficult to stay there for more than a few days. It wasn't that his sister and brother-in-law were unhelpful. On the contrary, they never even asked him to work and gave him a whole room to himself in their house. His home in Ghazipur had just two rooms and he shared them with seven other people and two buffaloes. Now was the first time he had slept all alone in a room, and he couldn't sleep the first few nights; he missed the sounds of other people breathing close to him; he missed the warm, strong-smelling presence of the buffaloes tethered close by.

No, he left because he felt he couldn't go on receiving his sister's hospitality while he was still without any hope of being able to repay it. In his family, he explained, it is brothers who take care of their sisters and not vice versa.

People from his caste and village had settled in Delhi. One of them owned a tea-shop in Shakarpur. Munna had his address; one day he presented himself at his place and asked for a job. He was hired on the spot. His job was to serve tea and clean used glasses; he also performed several other assorted tasks. For this, he was paid Rs 450 a month.

He slept inside the shop, bathed at the municipal tap, ate with the shopowner's family, but the money wasn't enough. He earned some more on the sly by collecting old newspapers, and then selling them when he had a pile of them.

I was curious to know what he had made of the places he had visited. What impression had they made on someone who had never travelled out of his village? But Munna could tell me nothing about that. In both Jalandhar and Delhi, he had found people from his region; he had stuck close to them, and had lived a small-scale, circumscribed life not much different from the one he had known in Ghazipur.

I wanted to know what was he doing in Udaipur.

He knew his opportunities in Delhi were limited; he had long wanted to leave. Then, he had come to know about someone from his village who worked in a factory in Ahmedabad, and who had helped two persons he knew find good jobs in the same factory. So, now he was on his way to Ahmedabad. Travel was expensive. Luckily, a truck-driver he knew from Delhi had given him a free lift to Udaipur; he had also given him the name of a driver who travelled frequently to Ahmedabad, and who could give him another lift. The driver came daily to this tea-shack. Munna had been waiting for him to arrive when I asked him if he was from UP.

What a life he had led! And what a story it was, so quintessentially of upcoming India. From that small village in Ghazipur district, people had fanned out in all directions. Slowly but steadily, they had established themselves in their presently secure positions in life. Success in their new settings had not made them discard their village ways. Their caste and clan loyalties were intact; and, it was the awareness of them, the knowledge that in those frighteningly strange cities there still were tiny oases of familiarity, that made it possible for others to leave. It was what had given Munna the courage to strike out on his own. Jalandhar, Delhi, and now Ahmedabad: his world had expanded fast enough to unman anyone; and to me he had at first appeared lost and adrift in it. But I was wrong. In the new world he had entered, he was more protected than most people. They had fallen out of the invisible network of old loyalties and patronage; he was still within it. And, as long as he remained there, he was safe.

7

I rejoined my friends and left Udaipur early in the morning of the year's last day, our departure hastened by the imminent New Year's-eve festivities.

The noise was already horrendous: loud pop music— *Saturday Night Fever* alternating with Pearl Jam—blaring out of restaurants. It threatened to get even more unbearable as the day progressed with almost every hotel promising, on big fluorescent posters, a 'grand gala feast'. Crude hand-painted posters held out invitations to private parties, almost all of these hosted, curiously enough, by mixed couples: Karen & Dinesh, Susan & Mohinder, Laura & Vivek. If the idea was to have a racially mixed crowd, it was well on its way to being hugely successful. At Rs 150 per person, every young hooligan one saw on the road shouting Hindi obscenities at passing white women was certain to be there, drunkenly tottering up to complete strangers, and earnestly asking them, according to the stories I had heard, if they would like to have sex with him. The Lake Palace hotel proclaimed its distance from such sordidness by first pricing its tickets at a steep Rs 1,500, and then pompously stipulating formal dress for all New Year revellers. All in all, it was a good time to leave for a quieter place like Bundi.

Bundi lies on the base of a hollow concavity formed by two steep hillsides. A sprawling fort looms high over the town; below it is the high-walled City Palace, majestic in its isolation and indifference. The houses are whitewashed with a sky-blue tinge in the Rajasthani manner. The streets in the new quarter are broad but, approaching a crowded intersection, abruptly narrow. On them, at unexpected intervals, are speedbreakers the size of hillocks. We had some trouble passing over one of them. The first time the car's underside scraped noisily against the absurdly high rump. We hastily reversed, and were just beginning to wonder if it wasn't more prudent to turn back and take another road when, in an instant, a crowd of advice-and suggestion-givers formed around the car. Some suggested an alternate road; others thought the speedbreaker could be negotiated. The latter were in a majority; they influenced us into another attempt.

More people came out of nearby shops and houses to watch us; boredom, from present evidence, was endemic here. From the expectant faces around us, we could have been stunt-jumping over a row of burning buses. A tiny hush of anticipation went around as we approached the speedbreaker; it seemed likely that bets had been quickly placed on our chances. I wouldn't have been surprised to know that the speedbreaker was a long-standing source of entertainment here.

The way up the rump was smooth enough. It was on the way down that we heard the sickening noise. It was still reverberating in our ears when we heard the applause and cheers behind us. The damage, whatever it was, had been done; and some consolation lay in the fact that we had made the onlookers' day.

Other people we met on the way made theirs by consistently misdirecting us to the point where we overshot our destination and travelled five or six kilometres out of town. It wasn't deliberate on their part—far from it. They looked over-eager to help; but they were without a correct sense of direction and distance; they ended up making wildly unspecific guesses.

After several divagations, we finally arrived at the palace-cum-guest-house to find the driveway barred by a set of massive iron doors. A small side-door was open; we got out of the car and went in through that.

There was a fenced-in garden to our right, melancholy and desolate in the fading light. To our left was the palace building, a squat, unmemorable affair, so designed that one could sit in any part of it and look out over the dully glistening lake—which was what I had intended to do after a bath and after writing in my notebook.

A lone decrepit-looking man standing at the top of the stairs to the palace regarded us suspiciously as we walked up. He was the chowkidar, and had the crankiness of his solitary occupation. I asked him if there were any rooms available. His reply was a harsh guttural 'No'.

I sought to challenge this. Who was staying in these rooms anyway on New Year's eve? And, where *were* the rooms?

'Judge sahib,' the chowkidar said.

Had he taken *all* the rooms?

He was even more disconsolately succinct this time: Yes, 'Judge sahib' had taken all the rooms for the night; he was about to arrive any moment; he didn't want us in his way; and so, could we get out as fast as possible?

We went back to the Rajasthan tourism hotel we had passed on the way. There was a big police bus parked inside the compound; armed policemen lounged about on the abraded lawn, playing cards, reading newspapers, munching peanuts. The man at the reception was sympathetic, but unhelpful. He had only one vacant room; the rest had been taken by 'Judge sahib'.

Judge sahib, it seemed, was travelling with a very large

entourage. I wondered if he was paying for any of his living arrangements. I wondered too if his reservations were decoys, made as if to deceive a potential assassin.

I asked the man at the reception about Judge sahib. Where was he from? What was he doing here in Bundi on a Sunday evening?

But he didn't know, or, if he did, wasn't telling me.

We drove back to the circuit house, our hopes of finding accommodation in Bundi rapidly dimming. The circuit house was the most likely place for Judge sahib to stay in. It would cost him nothing at all; it was where he and his family would be assured of maximum hospitality from the local administration.

And the circuit house, when we got there, looked as if it was full, waiting for Judge sahib to arrive. The driveway was blocked with government jeeps and cars. There were people on the lawn, lower-level officials rushing about, hysterical with authority, supervising the rearrangement of flower-pots, turbanned bearers obsequiously arrayed behind police and administrative officers, who sat there drinking tea in poses of serene arrogance that brought to mind images from both *Jewel in the Crown* and *The Music Room*, and made clearer the line of inheritance from feudal-colonial India to the administrative services.

The officers looked askance at us as we walked across the wide lawn towards them, shabby in our rumpled dirty clothes. They seemed to be considering whether to ask one of the servants to throw us out. In the end, they must have decided against it.

There was a moment's silence after we made our request. They looked at each other expressionlessly. I braced myself to hear about Judge sahib.

Finally, one of them spoke: Yes, there were spare rooms available. But they were expensive. Could we afford them?

How expensive? we asked.

He told us. It was much less than what we had paid at other places. The man either thought us complete scroungers or, spoilt by the cosy network of circuit houses, he had lost touch with the world of commoners, where one paid for the services rendered to one.

We said we found the fare agreeable, whereupon he summoned one of the lower-level officials hanging around in the background, waiting for just such summons. We were shown to our rooms. My companions got the room ostensibly reserved for visiting ministers and other VIPs; I got the room meant for their minions.

It hadn't been aired in a long time. The rug, grimy with dirt, smelt of mildew; there was algae on the bathroom floor; wide cracks ran down the walls; the towels and blankets were torn; the windows opened out on an uncovered drain.

Waiting for the hot water to arrive, I went for a stroll in the run-down weedy garden. There were policemen outside, trying to look watchful. They had been brought there by the same bus I had seen at the Rajasthan Tourism hotel. So, perhaps, Judge sahib was to stay at the circuit house after all.

The policemen eyed me warily as I went past them. One of them actually followed me, and then accosted me as I walked through the tall wild grass. He was a tall, thin man, with a strangely tormented expression on his face. You could imagine him being brutal in his exercise of power, as one of the frenzied *lathi*-wielding policemen breaking up a peaceful demonstration.

However, his manner with me was uncertain: he didn't as yet know who this stranger wandering in the garden by himself was, and until he knew, he couldn't act. I felt his appraising eyes on me, sizing me up, as he asked me where I was from, and I knew how abruptly his manner could change, how it could become, depending on my answer, deferential or aggressive.

Delhi, I said; and, as often happens, the word worked like magic on him. Instantly, he turned deferential, automatically slipping into the subservient role he adopted with his superiors. He asked me no other questions, and immediately retreated, a bashful, apologetic figure slinking back into the gathering dark.

How thin was the line between power and powerlessness in these towns!

After a brief, unsatisfying bath with tepid water, I sat in the lounge and read Iris Murdoch's *The Word Child*.

The lights were dim, barely enough to read by; they made the lounge look shabbier than it was, with its faded Rajasthan Tourism posters, its bulbous sofas, its threadbare carpet.

People kept passing through: servants, lower-level officials. Outside, they were constantly coming and going on mysterious errands. Cars slid up the driveway, and stopped, their engines running, on the portico. Doors clicked open; urgent voices rang out; then the doors were slammed shut, and the cars would move on.

A half hour of this, and then, abruptly, there was silence. The cars seemed to have gone away; the sound of voices and footsteps receded. I continued reading as I had through all the disturbance.

Presently, a shadow fell over the page I was reading. And when it didn't move across, I looked up.

It was the police officer I had seen on the lawn as we arrived. He hadn't talked to us then; he had just sat there, with his cap on his head, very upright in his chair, staring at us.

He was a thick-set, middle-aged man in his late forties

or early fifties. He could not have been a direct entrant to the police services; he had risen up the ranks to his present position. And, it was unsettling to think he had served, and been hardened, in those police stations one saw on the way, local centres of not law and order but atrocity, part of the horrors of small towns newspapers relegated to the inside pages every day, places where women were molested, suspects tortured and innocents harassed with appalling regularity.

'Can I look at your book?' he asked, in English.

'Yes,' I said. 'Certainly.'

He peered at the cover, then turned the book over in his hand, and asked me:

'This Eerice Murdoch. She is wife of Rupaart Murdoch, yes?'

The very idea was so amusingly improbable that it wasn't until later that the interesting fact sank in: the fact that this man had heard of Rupert Murdoch.

'No,' I said.

'But it is same name, no?'

'Yes, but they are not married, in fact, are not related in any way at all.'

He still didn't seem satisfied. He again turned over the book in his hands and examined it very closely.

He finally looked up and asked: 'What is your occupation in life?'

'I write,' I said.

'*Write*?'

He pondered that.

'Write,' he repeated, still looking at the book in his hand.

'What do you write?' he abruptly asked.

I said, 'I write articles.'

'Articles?' he echoed, now looking at me instead of the book.

'Articles,' I said.

He said nothing; he seemed to have mysteriously understood. He looked back at the book. He started reading the backcover.

He read; I waited.

He finished reading; looked at me, slightly puzzled; and then haltingly started reading out the backcover aloud, moving his finger along the text.

Hilary Burde, saved by education from a delinquent childhood, cheated of Oxford by a tragic love tangle.....

He stopped at the word 'tangle,' his finger poking at where he had stopped, looked at me and asked:

'Cheated? Why?'

I do not remember what I said.

'What is this book?' he asked again.

'It is a novel.'

'Novel?' He looked puzzled again.

'*Upanyas,*' I said.

But he did not hear me.

'What is the meaning of "cheated of Oxford"?' He started afresh.

'*Matlab woh Oxford nahin ja saka*, Meaning he couldn't go to Oxford,' I lied, switching to Hindi, hoping he would do the same and make our conversation a much smoother affair.

He persisted with speaking in English.

'Why not he go to Oxford?'

'Because he got injured,' I lied again.

He went over the backcover again, looked at me, and asked:

'What is there in this book?'

I considered a few uncomplicated replies, and then said, 'A story, plot, characters, situations.'

But he wasn't listening to me.

'Why are you reading this book?'

'For pleasure,' I said, beginning to get slightly irritated by the persistent questioning, and then added in Hindi: '*Apni khushi, apne maze ke liye.*'

He looked down at the book again, very intently this time, turned it over in his hand, examined the cover, his brow deeply furrowed with thought, and then, after a long pause, said, '*Yeh to badi moti aur difficult kitab lag rahi hai, isme kya maza aayega*? This looks like such a thick and difficult book. What sort of pleasure can you get out of it?'

The cars came back later, this time with wailing sirens and revolving lights, bringing the much-awaited Judge sahib with them.

I was in my room, driven there by the relentless police officer, and I heard the sirens when they were still some way off. They were meant to clear the traffic; but there was no traffic. It was a late Sunday evening, the last day of the year; the roads were deserted, with not even a cyclist or pedestrian on them; the sirens and lights were clearly unnecessary.

But they were a badge of status and importance on these provincial roads where there was scarcely a car or jeep that did not have a plaque in front indicating, in shiny brass letters, its owner's place in the local hierarchy of power. So far, only lesser people had needed them: Assistant Irrigation Engineers, Police Sub-Inspectors, Munsif Magistrates, Block Development Officers. But even higher authorities had now begun feeling that they were not being given the requisite amount of respect on the road. I had been reading about the High Court judge who demanded a siren for his car. The case went up to the Supreme Court which, firmly and correctly, disapproved of such vainglory.

Presumably, Judge sahib was on vacation and travelling in not his own but some local eminence's car.

I didn't see him arrive, but I heard the doors opening

and shutting in quick succession, and the sound of hard-soled shoes pattering up the steps to the lounge. I came out of my room to find a long convoy of cars lined on the driveway, and policemen rigid with attempted alertness.

I strolled over to where the two cars with the lights on top were parked. The boots were open, and one of the lower-level officials was supervising the servants carting the luggage inside.

As I had suspected, Judge sahib had come with his entire extended family. There were a large number of children outside on the lawn and in the garden, nasty little brutes in denim jeans and sneakers who shouted at erring servants in English—*Hey! You fool! You stupid!*—and while the lower-level official looked on indulgently, plucked off the few flowers that were there in the pots, ran screaming over the relaid garden-beds and their fragile plants, shattering the peace of the Circuit House, and converting it, in the process, into their personal playground.

The lounge was now full with people, with, presumably, Judge sahib's family and his reception committee, composed of assorted district officials. I heard their voices outside, urgent, authoritative, laden with instructions. I was dying to see Judge sahib by now; I decided to go in.

I had barely reached the short flight of steps leading to the lounge when I heard the sharp command behind me.

'*Rukko*, Stop,' it said.

I turned around to find a man pointing the serious end of his rifle at my abdomen.

I couldn't recall seeing him before. He looked bigger and fitter than the local policemen posted around the Circuit House, and was probably Judge sahib's personal bodyguard, lurking unnoticed in the shadows while I watched the luggage being unloaded from the cars. He must have seen me and wondered what I was up to.

'*Kahan ja rahe ho*, Where are you going?' He now wanted to know.

My mouth, as I now discovered, trying to speak, was dry. It was my second encounter this evening with a policeman, with the important difference that this one had a rifle with him. Swallowing with difficulty—the rifle still pointed at me—I croaked:

'*Andar*, Inside.'

'*Kyon*, Why?' was the succinct response.

I managed to say: '*Mein yahan rah raha hoon*, I am staying here.'

The rifle was instantly lowered. He said: '*Tab jaiye, mein to keval poochh raha tha*, Then you can go in, I was only asking.'

His voice held a subdued apology in it. I could not see the man's face in the dark; there may have been regret there. Or, it could be that he was used to such situations and felt, in their aftermath, neither regret nor apology.

In any event, he said nothing more and simply stood there, watching me. I realized my knees were trembling with fear. I was free to go in now; but all desire to do so abruptly drained out of me. Slowly, with a slightly wobbly gait, feeling his probing eyes on my back, I walked back to my room through the side entrance, and sat there for a long time, staring at my ashen face in the full-length mirror, attempting to steady my nerves.

I stayed there a long time, until Judge sahib and his family mysteriously left. Perhaps, he didn't find the Circuit House to his taste. Perhaps, he went to one of the two other places reserved in his name. Perhaps the kids got bored of vandalizing the Circuit House and wanted to vandalize some other place. I couldn't tell; it was all very baffling to me.

But I was grateful for the restored silence. Later, at night, we had a good satisfying dinner prepared on order by one of the Circuit House cooks. A couple of men in dressing gowns joined us midway through our meal. They were apparently government officials living in the nearby rest-house. They did not talk much among themselves, barely noticed us sitting at the same table, gulped their food down in a hurry, and left.

Afterwards, we went for a walk, hoping to find at least one New Year's Eve party we could crash.

But, Bundi, at even this early hour—it was barely eleven—was asleep. A few sounds of revelry floated out of the District Magistrate's residence; on closer listening, they turned out to be Doordarshan's year-end special. Other houses on the same road were silent and dark, the only sign of life being a lone guard at one gate whose curious gaze followed us long after we went past him. Further ahead, the road stretched empty and desolate in the sickly pallor of sodium streetlights. Muted TV sounds escaped through some half-open windows: more Doordarshan infantilia. The only things that moved were dogs, mangy and lame, nuzzling trash heaps that lay ready for morning's disposal vans.

We came back disappointed to the Circuit House. The New Year found us playing Trivial Pursuit—an appropriate beginning, one felt. Elsewhere in Bundi, the New Year began with a whimper: a dud firecracker that sounded like a plastic pop gun. No other explosions were attempted; silence swiftly moved back.

8

From Bundi I wanted to leave immediately for the South—that sun-lit place in my imagination, for whose old-world charm and civility I had developed a positive yearning after several months at a stretch in the barbarous North. I knew I would be 'working' there this time, but even then it promised all the relief and excitement of the many vacations I had taken there in the past.

There still, however, remained a journey in the North. I had long wanted to go to Hapur; it was one of the places that automatically chose itself when I embarked on my present travels. It could seem a strange choice: Hapur, a town grown rich on agricultural profits, distinguished itself in nothing, except its crime-rate.

But then, even stranger was the life of the friend from whom I had first heard about Hapur, and whose memory now encouraged me to go there.

His name was Rajendra, and he was my senior by a couple of years at Allahabad University in the mid-eighties. There were few students there from Western UP, and they tended to stick together even when all they had in common was a contempt for poor, backward, caste-ridden Eastern UP. I belonged to neither region, but still gravitated by choice to students from the West. Among them, I quickly noticed Rajendra. Unlike his compatriots— many of whom were still, in their mid-twenties, adolescent posturers, doomed to futility—he had an engaging earnestness about him. Unlike them, he realized his incompleteness as a person and strove to overcome that.

One of the ways in which he did that was by reading. He didn't read much, or too widely, but attentively, looking for instruction, hints for self-improvement, and he read serious books. He looked down upon fiction, and gave back, unread, the novels I so enthusiastically pressed upon him. His favourite book was Radhakrishnan's *An Idealist View of Life*; he was the only person I knew who had actually read Dasgupta's five-volume study of Indian philosophy.

The reading had come late in his life, and it only enhanced one's appreciation of him to realize how it may never have come at all. Rajendra belonged to a small notified backward caste where education so far was an unheard-of luxury. His father was a farmer; so were his brothers, and other close relatives. For generations now, his family had tilled the same soil, and none among them had gone beyond high school.

He couldn't recall why and how the decision to give him a proper education was made; but it must have coincided with the growing prosperity of his family in the early seventies. The Green Revolution's success in that region had prompted a lot of its beneficiaries to expand their horizons. Rich farmers were suddenly seized by a wish to send their sons to prestigious schools and colleges which until then were the preserve of the bureaucratic-business élite. Men in bright coloured turbans crowded their Victorian-Gothic portals. Many were turned away, but a good number succeeded, and among them was Rajendra's family.

After a few failed attempts, he was accepted at a public school in Rajasthan. He told an interesting story about his admission there. He was escorted there by his Uncle for the formal interview. The Headmaster had wanted to know if Rajendra had any English. His Uncle had immediately riposted: 'But that's why I have brought him to you. *You* will teach him English.'

And he had done remarkably well at school. From a shy, fearful fresher, he had grown into a natural leader: the bully of bullies. He excelled in studies; he excelled in sports; and, he had the charisma of people we can't place easily, people who come out of no known background, and who dazzle us by the unexpectedness of their talents.

After school, there was the university, where his success continued. He had just graduated, with distinction, when I first met him. By now he was certain that he would not take after his forebears. His family felt, and he agreed, that his education had to have a positive result. It was why he was sent to Allahabad: he was now expected to write the Civil Services exam.

A normal life, from all evidence; but derangement lay close to the placid surface, and often threatened to disturb it.

While in his last year at school, Rajendra had developed a homosexual passion for a junior boy. Sodomy was rife among his schoolmates; junior boys were often picked upon; and, in any other case, the passion would have been quickly consummated, and thus extinguished. But Rajendra was held back by some notion of feudal honour, and the repulsion he felt at his own aberrancy. At home, during his vacations, he had been exposed to the teachings of Swami Dayanand; they had left a deep impression on him. He couldn't bring himself to do what others did so easily and remorselessly.

.The passion deepened and turned into a torment. It became a tremendous strain to keep up the facade of the brilliant schoolboy. It was under great emotional and psychological stress that Rajendra wrote his final exams. Immediately afterwards, he had a breakdown. His father and uncle came to take him away from the school. They wanted to know what had happened to him; his friends asked him the same question. But he did not know: at that time, he denied his passion even to himself. Homosexuality, though rampant at school in various exploitative forms, carried an indelible stigma in his mind. Suicide was preferable to the prospect of his friends and family coming to know about his actual state. And it was of suicide that he preferred to think in his terrible loneliness.

His family, baffled by a condition they could not even name, took him to several doctors in Delhi. Finally, he was referred to a psychiatrist with whom some long sessions ensued. It was a new experience for Rajendra, for he hadn't even heard previously of this kind of healing. Fortunately, the psychiatrist was a competent man who made him feel revived enough to go to Allahabad.

But, once there, his troubles started again. This time he was referred to a local psychiatrist, and Rajendra met him on a regular basis for the next many years. Shrinks were, and still are, new to India. Rajendra's condition, however, wasn't new; it was, in fact, unsettlingly common. But it wasn't what anyone faced up to; and, if confided in someone it would have still been met with shock, incredulity, and, even, straightforward revulsion. Once again, he was alone, and these regular meetings with the psychiatrist belonged to a secret life of torment and obsession he concealed under a vivacious public self.

The meetings had grown infrequent when I first met him because Rajendra felt strong enough to dispense with psychiatric help. Aided by his random readings in religion and psychology, he had over the years arrived at his own peculiar interpretation of his last year at school. He had suffered there, he asserted, a total moral collapse. He hadn't spent enough time at home to be fully inculcated with the values of the Arya Samaj; therefore, at school, he had succumbed to the easy amorality of his peers. Had he been more secure in his ethical beliefs, he wouldn't have fallen for the junior boy.

The only solution was an urgent inoculation of Arya Samaj values, and accordingly, his room came to be full of pamphlets exhorting one to go 'Back to the Vedas'. A strange irony lay there. For his family, the Brahmin-dominated Arya Samaj could not have been little more than a promise of dignity, an attempt to shed their low-caste identity, a means to upward mobility. Rajendra, in his desire for stability, took it more seriously than they had ever done. But then, he was to remain an innocent about caste. He had been taken in by the deceptive castelessness of his public-school peers; like countless others, he had been lulled into believing the larger world to be an extension of his school.

The confusion, the contradictions, went deeper. Along with his revived interest in the Arya Samaj existed a vigorous curiosity about Bhagwan Rajneesh, 'Osho'. He read *Sex and Superconsciousness*, and quickly declared it a profound book. He read other books by Osho. Soon, he was blaming his troubles on the absence of a sexually mature society in India. His homosexual passion was now a perversion of healthy sexuality caused by unnatural repression.

University life has its illusions; early adulthood has its own. The former fosters a complacent inertia, a beguiling sense of timelessness; the latter dictates that the sorting out of the self is the most important task in the world. Often, the two coincide; and then you feel you have all the time in the world to sort out your self. The years were passing quickly for Rajendra; the pressures on him steadily accumulating. He went home to his family in Bulandshahr less often now; he wanted to avoid their relentless exhortations to live up to his promise and justify his expensive education.

In the meantime, he did nothing. He filled up a few

forms but flunked the tests. He was still looking for stability, and he thought he could find it in marriage. He began to court a girl from his caste. I began to see less and less of him. Shortly thereafter, he was engaged to be married. I left Allahabad soon after that. He came to see me off at the railway station. He was convinced he had done the right thing. His life was working out, he said. He could now plan his career, go places, do things.

There was something forced about his assurance; it seemed as if he was willing himself to believe in what he said, as if having come so far on his present path, he couldn't afford to backtrack or even stop to contemplate where he was going. But then it had always been like this for him. He was the first person in his family to step out into the modern world, and he hadn't always known where he was going. There had been no precedents in anything he did; every experience was a new experience for him. He had suffered, and, in his suffering, he had always been alone.

But I was to see this much later, long after I had left Allahabad, and lost touch with him. Back then, I may have only compounded his confusion by giving him the wrong kind of books to read.

I heard about his marriage. I received a card sent through a friend after it was over. A little later I heard he was in Allahabad, preparing in earnest for the Civil Services exam.

He unexpectedly showed up at my door one evening in Delhi. He was accompanied by his wife, whom I had never seen, and who turned out to be a rather pretty, vivacious, somewhat girlish woman. Rajendra was visibly nervous about the impression she would make on me. We went out for dinner with another friend. An awkward affair: Rajendra carefully avoided discussing his present and future plans, and looked anxious throughout over his wife's conversational performance. We talked of other things and never once referred to what he was doing these days.

Soon after this meeting, I heard he was taking the Civil Services exams. Then, the news from Allahabad was that he had flunked them again.

Months passed. News about him grew scarce, then stopped coming altogether as people he and I knew in Allahabad moved out into the larger world and lost touch with each other. I thought of him often during this time, and wondered where he was and what he was doing. Now, I was travelling to Hapur and one of my objectives there was to find out where he had been in the intervening years.

I went by bus. There were few other passengers at that early hour, and they sat sunk in the moroseness of an early winter morning, wrapped tight in shawls and blankets, unblinkingly staring straight ahead.

The road deteriorated immediately after we crossed Delhi's outer limits; the frequent jolting made it difficult to doze off. Fog obscured the passing wheat and barley fields outside. Men huddled over small fires of discarded tyres and tubes, and as we passed them, the stench of burning rubber briefly assaulted our nostrils. Already there were straggly queues in front of public taps, not of people but water containers in varying shapes and sizes, and of various makes: tin, steel, plastic, iron, and brass.

There were few uninhabited stretches; the area was almost continuously built up. Brick sheds euphemized into auto-repair shops cropped up at regular intervals. There were houses, built in the nondescript pan-Indian style, rectangular and squarish boxes of brick and cement, often unpainted and undistempered; and offices, mostly of real estate agents, who, judging by their number, were flourishing in these parts. Then, as if to remind one that this was indeed a prosperous area, and that land here was much desired, there were large, garishly-painted double- and triple-storied houses with paved driveways, enclosed by tall walls with barbed wires on top, two or three Marutis dully gleaming in the forecourt, water tanks and huge dish-antennas on the roof: the very symbols, as it were, of a confident self-sufficiency.

Immediately on arriving, I checked into a hotel close to the bus-stand. There was no power and, consequently, no running water in the bathroom, I was informed after filling up the register. The room I was taken to, by a long-haired urchin singing with annoying loudness some crude film song, was cramped and dirty. The dust looked as if it had been undisturbed for several days; there were damp patches on the walls; and it was piercingly cold.

All these deficiencies were sought to be compensated by the b/w TV in the room which the urchin switched on, as usual, the moment I entered the room. MTV was on; and there was Sophiya on the screen, mumbling in her London accent, looking more jaded than usual, swaying her pelvis in the slightly demented way MTV VJs have.

The urchin stood there transfixed before her as I washed my face with the ice-cold water he had brought in a small pitcher. He was still there after I finished; so was Sophiya, who was in a somewhat philosophical mood this morning.

I started a conversation with the urchin in the hope of eventually ushering him out of the room. I asked him if he liked Sophiya.

But he didn't know her at all. Nor did he know Nonie, Angela, David, Danny, and other pelvis-swayers, who, if metropolitan newspapers were to be believed, had become the role-models for an entire generation of Indian youth.

'Yeh saali videshi Chinese-Wienese pasand nahin aati, apne ko desi maal hi chalta hai, I don't like these foreign Chinese-Wienese types, I am turned on only by Indian girls,' he declared, with a bit of a swagger.

I ate a breakfast of *jalebi-dahi* and tea at a shop in a narrow lane behind the hotel. The dogs were already out in full force, frantically scouring, with mottled tongues, discarded earthen cups and leaf-plates on the ground; and people were now beginning to stir out of their homes, stout, hunched figures in the cold, holding milk-pails and *lotas* in gloved hands, newspapers protruding from under their armpits. Soon, a good crowd had gathered at the shop. An easy-going amiability existed between these people, who probably met at the same spot every morning. The tea seemed to lift their spirits; animatedly, then, they discussed the morning headlines: GATT, Dunkel, Kashmir, Mulayam Singh Yadav, the latest triumph in cricket, and the man found murdered in a cold-storage tank, his limbs chopped off, his genitals mutilated.

Its proximity to the national capital does nothing for Hapur. After breakfast I walked through its streets, and was confronted by exactly the same sights one would find in any town, big or small, in North India: broken roads which, choked with vehicular traffic and stationary *thela*-stalls, have no space for pedestrians, by their side open drains which go nowhere and remain festering in the heat until they evaporate, unpaved lanes where the slush is ankle-deep and impossible to negotiate on foot, rotting heaps of garbage which haven't been cleared for days, ponds covered with a thick film of algae, clusters of houses built to no particular design or order but simply plonked next to each other and lacking even ordinary ventilation, dense masses of tangled wires above street-corners, and emaciated cows serenely wandering through this assorted chaos.

I was looking for a cloth-shop; it was where I was to meet my contact in Hapur, a Mr Singh. It took a long time to find it. I didn't have the full address; it was hidden in a narrow bylane, one of many open-fronted shops in a row.

Then, when I finally arrived there, it turned out that I had come on a wrong day, and that Mr Bhatti was busy with his niece's marriage to be held the same evening. But, I was welcome to attend the marriage; there was to be a reception afterwards during which an orchestra party was scheduled to perform.

This was told me by the couple of young men in their mid-twenties manning the shop. When I arrived they were busy filling up a crossword puzzle in a local paper which required you to know, among other things, Zeenat Aman's first film and the name of Amitabh Bachchan's son. People in adjoining shops were doing the same crossword. They argued clamourously among themselves; they erupted in loud spells of shouting whenever they found a correct answer; their knowledge of film trivia exceeded anything I could have expected. Business looked non-existent, but this was as gay a crowd as one could have found anywhere.

The reception began at seven. I had a whole afternoon to kill until then. I hadn't thought of bringing a book along with me from Delhi. I now strolled over to the magazine stall I had seen before, hoping to find something to read.

But it didn't have anything apart from a stack of old issues of *Manohar Kahaniyan*. As I moved away from the magazine stall, the man inside called out after me.

I turned back to find him leering at me.

'*Kyon sahib, pondy-vondy chalega*?' he said, still leering.

At first I couldn't understand him, then I realized he

was asking me if I would be interested in porno magazines. Pondy: I had forgotten the word he used. I had never figured out its etymological roots, but it was the popular code-word for pornographic magazines in North India.

I hesitated, then said yes. He quickly fished out and handed me a bunch of magazines. I briefly glanced at them, and then, much to his disappointment, handed them back to him. They were in both English and Hindi, and badly printed. It was difficult not to burst out laughing at the prose, at twelve-inches-long penises and vaginas that could accommodate two such penises at the same time. The emphasis, wisely enough, was on photographs, which were blurred and hazy, and mostly of white women: of vaginas held apart with both hands, of globular buttocks and football-shaped breasts. There were no scenes of actual intercourse, no photographs of men at all. The magazines catered only to males, to a lonely desperate need, and it wasn't difficult to imagine the unemployed youth who is still a virgin and worries about his penis-size and the middle-aged clerk whose wife hates sex coming here in the evenings to pore over furtively, first with excitement and then with growing depression, these sad pictures and their promise of pleasures that are forever unattainable.

The venue for the marriage, I had been told at the cloth-shop, wasn't too far from my hotel. And I had no trouble finding it; I could have been anywhere in Hapur and still easily found it. I could have been in Delhi and still found it. One only had to follow the earthshaking noise, whose vibrations ranged over several kilometres, to its source.

The closer I came to it the more I wondered whether I had it in me to withstand it for a whole evening. In the end, only a sense of duty could prevail over an urgent desire to go back, to leave Hapur itself, and then Delhi, to put behind me, for some time at least, these Northern irritations and the outbreaks of anger and despair they provoked.

The most uniform and conspicuous feature of the towns and cities you travel through in North India, and also the most serious menace to civilized life in them, is noise. It accompanies you everywhere—in your hotel room, in the lobby, in the elevator, in the streets, in temples, mosques, gurudwaras, shops, restaurants, parks—chipping away at your nerves to the point where you feel breakdown to be imminent. It isn't just the ceaseless traffic, the pointless blaring of horns, the steady background roar that one finds in big cities. It is much worse: the electronics boom in India has made cassette-players available to anyone with even moderate spending power. Cassettes too are cheap, especially if you buy pirated ones. Together, they make up a deadly weapon in the hands of people desensitized by urban existence, who fill up the immense vacuum of their lives by a continuous production of sound.

I had spent some difficult weeks in Benares last year, dealing with just this problem. In the end, I had simply left. It was sad: I had great fondness for the place, but I had never felt so undermined anywhere else in India. There was nothing one could do about it, and it wasn't worth imperilling your sanity. My reactions were admittedly strong, even extreme; but they could not have been otherwise in the circumstances.

For, to be woken up at five in the morning by the devotional treacle of Anup Jalota, Hari Om Sharan and other confectioners, all of them simultaneously droning out from several different cassette-players; to be relentlessly assaulted for the rest of the day and most of the night by the alternately over-earnest and insolent voices of Kumar Sanu, Alisha Chinoy, Baba Sehgal singing *Sexy, Sexy, Sexy, Ladki Hai Kya Re Baba, Sarkaaye Liyo Khatiya* and other unspeakably hideous songs; to have them insidiously leak into your memory and become moronic refrains running over and over again in your mind; to have your environment polluted and your day destroyed in this way was to know a deepening rage, an impulse to murder, and, finally, a creeping fear at one's own dangerous level of derangement. It was to understand the perfectly sane people you read about in the papers, who suddenly explode into violence one fine day; it was to conceive a lasting hatred for the perpetrators, rich or poor, of these auditory atrocities.

The venue for the marriage was a small hall with a wide patch of bare ground in front. Tubular-framed chairs had been arranged in orderly rows, facing a raised platform on which were placed two tall red-cushioned chairs for the bride and groom. The backdrop to them was a tapestry of white floral decorations on which red roses formed the English words, *Awadhesh Weds Anita*. In one corner was the mandap where the marriage ceremony was to take place; in another, a small stage for the orchestra party, where microphones were being tested by a man babbling on in a cavernous voice, *Hello Testing, Testing, Hello, Testing*.... Inside the hall white-clothed tables had been set for the dinner afterwards. A tiny enclosure made by tent walls adjacent to the hall was the kitchen, where huge *kadhais* simmered over brick-and-wood stoves, and where the smell of *desi ghee* hung heavy in the atmosphere, overpowering even the strong aroma of incense-sticks.

I knew when I started that I would arrive too early, and so I did. The chairs were unoccupied, and the only people in sight were the hosts, menial labourers, electricians and various kinds of handymen. But I wanted to meet Mr Singh before he became even busier. With that intent, I asked around for him and was told he had gone out on some urgent business, but was expected back shortly.

There was nothing to do but wait. I sat well away from the speakers, but even then the music was deafening. Once again it was my lot to wonder why it did not impair the efficiency of people briskly darting in and out of the hall. Indeed, they looked energized by it—and no one more so than the restlessly wandering group of ten or twelve-year-old kids who sporadically broke out into fits of manic dancing, wriggling their torsos and thrusting their pelvises forward in imitation of their elders in Hindi films. All of them wore nearly identical clothes: denim jeans and jackets with Mickey Mouse and Sanjay Dutt patches on them, and peaked caps adorned with gold-coloured chains which, I had been told, were popularized by Amir Khan in the film *Dil Hai Ki Maanta Nahin*.

As conspicuous as the kids was one of the men scampering about the lawn. He wore a spotlessly white three-piece suit; his tie was red, and so was the carnation on his lapel. His trousers were very wide at the bottom, as though his tailor had persuaded him that the broad styles of the seventies were back, and flapped over his tan-coloured, peculiarly scaly, platform-soled shoes as he ran hither and thither with no specific purpose in view, except perhaps the appearance of great purposefulness.

There was another, somewhat younger, man in an achkan whose texture had the kind of silvery sheen you find on Bengali sweets. He had a red carnation too—so did, I was soon to notice, a lot of people—and he wore elaborately carved wooden Rajasthani shoes under clinging churidars. And, like the white-suited man, he was a picture of energetic activity, walking with short tripping steps all over the place, booming out peremptory orders.

Indeed, there was a lot of shouting of instructions; people yelled at the top of their voices to make themselves heard, but it occurred to no one to turn the music down.

Then, the guests began to arrive, and all activity rose to a feverish pitch.

The man in the white suit and red tie no longer ran, but sprinted from one end to another, his trouser bottoms flapping even more wildly around his ankles, his carnation slightly askew and in some danger of falling off. A reception committee quickly formed at the gate, mostly composed of elderly men in towering tie-and-dye turbans, dhoti-kurta, and white tennis sneakers worn over calf-length white socks. There was a lot of bowing and smiling as the guests trooped in. Amid all this, the music suddenly ceased.

The silence was thunderous.

A lot of the arriving guests were women, dressed in heavy glittering silk sarees and tons of gold jewellery, and giving off the cloying fragrance of cheap Indian imitations of Christian Dior and Chanel. A few years ago, they wouldn't have come like this; they would have slunk in through a side entrance, their saree-veils drawn very low over their heads, leaving the men-folk to walk in through the main gate. But then, a few years ago, there would have been no 'Reception' either. Mr Singh's family was of a low caste, and a few years ago, they would have only provoked high-caste opprobrium and ridicule for daring to host something as modern as a 'Reception'. They would have stuck to tradition; they would have had an old-style feast where people sit on covered ground to eat, neatly divided into caste-groupings, where Brahmins have the pride of place, and where women eat last, just before the dogs take over.

The only distinction I could see now was between vegetarians and non-vegetarians. Plainly, in Mr Singh's family, prosperity had promoted a confident egalitarianism. Unfortuately, in Mr Singh's in-laws-to-be, it had only promoted greed. There was much speculation going on among the guests about the exact nature and quantity of dowry paid to them. The amounts mentioned took one's breath away. One woman said: *'Sab mila ke pandra lakh diya hai*, In total, they have paid fifteen lakh rupees worth of dowry.' Another said twenty lakhs. Yet another pitched it as high as thirty lakhs.

And they weren't exaggerating. They were speaking of real amounts, such as they themselves had the capacity to spend. It wasn't too obvious, due to long-established habits of frugality and a superstitious fear of seeming too rich, but there was money here, in this crowd of overdressed men and women.

No one had questioned my presence as yet, but I was still nervous, and eager to establish my credentials lest I be identified as one of the freeloaders that slip into every dinner-party, and face disgraceful expulsion. And so I finally had someone point out Mr Singh to me. He was a short, balding man in his late fifties, convulsed with anxiety, shouting at all and sundry in the narrow kitchen, his forehead gleaming with perspiration. I went up to him and introduced myself. But he wasn't listening. 'Very good, very good,' he said, eagerly shaking my hand. I re-introduced myself. He said he hoped I would stay for the orchestra party's performance and dinner afterwards.

There was nothing more to be said to him at this stage, so I retreated to my seat. The orchestra party had arrived on the little stage in front, and was tuning, with sudden inspirational flourishes, the instruments, which consisted of a synthesizer, two electric guitars, a bongo drum, a pair of cymbals, and a drum set, the reverse side of which said, *Pappu Orchestra Party*. One of them, who looked like the lead singer in his satin jacket and knee-length cowboy boots, got hold of the mike, and started droning *Hello, Testing, Hello, Testing* into it. Somebody jumped on to the chair behind me; the next moment I felt a hand on my right shoulder. I looked back to see a ten-year-old boy, with a Malcolm X cap on his head.

'Hey, where you from?' he asked.

The English was as startling as the cap, but he had probably seen me writing in my notebook.

I said, 'I am from Delhi.'

He said, 'I from Delhi also.'

That explained the Malcolm X cap. They had become popular after the Spike Lee film. I had seen quite a few in Delhi, sported by people as unlikely to know about Malcolm X as this boy.

'Good,' I told him.

He kept staring at me, but said nothing more.

I turned back to find a young, short-statured girl had appeared on stage, and was talking animatedly with the lead singer. She could not have been more than fifteen years old, but there was a confidence about her that belied her age. The lead singer now turned to the audience, and muttered something incomprehensible into the mike. All I could catch were the words 'Baby Julie' which apparently referred to the young girl.

A few rapid rehearsals; and then, the lead singer and Baby Julie launched into their opening number. It was the risqué *Ham Tum Ek Kamre Mein Bund Hon* from the film *Bobby*. The acoustics were terrible; their voices were like the wailing wind in that narrow space, and only the instruments came through somewhat clearly. But no one seemed to mind: the orchestra party was only another one of the new marriage-rituals; their presence was enough; the music did not matter.

The lead singer and Baby Julie moved on to other numbers in their repertoire, which drew heavily from the seventies, with a couple of new hits thrown in for good measure. They paused after each song, as if waiting for the applause. But no applause came; the crowd was preoccupied. The men sat apart, busy discussing such masculine matters as crime and litigation; their wives, old and young, gossiped about the dowry and related things. Then, there were their shy young daughters who clung close to them or to each other; and, ogling them from a safe distance, gawky in their shiny new three-piece suits, the young popinjays of Hapur.

After finishing a song, the lead singer made an announcement in English. Again, I couldn't follow the exact words, and was still figuring them out when the orchestra party broke into a familiar tune. It was Madonna's *Papa Don't Preach*, a slower version sung by Baby Julie with much foot-tapping and hip-swaying.

The crowd remained as indifferent as before. But I felt the right hand on my shoulder again.

I turned back to find the boy with the Malcolm X cap.

He stared at me for an instant, and then, abruptly, his blank face broke into the widest grin possible.

'You *listen*?!' he said, gesturing toward the stage, 'You listen *English* song?!'

I didn't stay for dinner. The baraat was, as befitting its high current status, late. The orchestra party ran out of numbers to play and then began inviting young members of the audience to come up on stage and sing a song of their choice. This opened the floodgates, as it were, and one by one the pimply teenagers in three-piece suits went up and crooned out, with varying degrees of ineptitude, the hits of the season. As they did so, they gazed boldly at the girls in the audience who had provoked such an outpouring of emotion in their hearts, with the result that the girls shrank even further into their chairs.

After an hour of this, and with no sign of the baraat still, I decided to leave.

I ran into the baraat half a kilometre out of the reception venue. It wasn't difficult to see why they were late; the stench of rum preceded them by a good distance. Mr Singh and his family looked to be in some trouble from this mob. There were no women present, and the men had let themselves go. They were dancing dementedly when I caught up with them, holding aloft half-full or empty bottles of liquor, shaking their hips for all they were worth in beat with the assorted cacophony of the accompanying brass band. Some of them held wads of five- and ten-rupee notes in their hands, which they would periodically, with wide sweeping movements, fling up in the air. Blowing into their trumpets, the brass band members would follow with anxious eyes the notes fluttering down to the ground, where they were quickly snatched up by the nimble-footed petromax-lamp carriers. The groom sat on a horse in a yellow three-piece suit, illuminated from the side by two tubelights wrapped in flimsy blue paper, a trifle aloof from the high-spirited crowd before him, his mouth set in a tight grimace. Behind him, an ageing power-generator followed on a push-cart, noisily spluttering out thick smoke into the darkness.

I had managed to corner Mr Singh for a few minutes before I left. He looked as preoccupied as ever. I introduced myself. 'Very good,' he said, gripping my hand, and expressed the hope that I would stay for dinner.

I asked him without any further ado about my friend, Rajendra.

He looked blank for an instant, then searched his mind, and said:

'*Rajendra yahin hai Hapur mein, kheti kar raha hai,* Rajendra is here, in Bulandshar, doing forming.'

Kheti! Farming! After all the years at school and university! After all the time spent struggling to move away from that life!

But the news, in retrospect, shouldn't have been surprising. It had been a brave endeavour, Rajendra's passage from his feudal, low-caste background to the ultra-modern world of Osho. The courage wasn't immediately obvious, and then not to everyone; only those who knew the tremendous effort involved in absorbing contrary norms could see it. As long as he had lived, his life had been a perpetual war with himself. And he had lived with the kind of contrarieties that would have broken a lesser person. He himself had merely cracked, grown tired of his perennial rudderlessness. And he had retreated now to familiar ground, where caste and clan would anchor him, and give him the security and stability he had always craved.

His house was a few minutes' drive from where I was and it was open to me to visit him there. But something held me back. I spent the rest of the evening and most of the next day thinking about it; then, finally decided not to see him. I was part of a life he had put behind him for good. He would have been confused and puzzled by my interest in him; it would have been difficult for me to explain. It would have been too embarrassing for both of us.

9

A ramshackle overcrowded bus deposited me in Delhi the next day just in time for the evening train to the South.

Once again, I took the TN(Tamil Nadu) Express. It was the first train I remember travelling on as a child, and the years since then have not lessened my admiration for it. There are many more long-distance trains now, and the TN Express has not the same significance as before. Indeed, I was saddened to read in the papers recently that it has been rapped for chronic tardiness by the Railway Board. Still, few trains can match its bustling efficiency, its well-stocked pantry car, and the kaleidoscope of sights it offers as it snakes through more than 2,000 kilometres of varied territory. In comparison, Rajdhani is too quick and too impersonal; the Shatabdis have yet to shake off their parvenu airs; and, GT (Grand Trunk), Howrah-Kalka, Pathankot Express have all fallen into irreparable neglect.

With me in the AC II cabin were two other people. One of them, a Mr Rastogi, was a journalist for one of the major Delhi papers. He was in his mid-thirties, with glasses, diminishing hair, and an air of failure. His reading material identified him as a peruser of steamy thrillers. There were two fat novels on the table beside him. Naked buttocks adorned one cover; the other cover had buttocks on it too, but clothed in air-tight jodhpurs.

I had an early encounter with my other companion on this trip, a Mr Goenka, who turned out to be a Marwari businessman based in Madras. He was in his early fifties, oddly trim, and even somewhat dandyish in his green-and-red Proline T-shirt and Wrangler jeans.

He was busy rummaging through his suitcase when I came in. Mr Rastogi already lay asprawl on the other lower-berth. I put my magazines on Mr Goenka's berth so as to have both hands free to take my rucksack off my back.

He saw the magazines, and immediately spoke up, irritably: 'No No No No, Not here. Please keep your things on your berth. It is 10 p.m. Sleeping time, you know.'

Mr Rastogi considered me with interest, but no sympathy, as I removed the magazines from Mr Goenka's berth, placed them on the upper berth, and wriggled myself free of the rucksack.

Mr Goenka soon made it clear, after stretching himself comfortably on his berth, his stockinged feet giving off a terrible stench, that only dire necessity had forced him to travel by train. He told Mr Rastogi that his people in Delhi had been unable to procure an air-ticket for Madras. He was very upset, but what could he do? He hated trains; they were so slow, so uncomfortable, and so corruptly managed. For instance, he had wanted to go in AC First, but there were no vacant seats: they had all been sold by the ticket-conductor to daily commuters at black-market rates.

This last bit, I was in a position to ascertain, was a complete lie. I had myself toyed with the idea of changing my ticket and going in AC First after noticing the blank reservation chart for it. And the man at the booking counter had confirmed it possible. In any case, there was no question of anyone travelling illegally in AC First on the TN Express, which, I knew from experience, had a solid system of checks and counter-checks.

Mr Rastogi, who had quietly listened so far, and who seemed to me a reticent, uncommunicative sort, now revealed himself as a man of surprising garrulity. He took up Mr Goenka's lament about corruption in the railways, embellished it with some stories of his own, and then extended it to cover all government departments.

'I feel what Manmohan Singh is doing is good,' he concluded. 'He is taking away all power from government so that there is no scope for corruption.'

Mr Goenka agreed in principle. Some corruption, he however maintained, would always remain in India. Then, quoting Nehru, he swiftly moved on to the unacknowledged virtues of corruption.

'You know what Nehru said? He said what is wrong with corruption if the money doesn't go out of the country. Now, people call Harshad Mehta a corrupt person. Why is he corrupt? Because he made a lot of money? But did the money go out of India? No, it stayed here. I think he is genius. My son—he's doing MBA; he is very ambitious—he says Harshad Mehta has inspired him. He says one thing. He says: Can other people make so much money in same time? I say even if he is corrupt, he is inspiring younger people.'

Mr Goenka went on to accuse the media of sending out a wrong image of Harshad Mehta.

'Is media not corrupt?!!' he asked, angrily. 'In Madras, all journalists are behaving like *chamchas* of Jayalalitha. They only write praises of her. Everyone is corrupt. This is pure hypocrisy.'

At this point, Mr Rastogi introduced himself as a journalist, but Mr Goenka remained unembarrassed and unimpressed.

I would have expected Mr Rastogi to defend his profession, but, surprisingly, he tended to agree with Mr Goenka. He confirmed his allegation that journalists were corrupt. 'Allot them,' he said, 'a house in some good locality, send them on foreign trips, and they will write in your favour all their life.' He then assured him that

Harshad Mehta had plenty of admirers in the Indian press, even if they weren't too prominent.

When his turn to speak next came, Mr Goenka introduced himself as a Marwari businessman based in Madras.

Mr Rastogi confessed to feeling somewhat surprised by that. 'But I hear there is very strong feeling in Madras against North Indians,' he said. 'I never heard of people from North doing business there. You are the first one.'

Mr Goenka said, 'No, no, Marwaris are there. They have been for many years. You are right about anti-North feeling. It is very very difficult to do business with Madrasi people. They don't want to work. Very lazy people. I throw them out and then they try to create trouble. They say he is doing this because he is North Indian. It is all nonsense.'

Mr Rastogi concurred. 'Very strange people,' he said.

But Mr Goenka was not through. 'Completely inefficient,' he said. 'You see these waiters on the train. They are completely inefficient.'

This last accusation was so gratuitous, so much without basis, that I felt it could only be intended at me. Mr Goenka had seen me exchange greetings with a couple of waiters I knew from previous trips. He had looked curious at first, and then resentful. It was now clear that I had offended him far more than I realized by inadvertently placing my magazines on his berth.

Mr Rastogi kept glancing at me throughout his conversation with Mr Goenka. I couldn't tell: he may have wanted me to join it. In any event, I was happier recording it in my notebook.

Later, during a brief lull when Mr Goenka went to the toilet, he propped himself up on his elbows and asked me if he could borrow one of my periodicals.

I gave him the whole stack. Mr Rastogi briefly looked through them, and then holding up the

London Review of Books asked me:

'*Yeh kya London se chhapti hai*, Is this published from London?'

'Yes,' I said.

Mr Rastogi frowned at the list of contents, turned a few pages, and then commented:

'*Lekin badi ghatiya printing aur design hai*, But the printing and design are so bad.'

I said nothing, so after a brief pause he asked me if Iris Murdoch was Rupert Murdoch's wife (I was reading *The Word Child*; he must have seen the cover with the author's name on it).

Yes, I said.

'*Kya novel likhti hai*? Does she write novels?' he asked.

Yes, I said.

'*Kya combination hai*! Media tycoon and novelist wife!' Mr Rastogi seemed to like the idea.

He pondered that for a moment, then asked me if I was a journalist.

'No,' I said. 'I am a student.'

His interest in me immediately drained away. Retreating, settling his head back into his pillow, he asked me one last question.

'Where are you a student? I mean, which university?'

'JNU,' I said.

'*Achha*,' he gave a satisfied smirk. 'Leftist?' he said, still smirking, paused, and then strangely added: 'The god that failed, eh?'

Morning found us at Jhansi, running late by a few hours. We were not expected; the platform looked deserted from the window. No cries of *chai* could be heard, none of the sleep-disturbing commotion of early-morning arrivals was audible. And it was only when I got out that I saw people there, rows and rows of them in ungainly bundles on the grimy floor, wrapped from head to foot in assorted sheets, huddled close together for warmth.

Mr Goenka got out with me, looking for tea. He had rudely turned down the pantry car's tea, saying that Madrasis can't make decent tea. He traipsed down the long platform in his tracksuit ensemble, resembling an early-morning jogger, trying to find a stall that was open. He came back frustrated to his berth, complaining loudly to Mr Rastogi about the laziness and inefficiency of Railway caterers.

'The buggers are all sleeping outside. They don't want to work. Same story everywhere you go,' he said.

But Mr Rastogi wasn't listening. His whole manner had changed dramatically in the few minutes we had been out.

The reason wasn't hard to see. At Jhansi, we had been joined in our cabin by a mother-daughter pair. The mother was a tall stringy woman in her early forties with pageboy hair and a severe thin-lipped mien, which cracked when she laughed—a startlingly loud and rustic laugh—and revealed a row of large gleaming-white teeth. Her daughter, whom she addressed variously as Rita, Sunrita and Ritz, resembled her not in the least by being shorter, plumper, fuller-lipped, and with a curly mop of hair. She wore tight clinging black jeans and a loose creamish shirt. I was much struck by her resemblance, no doubt deliberate, to Pooja Bhatt, a cheesecake filmstar it was impossible not to know since her pudgy flesh bulged out of every magazine-shop display, and who presented, it must be said, a rather dubious, if trendy, model of attractiveness: short, chubby-cheeked, fuzzy-haired, uneven-toothed. But Rita's conformity to it was complete to the extent of accentuating, through eyeliner and mascara, the slight squint she may have been previously eager to hide, and which is now generally held to be 'cute'.

Certainly, it had its effect on Mr Rastogi. He quickly rolled up his bedsheet and blanket, and pulled up his berth for the ladies to sit, smiling gently and saying 'No, no, it is my duty' in response to Rita's mother's protestations.

It was when he was through, and settling back in his seat, still smiling and panting slightly from his efforts, that he noticed the novels with the buttocky covers, still on the table before him.

He froze for a full second before reacting.

His eyes, behind his glasses, became slits through which he looked sideways at Rita and her mother—no one had noticed; they were still arranging their luggage underneath the berths—and then, moving with feigned nonchalance, he reached out, gathered the two novels, and pushed them into the narrow space between him and the arm-rest to his left. He then dug deep into his pant pockets, produced a key-chain, bent down and, with swift fumbling fingers, unlocked the chain tying his briefcase to the table-legs. The briefcase was brought up and clicked open; another rapid movement of his hands and the novels disappeared inside it.

The whole manoeuvre took less than a minute, and it left Mr Rastogi looking slightly flustered. It wasn't the right time for him to notice that I had been watching him from above. Somewhat taken aback, he looked blankly at me for some seconds, and then I saw his right eye behind the thick glasses close jerkily. I looked more attentively; the eye opened and closed again. I kept looking; the eye went berserk, opening and closing in rapid succession. Finally, I realized that Mr Rastogi was winking at me.

He didn't wait for my response, but instead turned his attentions to Rita and her mother, Mrs Shukla. He offered to get tea for them, but Mrs Shukla had brought her own, in a thermos-flask. She offered some in turn to Mr Rastogi, who gratefully accepted, remarking, in the way Mr Goenka had done before him, on the inferiority of 'Madrasi tea'. Mrs Shukla tended to agree; she had spent some time in the South, and knew what 'Madrasi tea' was like.

A conversation now began between Mr Rastogi and Mrs Shukla that was to take up most of the six-hour-long journey to Itarsi. Despite Mr Rastogi's best efforts, Rita joined in only intermittently, and for most part kept reading *Stardust* and a novel whose name I could never see but whose back-cover declared it 'Sexier than *Basic Instinct*'. Mrs Shukla, on the other hand, more than made up for Rita's reticence by ceaselessly talking about herself, about her husband, her daughter, even, at one point, her dog.

I learnt, among other things, that her husband was a colonel in the Army, that she herself taught English at a primary school, and that she was a very active 'social worker', organising tambola parties, charity dances, fairs, and picnics.

'You have to do something these days,' she said. 'Otherwise life for an Army wife is *so* dull.'

She was escorting her daughter to Bombay where, she felt, a career in fashion modelling awaited her.

It looked like a hopeless venture. It did not need a fashion expert to tell that Rita's spoilt-girl looks and build were far too average for her to make it on her own as a fashion model. At best, she could be one of the extras in the crowd of westernized teenagers prancing about in the background to an advertisement for chocolates, ice-cream, or pimple-removers.

'She always liked to go on stage,' Mrs Shukla said. 'When she was young she won the Cinderella contest at school.'

Mr Rastogi wanted to know what a Cinderella contest was. Mrs Shukla explained.

'She was always very talented,' Mrs Shukla said. 'Very smart and confident.'

Recently, she told us, Rita had won the homecoming queen contest at the Army Club. She was voted the most beautiful girl in the entire cantonment.

Rita looked up briefly from her reading to smile uncertainly at Mr Rastogi, who beamed with pleasure.

'I feel it is time,' Mrs Shukla was saying, 'now for Indian women to throw off their chains. You look at these fashion programmes on STAR PLUS—how confident and bold those models are. Even though they are not beautiful. Why can't we become like that? After all, Indian women are the most beautiful in the world. Why don't we show our beauty on the world stage?'

She went on to add for Mr Rastogi's benefit that the press had an important role to play in the betterment of Indian women's self-image. One of the ways, she suggested, in which it could do so was by carrying more articles on fashion and modelling.

Mr Rastogi agreed. 'The press is now understanding the importance of modelling,' he said. 'In fact, every English newspaper in Delhi is devoting several pages to fashion these days. It is the new craze.'

I thought I detected some irony in the way he phrased his sentences. But I was mistaken; he spoke in earnest.

Later, after exchanging addresses with Mrs Shukla, he offered to arrange for some free publicity for Rita through his countless friends in the Bombay media.

Uncertainty appeared on Mrs Shukla's face. Rita looked as taken aback as anyone who hasn't got a single achievement to her credit would be, confronted by an offer as generous as Mr Rastogi's.

Mr Rastogi clarified. They weren't to think of it as a special favour. That was how things generally worked in the media world: through connections. You knew someone; you asked a journalist-friend to write a piece on him or her. Later, the journalist-friend would ask for a return-favour; he would comply.

'Mutual assistance, Madam,' Mr Rastogi intoned solemnly, his eyes opaque behind light-reflecting glasses, his countenance strangely aglow. 'That is how we live in this difficult world.'

He caught my eye as he spoke. He may have been winking at me. It was hard to see behind the glasses.

Mr Goenka abruptly broke up the mood of trust and good cheer. He had taken no part in the conversation, but had closely followed it, lying on his side, his back turned toward Mr Rastogi, Mrs Shukla and Rita. To the tradition-bound Mr Goenka—whose own daughters probably wore nothing more modern than a salwar-kurta, who hesitated for days before daring to ask his permission to go to a restaurant with college-friends, and who languished at home after reaching a certain age, embroidering old cushion-covers, waiting for marriage—to an old-fashioned tyrant like Mr Goenka, the fact of a mother encouraging her daughter into a dubious profession like modelling could have only seemed an appalling indecency.

He must have listened with growing repulsion. It now spilled over in a startlingly rude outburst.

While his back was turned toward her, Rita had tentatively propped her Bata loafers up on Mr Goenka's berth. In the interim, what with listening to Mr Rastogi and reading *Stardust*, she had grown inattentive. Now, as Mr Goenka abruptly turned over on his back, his legs collided with her shoes. Rita rapidly withdrew, but not before Mr Goenka had caught her in the act.

He was up in an instant, rubbing his pyjamas where Rita's shoes had touched them, and loudly admonishing her:

'*What is this?! What is this*?!' he cried. 'Why are you putting your dirty shoes on my berth?'

Rita was too shocked and fearful to react. So was Mrs Shukla who couldn't at first understand what had happened. Only Mr Rastogi knew, and he now tried to exercise his influence with Mr Goenka.

'*Bacchi hai, Goenka sahib, chhodiye bhi*, She's only a little girl, Goenka sahib, leave it.'

But Mr Rastogi had overestimated his influence. Mr Goenka by now had a very low opinion of him, and his words only provoked him further.

'*Bacchi hai to Bombay kyon ja rahi hai stage par dance karne*, If she is only a little girl, what is she doing going to Bombay to dance on a stage there?'

'Some people, they think they are very modern, but they have no manners,' he added, in English.

Mr Rastogi looked distraught; Mrs Shukla, even more shell-shocked than before; Rita, on the point of tears, but vengeful, swallowing quickly, trying to summon up a suitable retort.

But no further words were to be exchanged. Human responses are unpredictable; what could have caused in other circumstances a full-scale slanging match elicited not a word of protest in this case. Mr Goenka got up and left the compartment. He did not come back until after Itarsi. Mr Rastogi, Mrs Shukla and Rita remained sunk in a dreadful tense silence until the train stopped at Itarsi a few minutes later. Mrs Shukla and Rita were to leave us here to take the train to Bombay. Mr Rastogi helped them with their luggage. I saw him from the cracked tinted-glass window, saying goodbye to Rita with a broad encouraging smile on his face. I couldn't see Rita's face, but she couldn't have been smiling. Later, Mr Goenka slumbered and Mr Rastogi took out one of his novels from his briefcase and read. They did not speak to each other again for the rest of my journey.

A few miles out of Bhopal, the landscape begins to change. Gone are the flat treeless plains stretching to infinity on either side; gone is their dry indifference, their forbidding impersonality. The new landscape is on a much-reduced, manageably human scale, its thickly wooded, gently rolling hills and tiny brooks giving it an intimate quality that is rarely found on the plains. Long leafy branches of trackside shrubs caress the train as it slowly goes past; gleaming railway tracks snake in and out of tunnels, running circles round each other and themselves. Piles of thick logs await transportation at every small station where an amused-looking man stands with a green flag in his hand and where half-naked children come running out of the lone railway quarter to joyously wave at passing trains.

Another kind of landscape begins a few miles before Nagpur: flat, but crisscrossed on both sides by giant pylons. This is Vidarbha, the poorest part of Maharashtra, the parasitic cousin to sugar-rich Marathwada. But all things are relative, and Vidarbha, though poor, is still less so than parts of Bihar, UP and Andhra Pradesh. From the train, the land looks cultivated, and there are people here: men in eye-catching white, often with Gandhi caps, women in drab colours of the earth, with a blunter cast of features and darker skin-hues than most people in the north. But there is dignity here: people walk straight; even beggars don't cringe. And there is the striking presence, in even the tiniest village, of civic order. The red-tiled houses look attractive, the paths are well-paved, the courtyards clean, the streetlights unbroken.

My destination was Bangalore; and I went part of the way, unexpectedly, by plane. The train that was to take me to Hyderabad from Nagpur was reported to be running indefinitely late. There were other trains after it but taking them would have meant missing my connecting train from Hyderabad to Bangalore. The only way in which I would have reached it was by taking the evening Indian Airlines flight to Hyderabad from Nagpur.

The flight was, as usual, late. But there was mostly indifference on the faces of the crowd swarming the departure lounge; hardened travellers all of them, they were used to such delays. Some of them talked excitedly among themselves. Some sat on plastic chairs, impassively looking out on to the floodlit tarmac. Others paced the floor in what looked like growing anxiety. Still others unfolded their *Economic Times* and *Financial Express* and *Business Today*, and read.

There was an easy assurance about this crowd, a smoothness of demeanour that comes from the possession of either great affluence or power, and which in a country as poor as India could seem like arrogance. They were mostly business executives, and they looked the part in their button-down shirts and classic Oxfords, with their leather briefcases and electronic diaries. Here, under the fluorescent lights of the departure lounge, they were set apart, they were an exalted breed. Poor, backward, struggling India was somewhere else, part of the night behind the flood-lit tarmac. Here, they were with people like themselves, and their conversation only obliquely referred to the country in which they lived.

They talked of corporate intrigues, transfers, new appointments, government policies, salaries. They mentioned amounts which took one's breath away, and made one feel even more of an impostor in their midst: a penniless student whose plane fare had been paid for by his parents. I eavesdropped on at least three conversations where the name 'Manmohan' was repeatedly taken, with slightly varying degrees of casual affection. Only the first name was used; everyone knew whom it referred to: Manmohan Singh, India's finance minister, who, according to some Indian newspapers, was a cult figure in the boardrooms of the West for marketing India so effectively to multinational companies.

While this seemed highly unlikely, the work of grateful journalists who, Mr Rastogi would have known, had been taken on too many trips abroad, it was clear where Manmohan's cult status really lay. It was among these people, some of whom, especially those in their late twenties and early thirties, would have only recently made the long journey from the night outside to this brightly-lit oasis of wealth and stability.

They weren't difficult to identify in this crowd. They were the ones in Van Heusen shirts, with Rolex watches, and Cross pens peeping out ever so unobtrusively from their shirt-pockets, loudly bantering about Manmohan, eager to do the right thing, eager to claim access to the high and mighty, eager to assert themselves, to be rich, to be famous, to move *up*.

One of them sat across the aisle from me on the plane. He was a short, thick-lipped, earnest-looking man in rolled-up jeans, and he kept talking uninterruptedly all through the forty-five-minute long flight to Hyderabad, narrating the story of his life to the man in the seat next to him.

He was from Vijaywada, the son of a railway guard. He didn't dwell much on this past; he brought it in only to show up the contrast with his later achievements. By dint of sheer brilliance, he had first made it to the IIT, and then, the US. While there, he had done a course in Business Administration. He had been offered several lucrative jobs after he finished his course. Both Chrysler and Kelloggs had dangled salaries well over $100,000 per annum before him. But he hadn't been tempted. He had wanted to come back to India, and start his own business. That is what he was presently doing. He felt he had made the right choice.

'The sky is the limit in India,' he said, 'and I am very ambitious.'

It sounded like a boast, but he was stating the plain truth. And, he was following a general trend: suddenly, it was no longer gauche to flaunt one's ambition. 'I am very ambitious': one heard this line more and more often. Sportspersons, models, film stars, fashion designers, advertising executives—all of them liked to mouth it. The bland literalness, the banal self-regard, could be stupefying. But that was only because one looked for self-deprecating irony and wit in these assertions.

I sat next to a sober-looking middle-aged man who was reading *Gurus, Godmen and Good People* by Khushwant Singh. I had never heard of this particular book before. But then, keeping up with the relentlessly prolific Khushwant Singh is a full-time occupation in itself. I kept peering over the man's shoulders to read. I saw him grow self-conscious: he was reading the chapter on Bhagwan Rajneesh 'Osho'. I kept peering. Finally, he closed the book shut and offered it to me. I accepted with gratitude and browsed through the book before giving it back to him.

A brief conversation began. He turned out to be a fairly serious-minded devotee of Osho. His interest in him was recent, sparked off by a video recording of Osho's discourses that a friend had loaned him, but he was already planning to go the whole way: more readings in Osho, regular meditation, trips to Poona.

But there was a problem.

What?

'I don't know,' he said, and abruptly giggled—a shy, twitchy giggle. 'I don't know what to do with all this *sex* thing.'

10

'See, I told you! It's empty!' exclaimed my friend Sanjai as we walked into one of Bangalore's newest shopping malls. It was my third day in Bangalore. I visited the city almost every other year, and found something new each time. This time, it was the shopping malls on Brigade Road. There were several of them, built in a variety of adventurous architectural styles, and, seeing them from the road, I had first thought them larger, slicker versions of the 'air-conditioned markets' one saw opening up in big and small towns across India.

It was Sanjai who made me look at them differently. Sanjai was an old friend from Allahabad, who worked now for the Income-Tax department. We had gone together to Brigade Road one day for lunch; later, he had taken me to see the malls.

His contention was that, contrary to media images, Bangalore wasn't fully prepared as yet for the new money pouring into it. And the empty malls did bear him out. They had been mostly built by expatriates seeking to emulate in India what they had been impressed by during their time abroad, and they looked like serious miscalculations. People had either overestimated the city's spending power or were trying to fast-forward the place into the future through the sheer illusion and panoply of affluence. Whatever it was, it hadn't worked: more than a year after opening, the malls still awaited shoppers.

More accurately, they awaited shops. Very few people looked to have bought space in the malls. 'The rents are too high,' explained Sanjai, 'those who can afford them overprice their stuff, but people aren't willing to come here and pay more just for the escalator and the glass elevator. Anyway, they can ride them for free', he said, pointing to a couple of teenaged girls in jeans nervously gliding onto the escalator, 'and do their shopping outside.'

The malls, Bangaloreans proudly told me, were modelled on those in Los Angeles. There were other much-remarked similarities between the two cities. The temperate weather, for instance. Although the sun didn't always shine in Bangalore—it rained quite a lot—but when it did, it didn't scorch you as it did in Madras, Calcutta and Bombay.

Then, there was Bangalore's much-trumpeted cosmopolitanism whose greatest achievement, in the few days I spent there, seemed to lie in importing the latest Hollywood films faster than any Indian city. Another prominent sign of Bangalore's cultural pluralism was the accents on the fashionable Mahatma Gandhi Road—a beguiling mix of both Indian and American.

'C'mon *yaar*, Demi Moore was *there* in *We're No Angels*,' shrieked the young woman in black nylon tights, waiting outside a cinema-hall showing *Indecent Proposal*. 'Wanna have a bet?' her pony-tailed boyfriend in flared bellbottoms calmly responded.

The appurtenances of modernity were all very conspicuous: the kids in Reeboks and Nikes, chewing Wrigley chewing gum, clamouring to be taken to Spencer's open-air cafe. Yuppies, in loosened ties, sipping lager beer, talking stock-market jargon at Rice Bowl, the Chinese restaurant reputedly owned by the Dalai Lama's sister—the muzak on the sound-system appropriately by Nirvana.

Bangalore, I soon became tired of being told, had the

largest number of pubs in India; it was the only place to have draught beer, the best place to have Thai food. Many of its streets—a token few, I was to discover—were lit by solar-powered lamps. Bangaloreans were modern people, with sophisticated sensibilities. And the confirmation seemed to come one evening, watching *Indecent Proposal*, when not a squeak came out of the lower stalls as Demi Moore's breasts popped into view on the screen. Up in the uncivilized North, they would have been, I knew from experience, tearing the stuffing out of their seats.

Bangalore grew rapidly each year, but you still didn't feel the crush of massed humanity as you did in the other four metropolitan cities. The place had a general middleclassness about it: the one city in India where people had found some respite from poverty, and where their sensibilities would not be abraded by constant exposure to dehumanizing poverty. The serene self-possession of young executives at Bangalore pubs could not have been shared by most of their Bombay compatriots, by people who daily drove through Dharavi to reach their places of work. The slums in Bangalore existed, but were out of sight, unlike Bombay where they cower beneath high-rise buildings in the poshest of localities. Presumably, the poor couldn't afford to live in Bangalore.

For one, they would have had a problem getting around the city. I made the discovery every time I came to Bangalore: it simply had no cheap public transport worth its name. The sullen autorickshaw driver consented to take you only after a lot of persuasion and then tried to overcharge you. In that way, Bangalore could still seem to lack the frictionless efficiency which even a place as overpopulated and chaotic as Bombay had.

'It's an attitude problem,' Shinde, a software expert from Pune told me. 'The people who have been here from the beginning still don't think of themselves as living in a big city; they don't see themselves in the larger scheme of things.'

This may be true or untrue, but Bangalore, with its shopping malls, its new restaurants and five-star hotels, its health-clubs and designer boutiques, sent out a different message to the rest of India. It claimed to be up with the Joneses; it claimed to be modern and efficient; it proposed itself as the model Indian urban settlement, a place other upcoming Indian towns could aspire to. Bangalore, it could begin to appear, was where their future lay.

The only hitch was that Bangalore's own future was not too clear. Its problems were growing as population multiplied, and more and more industries came up, and they were the same as faced by other cities: power and water shortages, lack of proper transport, congestion, pollution.

Serious, probably insurmountable, problems. But one could be easily deceived by what was generally known about the place. In recent years, a lot of imported notions had come to stand for Bangalore: India's Silicon Valley, India's electronics capital. They belonged to the world of abstract finance, of gung-ho businessmen ever ready to pounce upon lucrative new territories, and they could almost completely ignore ground realities. In that world of cosy certainties, it was easy to forget, after all the talk about Silicon Valley, that Bangalore was an Indian city with Indian problems, which, given the experience of other Indian cities, had the odds stacked against it. It wasn't pessimism but hard realism which made one see that only time was of consequence, and that one only had to wait before Bangalore went the way other Indian cities had gone before it, letting entropy do its slow inexorable thing, turn this once elegant little cantonment town into another Indian urban nightmare.

But Bangalore still offered in full the metropolitan

excitements I had known in the past, and my days there fell into a pleasant routine. Mornings began with what must be one of the best breakfasts in the world: sambar vada, coconut chutney, upma and freshly roasted coffee. Later, I would loiter over to MG Road and read my way through a stack of newspapers, sitting on one of the benches lining the road. Then, it would be time for some book-browsing at Gangaram's and Premier's after which I would eat a light lunch of sandwiches. By late afternoon the newspapers from Delhi arrived, and I would now make my way through them over coffee at the Indian Coffee House. Later, I would go for a long walk in Cubbon Park before returning home to round off a day of perfect idleness with a TV dinner.

A few such days; then, early one morning in Bangalore, I took the bus to Tiruppur.

I had heard a lot about Tiruvalluvar Transport Corporation buses, but had never travelled in one. They were supposed to be the best in India, one of the positive outcomes of the populist policies pursued by successive administrations in Tamil Nadu, an exemplary success in a state where few public services could claim even ordinary efficiency.

It was proved true even before I started. At Bangalore Bus Stand, where buses from four states vied for attention, the Tiruvalluvar buses stood out with their clean and roomy interiors—quite unlike anything I had seen before on Indian roads. Now, as I travelled into Tamil Nadu, they were to become a familiar sight, visible at impressively regular intervals, a part of the landscape, strikingly blood-red against the surrounding greens and browns.

Unlike Bombay or Calcutta whose suburbs extend infinitely, and form separate cities in themselves, Bangalore quickly recedes. Instead of heavily populated settlements, there were factories on either side, each of them with walled enclosures and well-maintained gardens. There were few people outside at this early hour. There was a slight chill in the air even though the bus-windows were all closed. We left Karnataka and entered Tamil Nadu, where children in starched, ironed school-uniforms and young women with fresh flowers in their hair stood expectantly at local bus-stands. The landscape here was browner and drier; huge gravity-defying boulders perched on hillsides. Giant billboards loomed up, offering 'tiffin' meals and comfortable accommodation ("Hotel Nice: Fine Place for Nice People"). Water-logged rice fields and clumps of banana and coconut trees appeared after Hosur. At Dharmapuri, a sign-painted board welcomed one to an all-women police station, but the demonstration, a few metres ahead, of exuberantly noisy children led by a small group of adults was policed by males alone. There was at one tiny settlement a whole market devoted excusively, it seemed, to tomatoes. Further ahead, roadside vendors, shaded by large trees, sold coconut-water, the coconuts dangling at the end of long hemp-ropes coiled round branches.

Beside me sat Venkatesh Rao, a sanitary-ware retailer based in Hyderabad. He was originally from Tamil Nadu, but had now spent many years in Andhra Pradesh, and spoke Telugu better, he claimed, than Tamil. His Hindi, picked up, he said, from films and Doordarshan, was fluent too. He was in his mid-twenties, and wore a pink silk shirt and a prominent tilak on his forehead. He was new to the business: his brother, who set it up, had managed it single-handedly until Vankatesh finished his bachelor's degree.

Why was the bachelor's degree important? I asked.

He spoke frankly. His brother, he said, hadn't gone beyond eighth standard. The lack of education was a great handicap in a business where you had to travel a lot; then, you were also required to make a good impression on people so as to get better credit. So, he had wanted Venkatesh to acquire at least a bachelor's degree.

We talked about toilet bowls for some time. I asked him about the types he sold and whether the Indian-style bowls did better than Western ones.

Absolutely, he said. Indians, he said, weren't comfortable with western-style toilets. He knew many rich people in Coimbatore who had them installed in their newly-built houses, and then wanted Indian replacements. But the advances in toilet technology were all being made in the West. He told me about some of the new kinds of time-saving, effort-minimizing toilet bowls being developed: they came equipped with water faucets that hosed you at the touch of a button, warm-air dryers that dried you, and sophisticated sensors that knew when you had finished and flushed automatically.

He told me he had been to Delhi many times in connection with his business: Delhi was a big wholesale outlet for sanitary-ware.

I asked him whether he had liked Delhi.

But he didn't think of places in that way. He was concerned only with the business aspect of Delhi. He knew his wholesale dealers in Old Delhi; he did his work with them and then left. There was no time for anything else. On his first visit, he had taken the DTC-organized one-day bus-tour of Delhi, but he remembered nothing from it except the rudeness of the tour-conductors who openly ridiculed the South Indians in the tour-party, not realizing that some of them could understand Hindi.

He hadn't wanted to talk about it at first, but later he told me he had often felt cheated by the wholesale dealers in Delhi—so much so that he had almost ended his dealings with them, and had now found in Bombay dealers an honest and reliable substitute.

But, he added, I was not to take it too personally. Delhi wasn't an exception. There were frauds and cheats everywhere—he used the Hindi word for them: *chaar sau bees*. Only recently, a relative of his had bought a tin of Made-in-Singapore talcum powder in Madras at the imported-goods-market there. The seller had wanted Rs 150 for it. His friend had brought him down to Rs 40. Pleased with his bargain, he had taken it home to Coimbatore and presented it to his wife. She had used it only once when an ugly disfiguring infection appeared on her face. It had taken several trips to the doctor and much more than Rs 150 to cure.

Tiruppur, where I was presently going, had occurred early on my itinerary. A professor-friend in Delhi had first told me about it. Tiruppur, he said, was a boom-town, the site of some truly remarkable transformations in the last ten years or so. Along with neighbouring Coimbatore, it formed the centre of the hosiery business in India. It was to underwear what Sivakasi was to firecrackers. And now the market had expanded beyond India. Plane-loads of material for T-shirts were flown to Europe and America every week. The exporters had grown fabulously wealthy. Tiruppur's per capita income now was one of the highest in India.

Several other people whom I asked said the same things about Tiruppur. The versions never differed; they had the uniformity of something taken from common lore.

But there was to this fairytalish success-story a curious twist. Tiruppur, for all its wealth, had no water. The land was dry and arid, and too distant from any conventional sources. The nearest river was miles away to the north; no lakes existed nearby. Then, it was on a high plateau which made it even more difficult to pump up water from anywhere else. The government did its bit by periodically sending in water tankers. But they were never enough. Often, water was so scarce that it had to be bought—at ridiculous prices. And it was clear who suffered the most: the poor. The rich could afford to make their own arrangements—like those other affluent Indians who, in response to the growing contamination of tap-water, had started drinking bottled mineral-water.

I had left Delhi armed with a few names and addresses of people I could, I was told, meet in Tiruppur. But when I phoned them from Bangalore to seek appointments—for these were busy people—most of them turned out to be unavailable on the day I was to visit Tiruppur.

Only one name remained on my list. It was to see him that I was going to Tiruppur; and it seemed like a wasted effort when I finally arrived there, after a long exhausting bus-ride from Bangalore, and was told on the phone that he had been called away to Madras on urgent business.

But who are *you*? the boyish voice on the phone wanted to know.

I introduced myself as a writer-journalist.

Which newspaper was I working for?

I explained I wasn't working for any newspaper, but writing a book.

What kind of book?

A book about rich people in Tamil Nadu, I said, too tired to go into a long and elaborate explanation.

There was a pause at the other end. Then the voice introduced himself as my contact's nephew. His name was Kumar. He said he was sorry I could not meet his uncle. But did I want to see someone else?

Like who, for instance? I wanted to know.

Myself, he immediately said.

I considered this. I had planned to spend the night at Tiruppur, but there didn't seem much point in doing so now. I could press on for Trichur, and spend the night there. On the other hand, now that I was here, it didn't require much effort to meet this boy.

I said yes, but could he come over immediately? I didn't have much time in Tiruppur.

He was there in less than ten minutes: a boy, as I had guessed, in his late teens, dressed in what I was beginning to see as the distinctive style of newly-affluent provincial India, uniform and unchanged from Ambala to Tiruppur: Hawaiian shirt, stonewashed jeans, big white sneakers, a gold chain around the neck, diamond rings on fingers. There was also the regulatory fleshiness around the waist and face, a sign of uncontrolled gastronomic indulgences. Finally, there was the Maruti, no longer a car but a cliché.

His first words to me, spoken with a slightly disgusted look on his face, were: 'This place is very dirty.'

He was referring to the small road-side restaurant where I had asked him to meet me. It looked fairly clean to me, and I had just finished drinking, when he came in, some excellent coffee, served, in the South Indian way, in a tumbler.

Dirty? I asked, looking around.

'Yes, yes, all lower-class people coming here. It is not a decent place. Let us go to my house. I have my car outside,' he said.

I explained I was in Tiruppur for a very short while, and would prefer to talk to him where I presently was.

He sat down opposite me with some reluctance. I asked him if he would like a cup of coffee.

He was vehement in his refusal. 'No. No. No coffee,' he said. 'I don't take any refreshment from these places. They are very dirty places.'

Was he a Brahmin? I wanted to know.

The question took him by surprise. He stared at me for a moment, his thick lips parted and revealing a gleaming row of teeth inside, and then stammered: 'No...no....I am not Brahmin....Why you think I am Brahmin?'

I said his scruples about food and cleanliness had made me think so.

He first smiled—a broad naïve smile, showing pleasure

at my unintended compliment—but quickly grew grave again. 'You are talking about old times,' he informed me. 'There is no Brahmin or scheduled caste thing in Tamil Nadu now. There is no caste feeling. All are equal...'

He trailed off, and then came back with: 'I am not like Brahmins. They are pure vegetarian; they don't eat meat. I eat meat. Do you eat meat?'

I said I didn't.

'You must eat,' he said. 'Meat is very tasty, good for health also.'

I tried to make him talk about other things. I asked him about his education, his uncle's business. But I didn't get more than routine replies out of him. He went to college in Coimbatore; he planned to pursue a degree in Business Administration later. His uncle's business was 'very big'; he had houses in Tiruppur, Madras, Coimbatore and Ooty; he travelled regularly to Europe, America, Singapore, Hong Kong and Bangkok.

He himself had been abroad once. His one visit was to South-East Asia. He had accompanied his uncle; they had gone to Hong Kong.

What had he seen there?

He tried hard, but failed to recall any names from his sightseeing trip.

I persisted. What was his lasting impression of Hong Kong?

He thought for some time, gazing up at the ceiling. I thought I saw him smile to himself. Then, he was looking at me, uncertainly. He looked as if he had found his answer and was now assessing the effect it might have on me.

I tried to encourage him by smiling. He smiled back— a wide, complicituous smile.

He said, 'I liked the Hong Kong girls,' and then stopped, looking at me again with that keen assessing expression on his face.

I smiled. He smiled back, nervously at first, and then, as I kept smiling, more and more confidently, saying, 'They were very open. They were wearing very high skirts and showing their thighs. No shame at all. I took...' and here he giggled, remembering something, 'I took lots of sexy snaps. You come to my house, I'll show you.'

I politely declined his offer, and took the bus to Trichur.

I arrived there late in the evening, and went straightaway to the hotel Elite International that had been recommended to me. The lobby was modern, with thick carpets, sofa chairs, a gleaming elevator in the corner, and the overpowering smell, familiar from countless other hotel-lobbies, of floor-wax. But the rooms above belonged to another era, with their cheap foldable aluminium chairs, a formica-top dressing-table, wooden cots with tall mosquito-net rods—all of which could have constituted part of the dowry proudly displayed in a wedding in Meerut in the early sixties.

I quickly bathed, and then went down to the restaurant on the hotel's ground floor. It was, in the best traditions of up-market restaurants, sunk in darkness, the light barely enough to read the menu. Somewhere from an unseen radio emanated the grave, quaintly old-fashioned baritone of an All-India-Radio newsreader. There was no one else, apart from me and a couple of Medical Representatives, conversing in low Malayalam, giving away their profession with their harried travel-exhausted look and the names of medicines and pharmaceutical companies that cropped up repeatedly in their conversation.

I caught up with one of them at a fruit-juice shop outside the hotel. He was a tall slender man in his late thirties, with a melancholy elegance about him that made him someone more than what his profession hinted, that spoke of latent, neglected gifts.

He spoke to me first, asking me if I was from the North.

Was it so apparent in my manner?

He seemed for some reason to like my reply. He laughed heartily, and then said he knew about me because he had spent time in the North and could instantly recognize people from there.

We talked on. His name was George. He told me he lived in Cochin with his wife and two kids, and made weekly trips to Calicut, Palghat and Trichur. Being a Medical Representative was hard work: you were on the move all the time. Family life suffered. Your health suffered. No wonder, most of his friends were alcoholics. They would get back from an exhausting visit, and then drink themselves silly for the rest of the evening.

He himself staved off boredom through books. He was a reader; and, now as he spoke further, it became quickly clear that he was no ordinary reader, that his taste in literature ran to the most refined works. Borges and Calvino were his favourite authors. He had not read Proust, but he had read Gide, and possessed all the four volumes of his journals. He had read widely in modern European poetry. Valéry, Celan, Char, Montale, Saba, Cavafy—he knew their work intimately, and could quote accurately from the English translations he had read them in.

Did he also write? I asked. Kerala has some of the finest writers in the country, and I half-wondered if I was talking to one of them.

My question embarrassed him. 'No, no, I only read,' he quickly clarified, and then, as though realizing that he hadn't spoken the truth, guiltily added, 'Little things here and there don't count as writing. Everybody does that in their spare time. But that's not serious writing. It's just time-pass.'

I didn't press the issue. It seemed a sensitive matter with him, part, perhaps, of the other life of reading and contemplation he led, distant from his profession, distant from his life as a husband and father.

He had once spent four months in Lucknow many years ago on one of his first jobs. He had greatly enjoyed his time there. The street- and place-names were still fresh in his memory. He went promenading at Hazratganj every evening with friends. He saw a lot of English films at Mayfair. He ate countless meals at Kwality and Chaudharis', bought his books from Ram Advani and Universal. It was the first time he had lived outside Kerala, his first taste of freedom after years of parental supervision, and it was with unrestrained delight that he recalled his time there.

But as he spoke on, I began to notice a strange intensity in his reminiscing. It had been, after all, a typical life for someone as young as he was then; it was for most people an easily forgotten prelude to larger pleasures. But not so for George. His nostalgia for it was immense; and, listening to him, I wondered if a similar period had occurred again in his life, if these memories of early youth had grown more and more vivid and pleasurable through the course of an increasingly plain life, all excitement found only in books, in other lives, other worlds.

After breakfast the next morning, I went for a walk with George.

I had arrived the day before when it was already dark, and Trichur had been little more than a row of brightly lit shops along the road. Now, as we left the main market behind and plunged into the residential area, it quickly revealed itself as another place altogether. The contrast with Tiruppur couldn't have been more striking. Tiruppur had been all flatness: a drab exposed plain, dusty broken roads, low shacks and concrete-and-glass mansions. Trichur, on the other hand, was all stylish angularity: winding shaded lanes, hedge-enclosed tiled houses with wicket gates and spacious backyards, small churches looming up at unexpected bends. There was elegance here, in the fading nameplates, the bougainvillaea draped around mildewed walls, the old-style armchairs on cool porches, and it wasn't of a bygone world but one that was still preserved whole by people respectful of tradition and continuity.

Dark clouds abruptly gathered overhead. The sun disappeared; the light grew grey and dim, further emphasizing the luxuriant greenness of our surroundings. Soon, it began to rain. There was no preparatory drizzle; the rain came down all at once in thick heavy drops, reducing visibility to a bare minimum and making a deafening din as it pounded the various roofs in the vicinity.

We took refuge in a tiny coffee-shack we had passed before. George ordered two cups of coffee, and began a discussion about Thomas Mann. Other people came in, seeking shelter from the rain: two labourers, their wiry torsos bare and streaming with water; a short-statured man in white shirt and pants, probably on his way to work, who held a rolled-up copy of *Indian Express* in his hands. Wordlessly, they stared into the falling rain, locked in a trance, the moment of temporary repose the rain had created in the middle of their routine-led lives. I watched them, listened to George. This was what perhaps I had long wanted to do—discuss Thomas Mann on a rainy morning in Kerala over genuine South Indian coffee—— and I was happier than at any other time on my travels so far.

The rain stopped just long enough to allow me to get back to my hotel. Then, it began again, and I stayed in my room, ate a lunch of rubbery chapatis with greasy dal and a plate of overcooked vegetables called 'Vegetable Jhalfrezi,' and watched *Donahue*.

The subject today was polygamy. In the dock was a corpulent young man who had married five women. He had come with his current fiancée whose hand he held on to tightly all through the severe arraignment that followed. His ex-wives too were present, all rather on the heavy side themselves, and barely able to control their hatred for the man they had married. Their abuse often went beyond limits permissible for TV, with the result that Donahue today looked even more like a man walking over hot coals, hopping across from one speaker to the next: the quintessential TV sage, but without the wisdom, and with only some second-hand trendy prejudices of his time.

The matter was more complicated than he made it seem: the polygamist was a damaged man, who had been brutally abused in his childhood. And he had no money; marriage was for him a means to survival.

But compassion wasn't what came pouring out of the audience, which mostly comprised of upper-middle-class women, all of whom looked carefully gussied up for their appearance on the show, dressed in eye-catching colours, their mouths painted a bright red. They were a fierce bunch, snarling, full of scorn for the polygamist, and with the spontaneous cohesion—and subtlety—of a pack of hounds. 'You're a sleaze Mark, ged some help,' one of them yelled. Another asked Mark's current fiancée, who looked ready to faint with fear, 'Can't you do any bedder? Why dontchu play the field?' Yet another suggested to his wives: 'Ged a pair of scissors and ged him where he's haat.'

11

When the rain stopped, I took a taxi to Kottayam. I went via Cochin, where I had planned to stop awhile and eat. But I had misremembered the distances between these places, with the result that I reached Kottayam very late in the evening.

The traffic was light: an occasional truck or car. There was an almost uninterrupted series of settlements along the road, mostly residential buildings, clean and well-tended, nestling amid banana and coconut trees, and completely without the desolating quality of roadside towns in the North. At larger settlements, the road broadened instead of narrowing; no part of it looked encroached upon. And the women outside easily outnumbered men: mostly long-skirted, college-going girls with fresh flowers in their hair and books pressed to their bosoms, who giggled and pointed indecisively when asked for directions.

The road after Cochin—where I ate a hurried meal at Woodlands—suddenly deteriorated. The car lurched from side and side as it went over potholes; passing buses churned up thick clouds of red dust behind them. Then, just as suddenly, the road improved. The land here was hilly and less populated, the few houses were set well back from the road, and the vegetation was denser. Large fenced-in rubber estates lay on either side, with, sometimes, a shaded uninhabited-seeming bungalow on top of a hill. Teak forests and coffee plantations intervened to lend a few more shades of green to the scenery. Going endlessly up and down the twisting deserted road felt, in my fatigue-induced daze, like slowly penetrating to the core of an exceptionally lush and welcoming landscape.

At Kottayam, I checked into a hotel on the busy K.K. Road, quickly bathed, and then went out for a short walk.

I had noticed, while looking for my hotel, a number of new-looking readymade-clothes shops, their pastel interiors gleaming behind glass doors and windows, conspicuous in a street full of churches and old-fashioned, open-fronted shops. It was where I now went.

The shops—some called themselves 'boutiques'—were, as I had thought, new, and, without exception, deserted. I went into one with the bright name of 'Pretty Joanne'. The shop staff looked up with wide-eyed interest as I walked in. The interest turned into suspicion as I examined some outrageously gaudy 'designer' versions of the North Indian salwar kameez. Soon, one of them was breathing down my neck and demanding to know what I wanted.

'Just looking,' I said.

'But this is ladies boutique,' he said.

I hadn't known that. With as much dignity as I could muster, I made a quick exit.

I didn't go into any of the other shops, and merely observed them from the road, especially the people manning them, who, listlessly looking out from amid their brilliantly-lit enclosures, gave off a strange forlornness. It couldn't have been just the strain of waiting interminably for customers who never arrived. It was more the alienness of their setting: these shops which with their clean-cut lines, their dust-free interiors, their glass fronts, their air-conditioning, created an oppressively unfamiliar world for their inhabitants in a small place like Kottayam. It was something I thought I could recognize from the past. I had been living in Allahabad when its first 'fast-food' restaurant opened in 1987. The owner had been inspired by Nirula's of Delhi—inspired in turn by McDonald's of America—and he strove to recreate it in every way he could in Allahabad—down to the plastic vines and plants. But what at first looked strange and incongruous in Delhi was even more so in Allahabad. There were prospective customers I knew who would not dare to step inside the restaurant for fear of being intimidated and embarrassed. And the staff, most of whom were locals, had not ceased for months to give an impression of total unease in their alien Americanized surroundings, always looking, in their jaunty peaked caps and monogrammed uniforms, like people trapped in an overly elaborate and pointless masquerade.

In the morning, I called upon Mrs Mary Roy, famous litigant, and, currently, Principal of Corpus Christi School, Kottayam.

Mrs Roy, in a celebrated court case in the mid-eighties, had taken on the entire Syrian Christian Church, and won. She had contested the legality of a pre-independence Succession Act that denied women their rightful share in paternal property, allowing them only a pitiable fourth of the son's share. Amazingly, this Act, which stood automatically repealed after India became a republic in 1951 and promulgated its own Succession Act, had been allowed to govern property distribution for thirty-five more years. Finally, Mrs Roy took up the cudgels on behalf of Syrian Christian women, and filed a public interest litigation in the Supreme Court. That was in 1983. In 1986 came the historic judgement declaring the old Succession Act null and void.

The litigation attracted a fair amount of publicity, even if hardly as much as the coterminous Shah Bano case.

Emerging from relative obscurity, Mrs Roy became for some time a national figure, her bold views on men, marriage, and feminism featured prominently in women's magazines.

And I first thought I had not properly realized the true extent of her fame when I tried calling her and found that she was as well-shielded from nosey journalists as any Bombay filmstar.

Three different voices interposed themselves between Mrs Roy and me. The first one told me that Mrs Roy was ill, and therefore unable to meet me. However, it asked for my hotel number in case, the voice said, Mrs Roy felt better and inclined to see me.

The call came ten minutes later. It was another voice this time, demanding to know, in not very clear English, my credentials.

I explained. I said I had come with an introduction from Mrs Roy's daughter, Arundhati—a Delhi-based filmmaker, whom I had briefly met through a mutual friend—and if Mrs Roy wasn't too indisposed, could I at least speak to her on the phone?

But this was almost instantly rejected, and the voice resumed its questioning. How did I know Arundhati? What kind of book was I writing? Why did I specifically want to meet Mrs Roy?

I patiently answered. Then the voice broke off without explanation.

There was another call after just five minutes. It was the third voice. The interrogation began anew. What was my book about? Why...

I replied with weariness and a growing impulse to put the phone down.

Finally, I was told to come round in an hour's time. I was given directions to Corpus Christi school; I was warned not to pay more than ten rupees to the autorickshaw driver.

Contrary to what I was told on the phone, Mrs Roy, when I was finally ushered into her office, turned out to be in reasonably good health. She was a large matronly woman in her late fifties, with prominent black bags under her eyes, an affable manner, and an impish smile that was startlingly like her daughter's. Unlike her three assistants, she asked me no questions at all about myself. Perhaps, she was satisfied by what she had been told by them. Perhaps—and this seemed more likely after three hours in her company during which she addressed me variously as Pankaj, Pradeep, Sunil, and Ashok—she was simply incurious about someone who after all was only the latest in a long line of interviewers.

She said she was going out to the bazaar for some urgent shopping. Would I mind accompanying her? We could talk on the way, she said.

She wondered, as we walked out to the waiting car, why I was interested in Kottayam. She said, 'It is such a backward small town. Nothing happens here.'

But that was only a bit of instinctive self-deprecation before the visitor. For soon after, in response to my mentioning the readymade clothes shops I had visited the day before, she said, 'Oh, Kottayam is a very modern place. You'd be surprised. All these people are incredibly rich. There is a lot of money in this town, even if it's not too apparent.'

And once we were out, and driving into downtown Kottayam, her manner changed, became more expansive. 'Look,' she said, pointing to a church, 'the church has some of the most valuable property in Kottayam. Do you know there are about five hundred bishops in Kottayam alone? They are always fighting each other because all of them have such grand notions about themselves. They even dress like the Pope!'

And when I made a remark about the number of

women I had noticed wearing salwar-kameezes, something that seemed to me an interesting departure from traditional modes of dress, she said, 'But you know, this part of India was always very different in these matters. We had women going around bare-breasted before the British came and put an end to that. There was a whole agitation against the British on this issue.'

Later, as we waited for the girl who drove us to find some parking space, she said, 'Arundhati is thrilled by that girl. She came from a very poor background, but look at her now: how self-confident she is.'

I followed Mrs Roy on her shopping round. Despite what I had heard about her unpopularity, she appeared to be a well-respected figure. We went first to a large saree store where the men behind the counters rose to their feet as Mrs Roy walked in.

One of them, a tall, spry, spiffily-dressed young man, was her ex-student. We were introduced. His name was Vasudevan. He asked me what I was doing in Kottayam.

Just passing through, I said.

But there is *nothing* here, he said.

That was the second time in a day that I had heard this. 'But how can this be true?' I tried to protest, 'The largest-selling newspaper in India has its offices here. Then, it is the centre of Malayalam publishing. You have the Syrian Christian community here, so many denominations, so many churches. It is a *fascinating* place.'

Mrs Roy looked amused at my response. Vasudevan permitted himself a brief smile.

'That is all for tourists,' he said. 'For people who live here there is very little.'

Mrs Roy told me more about Vasudevan as he busied himself with her order. He was one of her success-stories. After graduating from her school, he had gone on to study at Sydenham College in Bombay. He had then come back to take charge of his father's saree shop.

The saree shop, she added in a lowered voice, had fallen on bad days lately. There were three floors in all when the shop first opened, and it had a monopoly on the wedding-saree business. Now, after the opening of Rehmanika in Cochin, it had gone into rapid decline. Just as it had decimated other saree-businesses in the region ten years ago, so it was being decimated by Rehmanika now.

I had been to Rehmanika on a previous visit to Cochin, attracted by its claim to being the largest saree store in Asia, and had come away quite impressed. It was gigantic all right, but it was also generous. Instead of being unceremoniously ejected, a casual stroller like myself had been presented with a soft-drink. In the air-cooled waiting space for impatient males, there had been a stack of the very latest magazines.

Vasudevan, overhearing me talk about Rehmanika, piped up; 'Do you know it is owned by a man from Kottayam?'

Mrs Roy turned to me and said, 'Didn't I tell you? People think big in this town.'

She asked Vasudevan to show me round the shop. He looked hesitant. The reason became quickly clear: there was nothing to see.

We went up unsteady wooden stairs to a dark hall full of dusty overturned furniture and musty smells. Vasudevan switched on the light. I looked. He waited. I thought hard of something to say.

Some time elapsed before Vasudevan said, 'This floor was operational until sometime back. Now we are trying to turn it into a readymade clothes section.'

'Oh,' I said.

We stood there in some embarrassment, both of us at a loss for words.

Then, as we were going down the stairs, Vasudevan said, apropos of nothing, 'Actually, I am from Bombay.'

But he wasn't. He had only studied there. I knew that already from Mrs Roy.

Slightly puzzled, I said nothing. There was a strange poignance in his claim. It was intended for me: the visitor from the metropolis. But I didn't realize this until much later.

It must have been as a young man full of promise that he travelled to Bombay. His years there, in the company of other big-thinking students, must have further enhanced his ambitions. And things might have seemed to be going his way when he came back to his father's flourishing business in Kottayam.

But then Rehmanika had arrived, and forced his shop into decline. It could not have been an easy thing to take for a man whose notions of success were formed in Bombay, and who probably always thought his proper place was there. It must have revived all his latent dislike for small-town efforts. And it must have revived his desire to reconnect himself with the larger world, a desire, which, in the present circumstances, couldn't go beyond an attempt to distance himself from both Kottayam and the failure the upper floor spoke of.

Back at her office, Mrs Roy told me about her continuing harassment by fundamentalist elements within the Syrian Christian Church. It didn't seem likely that they would ever forgive her. Most recently, they had denounced as blasphemous the Lloyd-Webber play *Jesus Christ Superstar* which the children at her school had put up. On their prompting, the District Collector had raided the school twice to prevent the play from being staged. A close contact in the police department had warned her that drugs might be planted on the premises during the raid, and she had had to take anticipatory bail in order to avoid arrest.

She pointed out the anticipatory-bail order to me. It had been framed and hung just above her chair.

'Look carefully,' she said. 'Do you see something strange in it?'

I couldn't. It was too far from me to read.

'Look carefully,' she said, with a triumphant note in her voice. 'It is an order without any dates on it!'

She received a regular supply of hate-mail. Much of it concerned her daughter, Arundhati, who had outraged fundamentalist opinion by openly living in sin with a Hindu man in Delhi. She was alleged to be promiscuous, flitting from one man to another. Others thought her a prostitute. All concurred in thinking her a morally debased woman.

'All this small-town pettiness,' Mrs Roy said, 'I am so glad I sent my daughter out of Kottayam. I didn't want her growing up here.'

As we talked, a maidservant came in, wearing an immaculately clean apron, and holding a tray with two glasses of Thums Up. While I took an occasional sip from my glass, Mrs Roy never even touched hers. As the afternoon wore on, she grew more voluble, and I was called upon to say less and less. Her range of topics expanded; she turned out to be full of opinions on a variety of subjects.

A common strand ran through them: her desire to separate herself from Kottayam and its backwardness. It wasn't easy to understand at first how she differed from Vasudevan in that. But then, unlike him, she had no cravings for metropolitan success. She was a well-established prominent citizen of Kottayam, the principal of a prestigious school. In however mixed ways, Kottayam offered her a stable existence; the place could even be, as I had seen, a source of pride. Her wish to be distinguished from it clearly had different roots. And it mostly seemed as if by repeatedly emphasizing the stultifying aspect of her surroundings, she was trying to throw into even sharper focus her own struggles for an independent modern identity. Kottayam and its backwardness were, in effect, merely the backdrop—albeit, an essential one— to a long and difficult process of self-creation.

The locals, who had witnessed it from close quarters, could take it for granted; it was the outsider, to whom it wasn't always apparent, who needed to be told about it. Thus, the manifold opinions, which were like cryptic assertions of her independence and modernity.

She talked about sex. She thought it a wonderful thing, and deplored the Christian attitude to it. 'I think Hinduism has a much more positive view on this. I mean, they even tell you how to have sex. And, look at Krishna! How sexual he is!' she said.

She talked about television. She liked the new satellite-TV serials. 'Serials like *Santa Barbara* and *The Bold and the Beautiful* are so much better than anything on Doordarshan. The story is all trash of course, but they are technically very good.'

Technically very good?!! *Santa Barbara* and *The Bold and the Beautiful*?!!

It seemed a strange thing to say, coming from the mother of a fairly accomplished filmmaker.

But just before I left, she said something even stranger. She said, apropos of nothing, with an unexpected passion in her voice, 'I think white people are a curse on mankind. Wherever you look, they are busy causing destruction to something or the other. And they think themselves so superior to everyone else! They are really awful!'

I was still pondering over that remark when I went to Kovalam Beach and found a good reason why white people, for admittedly no fault of theirs, could soon find themselves resented by more Indians.

On a previous visit to Kovalam with a friend I had noticed a hotel called 'Searock'. It was right on the beach, closer to the water than any other hotel. We were then staying at the Hotel Rockholm, a far more clean and pleasant place, but slightly expensive; and we had decided to ask at the Searock, which we knew to be cheaper, if there was anything there for us.

A tall broad-shouldered man with a gruff stentorian voice and absurd accent had met us at the reception. No, he had boomed out. There were no rooms available at his hotel. He had full bookings for the entire season.

It was then the month of October; the season hadn't even commenced. And, I knew that irrespective of which month of the year it was, the hotels in Kovalam were never quite full.

There was something else going on, and a British couple I met on a train had confirmed my suspicions. The Searock, they said, didn't admit Indians. They had come to know this from a French couple on the beach, who were also staying at the Searock and who fully approved of its policy of barring Indians. The British couple, to their credit, had been horrified by such blatant racism. They had left Searock the same day and moved into another hotel.

I had heard about similar hotels in the Caribbean, the playgrounds of rich white Americans, where local blacks, no matter how wealthy, were not welcome. And it had seemed a distinctive feature of the Caribbean's tourist economies: the self-abasement before foreigners, the frantic wish to please at any cost, the desire to be more white than the whites, the lust for dollars, the distrust and contempt for one's compatriots.

But India wasn't a tourist economy—at least, not yet.

All the more disturbing, then, it was to know about places where the shoddy practices of poor parasitic nations had crept in. In India, they were an unpleasant reminder of old colonial hierarchies: whites at the top, Indians somewhere at the bottom, finding their own different levels of degradation. They spoke, at least in certain quarters, of the growing damage, after just forty-seven years of independence, to national self-esteem; and they were the unexplored darker side of globalization, the social consequence of joining the global market as a pavement beggar.

It was the same man at the Searock's reception when I went in. He had two friends with him this time: as tall and broad-shouldered as he was, and with the manner of bullies.

It was some time before he noticed me, standing there with my rucksack.

'Yes? What do you want?' he boomed out.

I said I was looking for a room.

'Single or double?' he asked.

'Single,' I said.

'Sorry,' he said, with an air of finality, 'we have no single rooms.'

I persisted. 'What about a double room?'

'We have them,' he intoned, 'but they are too expensive.'

'How much?'

'Two hundred rupees a night.'

'That's fine by me,' I said. I was expecting a much higher tariff.

But he wasn't listening to me. He had already turned to his friends and was conversing with them in rapid Malayalam.

I said in a louder voice, 'I'll take the room.'

He turned and looked at me, impatience writ large on his face. 'You take my advice and go to the main beach,' he said, in a commanding voice, 'you'll find much cheaper places there.'

'Thank you,' I said, 'but I like it here.'

For some reason, he didn't offer any more resistance. He did look vaguely regretful as I signed the register and paid out the advance, as if berating himself for not having told me that the entire hotel was booked for the season.

I was walked over by a servant to a small room at the end of the corridor facing the reception. The two beds left barely enough space to stand; in the bathroom was a torn towel with a scruffy surface, and a small bar of Hamam soap. I quickly undressed, and went in to bathe.

Two minutes later, the light went out. I finished my bath, dressed, and went out to the reception. The man smiled when he saw me, and exchanged a look with his friends.

'Yes? What do you want?' he asked.

'There is no power in my room,'

'Yes, I know,' he said. 'There is some fault in the fuse. It will come back after two hours.'

I walked back to my room and lay on the cool bed. It had been a long and tiring journey from Kottayam, and I was tired. I must have drifted off into sleep, for when I woke up it was fifteen minutes later, with the sounds of heavy pounding coming through the thin walls from the adjacent room. The noise was deafening; I must have woken up almost immediately after it started.

I got up and went out to the reception. He was still there, but without his friends, and there was a stern expression on his face.

'Yes? What do you want?' he asked.

I told him about the hammering sounds, and how they had disturbed my sleep.

'That will go on,' he said. 'My work cannot stop.'

'Do you have any other room?' I asked.

'No.'

I looked at him; he, at me.

And then without any warning, he took out two hundred rupee notes from his shirt pocket, and, handing them to me, said, 'I told you in the beginning. Take your advance back, and find another hotel. This is not the right hotel for you.'

I checked into another hotel, slept, wrote in my notebook and read an old collection of stories by Vaikkom Mohammed Basheer that I had picked up in Kottayam.

Later on the beach I ran into someone I knew from my last visit. He was a sixteen-year-old boy from a nearby Muslim fishing village. He had dropped out of school at an early age, and, while I was there, seemed to spend all his time soliciting beach-side tourists for business.

The business he offered was deep-sea scuba-diving. The vision he painted of it was exact in its details: the motor-boat drive before dawn, the lonely spot miles away from the shore, the Made-in-Germany scuba-diving equipment awaiting one in the boat, the army of expert swimmers ready to help in case something went wrong.

Moving from person to person on the packed beach, he retailed the same vision, making it all somehow sound like child's play. But I don't believe he ever got any customers. The reason was obvious at first glance. For such a glamorous-sounding sport as deep-sea scuba-diving, he was an extremely unconvincing salesman in his torn vest and lungi, all of whose talk about motor-boats and Made-in-Germany diving equipment could seem to be part of the idleness of the beach.

I met him everyday while I was there. He talked of different things to me after I had quickly discounted myself as a prospective scuba-diver. His ambition was to go to Saudi Arabia, and earn a lot of money there. Many people he knew had already done so, and he was determined to emulate them. As for now, he was content to earn a little money here and there, doing odd jobs.

I never asked him what those odd jobs were, but toward the end of my stay he gave me a truer idea of them. He asked me one day if I liked boys or girls.

I didn't at first understand the true import of his question.

'Both,' I said.

'Boys,' he said, 'you like boys?'

'Yes,' I said, still not understanding.

He said, 'You want to fuck boys?'

So great was the shock that I couldn't bring myself to say anything for some time. I saw him looking expectantly at me, without fear, without embarrassment. It was clearly not the first time he had asked someone that question. I finally managed to weakly blurt out, no. He appeared content with that, and did not offer me girls in place of boys. It was possible, of course, that there were no girls to offer, that there was only him and a few other boys who, struggling with desperate poverty, had fallen back on an ancient profession.

He was in the water, a few feet to my left, when I saw him. He was with a tall skinny girl in a flourescent-green bikini, whose hand he held onto tightly as they dived headlong, shrieking with delight, into the base of a looming wave. He saw me, and his face broke into a smile of recognition, but he appeared unwilling to let go of the girl's hand and swim over to where I was.

He did so after the girl left. He had grown slightly since the last time I saw him. There were the wispy beginnings of a moustache above his upper lip; an Adam's apple bobbed in his throat; his shoulders looked broader. And he was wearing a skimpy Speedo swimsuit, a gift, no doubt, from one of his tourist-friends.

'See that girl,' he shouted above the roar of crashing

waves, pointing to the figure wading back to the beach, 'she's from Israel. She's my girlfriend.'

'What about Saudi Arabia?' I shouted back.

But the sarcasm, in poor taste as it was, was lost on him. His blank face told me he had forgotten about Saudi Arabia, forgotten that he once wanted to go there. It was part of the now-discarded fantasy about motor-boats and scuba-diving; it had never meant anything.

We didn't talk much. He looked restless and distracted, eager to get away.

I commented on that. 'You look like a busy man,' I said.

'Yes, yes, very busy,' he said. 'Too much people wanting me these days.'

The imprecise English inadvertently expressed a kind of truth. Business had finally boomed. From being one who solicited, he had rapidly moved to being one who was solicited. He didn't have customers any more; he had girlfriends. And he was only seventeen, his body yet to achieve its full muscular development, yet to ripen into the bronzed glory which for many winters to come would keep finding new admirers, if not also bring old ones back to these shores.

In the evening, a band came over from Trivandrum to perform at one of the restaurants on the beach. It was a college band, and their repertoire didn't go beyond the perennial college-function favourites: Eric Clapton's 'Cocaine', 'I Shot the Sheriff', 'Wonderful Tonight', Dire Straits', 'Sultans of Swing' and 'Money for Nothing', Deep Purple's 'Smoke on the Water', Santana's 'Black Magic Woman', and a few other hits from the seventies and early eighties.

The audience, all of which was non-Indian, was too

young to have known most of these songs. They lapped
it up nevertheless, swaying their hips, whenever standing,
and tapping their feet, laughing at the funny accents of
the lead singer, raising their empty glasses and bottles
and loudly clamouring for more beer, grateful for a bit of
excitement after a long somnolent day.

They sat under strings of coloured electric lights in
small national groups: the French here, the Israelis there.
The voluntary segregation was one of the interesting things
I had noticed on the beach. It looked even more
pronounced in the small space where guttural German
voices competed with open-throated Dutch yells.
There was a sweet smell of marijuana in the air, but since
a lot of people were smoking cigarettes, it was hard to tell
from which group it emanated. Moving tirelessly from
group to group, as a kind of international coordinator,
was a short, middle-aged Malayali-American man in
Bermuda shorts I had noticed early in the day,
his Californian accent—one that turns every sentence into
a question—the most conspicuous thing about him. He
had appointed himself the master of ceremonies,
periodically seizing the mike and exhorting the crowd
'to give this awesome band a big hand'. Indeed, it looked
as if he had arranged for the band because he was now
going around entreating people to come on the 'dance
floor'.

The 'dance floor' was a tiny bit of sand-covered space
beside the band. Predictably, the first people to appear on
it were two British girls, who had been the cynosure of all
eyes on the beach with their hourly changes of identical
thong-bikinis and brightly-coloured sarongs. They never
went into the water, but merely promenaded upon the
shore with a rather provocative come-hitherish gait,
aimlessly, restlessly, hour upon hour in the blazing sun.
They now wore tight identical halter-tops over even tighter
identical shorts which barely covered their buttocks, and

which, as their bodies went into frantic convulsions in response to 'Hound Dog', slid up to reveal even more.

Other people soon joined them: the Israelis, lean and tanned, the Scandinavians, their skins potato-white and untannable, the disgracefully drunk British, and finally, the Germans, residents still, it seemed from their long hippiesh hair and ragged clothes, of the nineteen-sixties. The sandy floor didn't allow for quick feet movement, and most people were content to simply sway their bodies, their heads loose on their shoulders—a kind of semi-mystical trance that brought to mind, bizarrely enough, calendar-art images of Chaitanya Mahaprabhu going on his rounds through the villages of North Bengal.

There was a short break when the band-members refreshed themselves with beer. The Malayali-American fellow took this opportunity to thank various 'fantastic' people for their efforts toward making possible a 'fantastic' evening. A young American with a guitar came on next, with a song dedicated to the memory of the environmental activist, Chico Mendes. He sang well; the lyrics hinted at a feeling for words. But the audience wasn't interested. In this crowd of beach-drifters, where the talk was of Goa and Bali and other cut-price beaches, there would have been few people likely to have heard of Mendes. And they turned to talk among themselves; they called for more beer; a large number left to let some beer out from their systems.

The dancing continued; and one of the dancers this time was an American man I had met at lunch. There, in the crowded restaurant I had gone to, where people were reading either Judith Krantz or Jackie Collins, I had noticed him perusing *The Susan Sontag Reader*. We had got talking. He had been quick to distance himself from his book, introducing himself as a committed Marxist, with a special aversion for Susan Sontag's brand of 'post-modern politics'. He had then, apropos of nothing, gone on to denounce her son, David Rieff, and his friend, Christopher Hitchens. He had firmly declared himself against any kind of Manhattan-style 'milk-and-toast' liberalism. He had talked about the need for a Bolshevik-type revolution in the US. 'Clean up all the dirt at one stroke,' he had declared, arms flailing.

Arms still flailing, he now looked cleaned-out of everything except beer, dancing with a petite gazelle-eyed Italian girl I had noticed him keenly eyeing during our conversation at the restaurant, bumping his hips against hers, thrusting his pelvis toward hers, a look of almost lunatic ecstasy on his face.

12

At Kanyakumari, where I went the next day, I fell in with a Bengali family. They were delighted to know I understood a little Bengali and even spoke some, haltingly. I was grateful for their company. Their perennial good humour and high spirits did much to relieve the joylessness of the place.

Kanyakumari is where India begins. Visiting travel-writers who point that obvious fact out then move on to a rhapsodic celebration of the great land mass stretching northward: the endless plains, deep forests, wide rivers, eternal snows and so on. Other distinguished visitors have confessed to similarly uplifting reflections. Every Indian schoolboy in my time knew Swami Vivekanand came here before setting off for the Parliament of Religions in Chicago in 1893 to impress upon assembled delegates—if not the world at large according to overly patriotic history text-books—the indubitable superiority of Hinduism. For those who may have forgotten this, a building of hideous design set upon a huge rock commemorates the visit. Mahatma Gandhi was another visitor who found it a congenial place for meditating on such momentous subjects as India's character and destiny.

Modern-day Kanyakumari, however, inspires a different set of meditations. India begins here, and it begins

with a beach rendered uninhabitable by early-morning
squatters; it begins with piles of unclaimed trash and open
drains alongside the roads; it begins with the ear-splitting
noise from assorted loudspeakers on electric poles; it
begins with the ugly clumps of squat concrete-and-glass
buildings. Urban India begins in Kanyakumari, and
doesn't end for thousands of miles inland; and all its
misery and squalor is encapsulated in this tiny town on
the tip of the subcontinent.

The Bengali family I was with had come from
Durgapur. Like all other Bengalis I was used to meeting
in places remote from Bengal, they were veteran travellers.
I had grown to admire their type, for they weren't rich,
merely middle-class, and only curiosity and a wish for
adventure led them to spend so much money each year
on their travels. This was their second trip to the South.
They had been to all the major hill-stations in the North;
they had travelled through Rajasthan; they knew Orissa
like the back of their hands; and only financial constraints
seemed to keep them from exploring the world outside
India.

But it didn't keep them from having an ebullient wide-
eyed curiosity about it. I spent most of my time with them
discussing with the seventeen-year-old son, Basab, the
complications surrounding the Maastricht treaty in Europe.
As I didn't know much about recent events on that score
it was he who did most of the talking and filled up gaps
in my knowledge. He reminded me of the narrator in
Amitav Ghosh's *The Shadow Lines*. And when I told him
that, he turned out to have read all of Ghosh's books.

A year older than him, his sister, a slim serious girl in
glasses, planned to study Sociology at the Delhi School of
Economics before going abroad. Two years into her
undergraduate course, she already had a good idea of
what she would do her doctorate on. She wanted to work
on non-resident Indians abroad, probe into their

backgrounds and the metamorphoses their culture underwent in a foreign setting.

Then, they took the bus to Madurai, and I was left alone once again. I would have left immediately had I not got a train ticket to Bangalore for the following day. I now had a whole afternoon on my hands with no further interest in exploring Kanyakumari. I went back to my hotel room—a gloomy, dimly-lit, low-roofed affair—and tried to read. But the noise made it difficult to concentrate. I closed all the windows, drew the curtains, and it still seeped in like a distinct murmur.

Later I watched the sunset, periodically disturbed by sun-glass-vendors who offered me Ray Ban glasses for a special discount price of Rs 100. 'You'll look *very* smart, *very* handsome,' they choused, 'just like Rambo. Guarantee!' They carried hand-held mirrors and pictures of Sylvester Stallone wearing sun-glasses for instant comparison. I tried one of the proffered pairs. The lenses were cloudy and badly specked; it wasn't Rambo, but a blind person that one was likely to resemble after prolonged use. I bought instead a shoulder-bag with an embroidered portrait of Stalin on it, his moustache the closest equivalent I have seen to the cockroach in Osip Mandelstam's ill-fated poem.

At dinner my companions were four young men from Kanpur. I had seen them earlier in the day at the beach, wearing the same brand of Y-front underwear, tremulously dipping their feet into the water, their paunches helplessly exposed and quivering as they ran back from an approaching wave. The underwear had made me think they were brothers; they turned out to be close friends. All of them owned businesses in Kanpur (businesses was a euphemism for shops), and annually came on a pilgrimage to the South. I had expected them to be full of anti-South prejudices; but I was wrong again. They were indifferent to their surroundings. They had found people from the North wherever they went. Tirupati, Rameswaram, Kanyakumari, Madurai, they said, were full of North Indians. In a way, they had never really left home.

Two of them were now planning a far more ambitious trip: they were going to England.

This took me completely by surprise.

What for? I reflexively asked.

'*Ghoomne*, Sightseeing,' they said.

My amazement grew. Obviously, these men were far richer than their clothes and conversation made them seem. But a visit to England implied the shedding of inhibitions other than the merely financial. For a resident of overcrowded, congested, polluted Kanpur, it meant a gigantic leap into a world where few of their compatriots had gone before; it meant the overcoming of several psychological barriers; it denoted a cultural confidence one would not have expected to find in the narrow bylanes where they had their shops.

But some anxiety still remained. Sushil, the more articulate of the two, worried about 'manners'.

'*Sunte hain manners bade jaroori hain wahan*, I have heard that manners are very important there,' he said.

His friend, Vikas, solemnly nodded in agreement. '*Thank you, sorry, sab hamesha theek samay pe bolna chaiye*, One should say "Thank You" and "Sorry" at the right time,' he said.

'*Varna saale sochenge Hindustani abhi bhi junglee ka junglee bana hua hai*, Or else they would think Indians are still as uncivilized as before,' said Sushil, giggling uncertainly.

They asked me if I knew what English 'manners' were.

I said I did not since I had never been to England.

Sushil said he had consulted some books on the matter. He had even tried out some of their suggestions when he went to the British High Commission in Delhi for his visa.

He had been interviewed at great length about his purpose in visiting England. He'd had to produce all sorts of evidence to prove that he did not intend to stay on in England, and that he was going as a mere tourist. Finally, he was told his application had been accepted.

'*Bada khush hua main*, I was very happy,' Sushil said. There had been many Sikhs outside with rejected applications, and he felt himself to be tremendously lucky. He had come prepared for the occasion, having memorized beforehand a few expressions of gratitude. So that when the woman in charge gave him the good news, he immediately bowed low to the ground and said: 'Respected Madam, I am much beholden to you for your warm and kind cooperation and assistance. I shall forever remain your humble and grateful servant.'

Trouble awaited me at Kanyakumari railway station where I was to take the train to Bangalore. It arrived at the platform half an hour before departure time. I had a confirmed ticket in my pocket, and so, I took my time at the magazine-stall before complacently strolling over to the AC II coach.

I did not bother to check my name in the reservation chart. I walked straight to the compartment mentioned on my ticket, and found my berth occupied by a large family eating what looked like an enormous dinner.

The compartment was full of the pungent aroma of pickles. I stowed away my rucksack with some show of impatience, and then said, as politely as I could, that I hoped my berth would be soon vacated.

'What is your berth number?' A male voice asked.

I told him.

'But how can that be?! That's ours! This whole compartment is ours.'

I was beginning to say that he was in the wrong compartment when he produced his ticket, gripping it with oil-stained fingertips, and pushed it in my face.

'See. Coach no: A2. Berth no: 24.'

I saw. I fished out my own ticket and looked. Coach no: A2. Berth no: 24.

'But, look at this,' I said, showing him my ticket.

He looked. His face grew puzzled for an instant, and then rapidly regained composure.

He said, 'But my name is on chart. Have you seen it?'

I had to concede I hadn't.

'Please see then,' he said, smiling. He was beginning to take some pleasure in my discomfiture. So were other members of his family, who, momentarily perturbed at the thought of having made a mistake, were beginning to relax again.

I went and looked. The man was right. The name Vijayan occurred at six places, including berth number 24.

I looked, with growing dread, for another AC II coach. There wasn't any.

Five minutes remained for the train to leave. I went in to request Mr Vijayan to mind my luggage while I spoke to the ticket-conductor. Mr Vijayan was positively magnanimous in his consent.

But the ticket conductor was not to be seen anywhere on the platform. The coach attendant said he hadn't arrived.

Two minutes now remained. I saw the signal turn to green. The coach attendant said that sometimes the conductor boarded the train at one of the lesser stations after Kanyakumari.

Then I saw the familiar black-jacketed figure with the clipboard in his hands striding toward us. Dizzy with panic, I ran up to him; he, a tall, swarthy, stern-looking man, regarded me as ticket-conductors regard supplicants who run up to them, pleading for berths: with calm contempt.

But I wasn't going to put up with it today. For one, I wasn't a supplicant; I already *had* a berth, according to my ticket. And, I was being put to unnecessary inconvenience and anxiety by the fault of some railway reservation clerk who had unthinkingly issued two tickets for the same berth; I was burning with righteous zeal.

And, holding my ticket under his chin, walking fast alongside the conductor, I indignantly blurted out my story and demanded an explanation.

He heard me out, barely looking at my ticket as he did so, and then said:

'I shall check on train.'

But, I said, this is *urgent*.

He said, 'You say you have confirmed ticket. Why are you worrying? I'll adjust you.'

Feeling somewhat consoled by that, I went back to where I had left my rucksack. Mr Vijayan, in my absence, had taken it out from under his berth and placed it in the corridor where the shoes of passing people had already left several muddy imprints on it.

'It is causing inconvenience to us, so I have put your luggage here,' Mr Vijayan explained.

The train left on time. I saw the conductor come in from the other end. I hurriedly walked up to him, ticket in hand. He looked at me, abstractedly.

I said, 'Can you check my ticket now?'

He seemed to have difficulty recognizing me.

'Yes, tell me,' he said, accepting the proffered ticket and settling himself on a vacant berth, 'What is your problem?'

I told him, far more composedly this time, conscious of other people listening in the compartment.

I finished my account. I noticed the faces around me

looking sympathetic. I waited. The conductor was peering at my ticket. He was peering at it very closely.

Finally, he brought his face up. There was a strange triumphant look on it.

He said, 'But your ticket is for next month.'

What?

'Look.'

I looked at where his thick finger was pointing on the ticket, and the dread which had been slowly ebbing in the last few minutes spouted up within me with debilitating force. He was right. The ticket *was* for next month. I hadn't checked the date at all, neither at the time of issue nor later.

The conductor was already withdrawing, handing back my ticket as if he didn't want anything more to do with it, relegating me to the lowly ranks of berth-seekers.

He busied himself with other passengers. I was told to wait. I would have to buy a new ticket, I was told, but only if there was a spare berth left over after accommodating wait-listed passengers.

So I waited for the next hour in a growing agony of suspense, watching from afar the conductor go on his rounds, fervently hoping there was a vacant berth for me somewhere. In the end, my prayers were answered. I was issued a new ticket and allotted a berth in the compartment where he had first examined my ticket.

Thus I found myself in the same compartment with Mr Mehrotra, who had followed my case with keen interest, and who, at one point, had suggested that I bribe the conductor.

'Give him half the ticket money. He'll take you free to Bangalore.'

Then, he had asked me where I was from. My reply had him promptly holding out his hand, and saying:

'Let's shake hands then. I am from Delhi also.'

His fierce military grip had left my hand hurting. It now turned out that he was a Captain in the army.

'One has to serve,' he was telling his companions—a mild-mannered young computer engineer from Bangalore and a bulbous-nosed middle-aged contractor from Warangal—when I came in. 'And I could not think of any better place than the Army.'

'What do you mean by serving?' the computer engineer asked.

Mr Mehrotra ignored the question. 'You see,' he added, looking at the computer engineer, 'a lot of avenues are now opening up in private sector. But the Army has something like organizational support....'

Saying that, he bent down, unzipped his bag and produced a big-sized bottle.

'You see this bottle?' he held it up for everyone to see. It was the new Indian champagne, inexplicably named Marquis de Pompadour.

'This bottle costs over four hundred rupees in open market,' he said. 'But if you buy it in Army canteen, it is only costing two-hundred-and-fifty rupees. You see what I mean?'

He had recently served in Kashmir, and had definite views on the subject.

'We can be more tough but there is too much political pressure. It is always there, otherwise the Army can set Kashmir right in one month if politicians give us free hand,' he said.

This brought him to the problem of human rights.

'I am very religious, I go to temple very regularly and I think human rights is fine. But when it comes to the unity and integrity of the country, human rights are no consideration. I don't care. The country is more important than human rights,' he declared.

The contractor from Warangal agreed with him.

'Human rights, human rights, people are talking

bloody nonsense! What is human rights when there is terrorism from Pakistan side?!'

He went on to say that Hindus should migrate in large numbers to Kashmir so as to turn the Muslims there into a minority.

Mr Mehrotra called upon the computer engineer, who had merely listened so far, to express his views on the subject.

The computer engineer thought for some time, and then softly suggested that perhaps the Kashmiris should be allowed to decide their future.

Dismay appeared on Mr Mehrotra's face. But, it was the contractor from Warangal who spoke first.

'Sir, may I know your good name?' He abruptly demanded of the computer engineer, bringing his face forward, his mouth drawn into an expectant snarl.

Mr Mehrotra looked puzzled. The computer engineer was himself taken aback by this unexpected turn to the conversation. He nevertheless replied: 'Narayan Hegde.'

The contractor looked disappointed. The snarl vanished from his face. Leaning back, he said, in a somewhat plaintive tone, 'That means you are Hindu, sir. But views like yours are spoken by only Muslims.'

Mr Mehrotra did not seem to much appreciate this new communal slant to the discussion. He said, 'I disagree, boss. The question is not of Hindus and Muslims. India is a secular country and there is no such thing as Hindus and Muslims in it. All are equal. The question is about the unity and integrity of the country...'

He went on to relate his various experiences in Kashmir, fighting terrorism. There were some things he said he was sorry he couldn't tell anyone: they were state secrets.

In between, he noticed me on the upper berth, frantically scribbling in my notebook—I was recording the conversation, word by word—and abruptly asked me:

'Mishra, what are you writing?'

'Oh, nothing,' I said. 'Just my personal diary.'

He said he understood. He himself, he told me, kept a personal diary, and was much 'bothered' if he was unable to write in it everyday.

Later, I read *Hinduism Today*, which I had bought at Hyderabad railway station, impressed by its masthead ('The Hindu Family Newspaper Affirming the Dharma and Recording the Modern History of Nearly a Billion Members of a Global Religion in Renaissance'). Published, it claimed, in seven editions, including one in Dutch, it had its editorial offices in Hawaii, and correspondents in places as far-flung as Mauritius and Surinam.

I read about the Fifth Annual Bharat Natyam Summer Camp in Virginia, USA ('Intense, life-changing, fun'). In the letters column, one Mr Hari Babu Kansal from Delhi aggressively demanded to know why one Mr Narendra Kumar 'trembles while uttering the word Hindu'. Then there was a report on an *Ashwamedha Yagna* performed in Los Angeles, and attended by 25,000 people, for 'purification of subtler atmosphere and restoration of ecological balance'. A 'western scientist' was quoted as saying that: 'Mixing ghee and sugar and burning them creates smoke which kills the germs of certain diseases and secretion takes place from some glands related to the windpipe which fills us with pleasure.'

13

From Bangalore I had planned to take the early-morning train to Shimoga, but when I phoned the railway station to confirm its timings I was told it had been temporarily discontinued. So I went by bus.

On the way I read in *The Deccan Herald* that the state government planned to set up nine more branch libraries in Shimoga and Bhadravati. It wasn't the kind of news-item one was likely to come across in, for instance, UP, where some of the best old libraries in India—including the one in Rampur which had priceless manuscripts dating back from Dara Shikoh's time—had been allowed to go to ruin; and it confirmed what I had been told about Shimoga being the centre of education in Malnad region of north-west Karnataka.

The road narrowed a few miles out of Bangalore. Tiny shacks sprung up on either side, selling tea and biscuits, offering auto-repair services. Behind them were sunflower fields and grape orchards, in the midst of which, blending well with the colour of the earth, would be set an attractive red-tiled house. At Tumkur, I had the cheapest glass of grape-juice anywhere in India, watched a browser at the magazine-stand stare stupefiedly at the cover picture of a topless model on *Glad Rags*, and bought a copy of *Hanuman Chalisa* from an importunate vendor.

For lunch, the bus stopped at a road-side shack miles away on either side from any settlement. My initial scepticism gave way to pleasure as I ate a rather delicious thali, and then washed it down with coconut water. The bus went inexplicably faster after lunch-break. Just before Birur, passing a row of shops, it nudged an oncoming bullock-cart off the road. I heard a metallic scraping sound; I looked out and saw the bewildered-looking bullock-cart driver attempting to control his frantic animals; I saw the people in adjacent shops rise to their feet in consternation; and then they were behind us, lost in a cloud of dust.

At Birur, I took out my notebook and wrote in a jerky hand the name of a school we had just passed: 'Bright Future English School'. The number of arecanut trees rapidly grew till they dominated the landscape, tall and elegantly half-bent with their weight. Low hills appeared on the distant horizon. Water glinted from unexpected nooks and crannies in the ground. A glutinous overpowering smell from sugar refineries announced the twin towns of Shimoga and Bhadravati. Most of the passengers got down at the heavily industrialized stretch of Bhadravati. Then there was a long wait before the bus hurtled down to Shimoga with its reduced load.

I got a room in a hotel opposite the bus-stand. The room was clean, with attached bath, and the bell-boy made no attempt to switch on the TV set as I came in. I bathed, rested, and then went downstairs to the lobby, where the hotel staff was watching *Baazigar*, to make some phone-calls.

It was Dr U.R. Ananthamurthy, author of *Samskara* and leading Kannada writer, who had encouraged me to go to Shimoga. I had met him at JNU where he was teaching a course on the Indian Novel for a semester. A short dapper man in his early sixties, he wore a salt-and-pepper beard, and exuded a quiet charisma that no one who spoke to him for more than five minutes could feel untouched by. He spoke to me for well over an hour, and Shimoga was thereby placed on my itinerary.

He told me he was born in a small village near Shimoga, and that he had spent his formative years in and around the town. Though now it had been decades since he left it, and started living the life of an itinerant professor, his links with it were intact. Part of his family lived there; he himself went back very often. There was much affection and regard in the way he spoke of it; there was also much in his account that struck me as unique.

For one, it was exceedingly rare for an Indian intellectual to credit his small-town beginnings for his later growth. It was usually the exposure to the metropolis, whether in India or abroad, and all its possibilities for self-improvement and advancement, that was the crucial experience for most people. One's small-town origin was usually something to grow out of as fast as possible.

But it hadn't been so for Dr Murthy. He, and several others of his generation, had been made by an important event that occurred in Shimoga when they were still in their twenties. It had marked them in a way that no other later experience could. It had given them a set of ideas and convictions that, being borne out of an engagement with the real world,   had proved more durable than those that campus radicals pick up from trendy textbooks.

Shimoga had witnessed in the mid-fifties one of the first peasant agitations anywhere in post-independence India. Using Gandhian methods of satyagraha, the peasants had lain claim to the big estates of local landlords, the land they had tilled since time immemorial without any rights of ownership. The movement, organized by Gopal Gowda of the Socialist party, had quickly brought people other than peasants in its fold. Students, workers, lawyers, even some landlords, had joined in. For a brief while, Shimoga had been the centre of national attention.

The movement itself, as it developed, had got bogged down in legislative and judicial procedures. But by then, it had had its impact on Dr Murthy and many of his young coevals. They had joined the movement as students, swept away by its egalitarian passions; it was to offer them their first serious awareness of the world. Few things learnt then—about inequity, about injustice—were to be ever unlearnt by them. And this generation, so radicalized, was to go on to produce some of the best writers and artists in Karnataka.

Most of them now had moved out of Shimoga, and lived in Bangalore or Mysore. But there were other people there whom Dr Murthy had come to know during the movement. Before leaving Delhi, he had supplied me with a list of their names and addresses. One of the first names was of a printer, a Mr Rao. I now called him. He wasn't in but the person on the phone said he'd be back shortly. He gave me directions to reach his office from my hotel. It wasn't far at all, he said.

I walked across a vast field which may have been the town's dumping ground if not for the empty trucks that stood there, awaiting cargo. The picture it presented was of unremitting desolation. The earth had turned black with soot and leaking oil in several places; filthy rags lay strewn everywhere, slowly decaying into the dust. Shimoga in every respect looked like the towns that I had travelled through in the morning: dirty, congested, its inhabitants seeming to adjust themselves unprotestingly to every abrupt fall in their living standards.

Mr Rao, an affable man in his sixties, concurred when I raised the point with him. He had known Shimoga when it had a population of 20,000. The figure now was more than ten times as much. Everything in the town, he said, had been depleted, except the population. He could not recall a time when he suffered from a shortage of water. But that was now an everyday story. Despite this, real estate prices could compare with those of Bangalore. The town had seen no industry; the old trade in arecanut still accounted for its wealth. There was little potential for anything else; yet the number of inhabitants grew every year.

We sat in his office overlooking a tree-lined lane. The room was simply furnished, with a glass-topped table, a few chairs, a steel cabinet, and two calendars on the wall. Behind me was the printing press, its muted noises the steady accompaniment to our conversation. Outside, in the narrow driveway, stood an old Fiat, curiously emblematic now, as swanky models made with foreign collaboration take to the road every month, of good taste and elegance.

We talked about Shimoga for a while. Mr Rao told me about the changing ways of arecanut merchants. Previously content to hoard their money, they were now turning into large-scale consumers. Their sons went round in new Marutis and Hero Hondas; they owned houses in Bangalore and Mysore.

In between, Mr Rao unexpectedly disclosed that his father had died of the plague in 1945.

The plague! I had thought it one of the eradicated dieseases, its eradication one of science's enduring triumphs. But Shimoga, Mr Rao informed me, had long suffered from a massive population of rats. So much so that people left their houses and set up tents outside the town's limits.

I was still digesting this when he asked, 'Do you want to meet someone from Gopal Gowda's movement?'

I said yes. He picked up the phone and spoke to someone in Kannada. A little while later, a short, slight, worried-looking man in a long-collared shirt and flared trousers arrived. Mr Rao introduced him as Mr Bhatt, a former landlord, who, when the agitation began in the nineteen fifties, gave away all 200 acres of his land to landless peasants.

This was how Mr Rao introduced him. But Mr Bhatt was quick to correct him. He hadn't given away all his land; he had kept five acres with him.

He interested me. He was now a notary clerk at the district courts. He had taken up various occupations after giving up his land, all of them several rungs below what had been his original position as an eminent landlord of the region. He had led a hard life out of his own volition. It was the price he had paid for his renunciation. But, and this struck me as unexpectedly moving, he wore his renunciant's aura lightly, without show, without pretension.

It wasn't his own story that he wanted to tell me, despite Mr Rao's exhortations. He was more interested in rendering the precise details of the movement's origin. Patiently, he began explaining to me the difference between wage earners and tenants.

Mr Rao kept interrupting him. He would say, 'That's not what he wants to know.'

Mr Bhatt would turn to me and ask, 'What exactly do you want to know? The movement's origin or its later development?'

And before I could reply, Mr Rao would turn the conversation in a different direction altogether. When Mr Bhatt came back to his topic, Mr Rao would interrupt him again and so on.

He was playing, and I was part of the play: the visitor from Delhi, curious about an event so part of their lives as to be almost invisible. My questions, by referring to a world he took for granted, amused and flattered him. They demanded an intellectual distance from that world, but he found in humour an easier response.

Mr Bhatt, on the other hand, was all earnestness. He hadn't been prepared for my presence in Mr Rao's office when he came in, and it took some time for him to assemble his memories. It accounted for the disjointed nature of his reminiscences where he would leap back and forth across decades, explaining this and that point, suddenly recalling something important he had missed earlier, and going back to re-explain a particular point.

But there was no doubting the goodness of the man. 'Feudalism here,' Mr Rao had said earlier, 'was never as cruel as in Bihar and UP.' But Mr Bhatt embodied more than just some negative virtues. There was true nobility in him, and it came not only from his exemplary renunciation of decades ago, but also from the dignified modesty with which he spoke of it; it came from the complete absence of regret and longing one saw in him; it came from the living of a life governed by not fate, but individual choice.

Other people came in as the evening wore on. They were mostly of Mr Rao's age, and memories came bubbling out of them as soon as they were introduced to me. They talked of the times when Shimoga alone published about 30 evening papers. There were more colleges now, more education, but few readers. People had fewer wants then; there wasn't the frustration one saw among the younger generation now. Alongside these changes, some things had remained constant. Middle-class people still preferred government jobs. Those with money still invested in small-scale businesses. Shimoga had produced no ambitious entrepreneur. And there was a lot more corruption now.

The next morning, I went to visit Kuvempu University, which was a few miles out of Shimoga, and accessible only, it turned out, by a local mini-bus.

A straight narrow road in dappled shade; sugarcane fields on either side, broken by clumps of arecanut trees;

red hills in the distance; tiny villages in dusty clearings with neat-looking high-roofed thatched houses; smoke rising from earthen stoves. The further we went—into thicker woods, past the villages and their columns of smoke, closer and closer to the hills—the more my fantasy grew of the university as part of a pastoral world, where education was a daily adventure, beginning with the morning bus-ride from the ugliness of downtown Shimoga to this scene of edenic beauty.

The bus was packed with huge coir baskets full of fresh vegetables, and a powerful smell from beedis hung in the air. Apart from a few students, conspicuous in their freshly ironed clothes, all the passengers seemed to be from nearby villages, travelling to local markets with their produce.

My companion was Rajendra Chenny, a pleasant, soft-spoken man in his thirties, who was the head of the Department of English at Kuvempu University. I had met him just that morning at his house in Shimoga, in a room with heavy wrought-iron chairs, an Onida TV and paperback editions of *Mimesis* and *Structuralist Poetics* on the shelf, along with a Mono tape-recorder, greeting cards, and framed photos. His wife, also a teacher of English, was present, and we had made some small talk before starting for the University.

Mr Chenny told me about his students on the way to the University. They were a peaceable lot, mostly from the nearby provincial towns of Chikmagalur, Arsikere, and Chitradurga, and generally had good relationships with their teachers. They were serious about literature, and in particular about Kannada literature which they loved passionately.

But, unfortunately, their inadequate English came in the way of a similar passion for English literature. Most of them had studied at Kannada-medium schools where only the barest grasp of English was deemed necessary.

He didn't wholly disapprove of such a thing: English, on the whole, held a disproportionate amount of importance in India. But it meant that he was less a teacher of literature than a language instructor to his undergraduate students. Indeed, many students took up English literature only to improve their communication skills in the language.

But there were always exceptions, he later said in his office—a small cubicle in what was, disappointingly, a modern, soulless university building. He introduced me to two doctoral students under his supervision, who came in as we sat talking. One of them was doing his dissertation on Saul Bellow; the other was about to finish a comparative study of Ralph Ellison and the Dalit novelist, Mahadeva.

Mr Chenny had also been able to revise his syllabus, to include more Indian works, more translations. His students now worked on Salman Rushdie and R.K. Narayan along with T.S. Eliot and Jane Austen. The experiment had worked; he had found them responding far more keenly to *Midnight's Children* than *Pride and Prejudice*. He had successfully introduced books like Gunter Grass' *The Tin Drum* into the curriculum. As time passed, he believed, the old emphasis on purely English works of fiction would gradually lessen till only a few token works from England were studied.

Then Mr Chenny excused himself for a class, and I wandered around the department, reading notice-boards, copying in my notebook this sentence I saw scribbled in coloured chalk on a blackboard, underneath the sketch of a crossed skull: 'For Freshers: Welcome to this undiscovered charnel dungeon from whence no Angel returned.' I mused over the words, 'undiscovered charnel dungeon'. Did they refer to anything at all or were they simply used for their effect? Was some sort of oblique statement being made about the department?

I went down to the library where a young man was asking for *Beyond Deconstruction* at the issue counter. I browsed through the shelves, surprised slightly by the large number of Balzac's and Zola's novels they held, before settling down with a collection of translated poems from Kannada.

Mr Chenny asked me, when I went up to his office again, if I would like to speak to his students. He could arrange for it immediately. I thought for a second and said yes.

Little inkling I had then of my forthcoming embarrassment.

Mr Chenny escorted me to the classroom where about twenty-five students sat around a large table in expectant silence. Mr Chenny sat at the head, and briefly introduced me as a visiting writer from Delhi. He then called out the names of each of the students present; as their names were called, the students looked at me and nodded. Then, the introductions were over, and Mr Chenny said I could now speak.

There had been little time to prepare anything beforehand. Even as I was being introduced, my mind was busy considering possible topics. Finally, I chose something I had been discussing with Mr Chenny just as we went in. I began speaking on the problems of teaching English in a post-colonial setting.

Two books had recently appeared on the subject in Delhi, and had caused much debate and controversy in the tiny world of English departments. The so-called problems weren't really different from those faced by every Indian trained abroad. They were the problems of people seeking to put to good use their sophisticated skills in an Indian setting. And they were confined to the small set of foreign-educated academics in metropolitan universities. For teachers like Mr Chenny, the problems were of a different order. They were of such mind-numbing simplicity as his students' imperfect knowledge of English, and no book was likely to be written about them.

In any event, I had chosen a highly unsuitable subject to speak on. Half-way through my speech, I began to notice the puzzled incomprehension on the faces round me. It was too late by then but I still attempted to switch tracks by beginning to talk about the greater benefits of studying Indian writers as opposed to English ones.

Still the frowns remained. I tried humour; it didn't work. Then, unexpectedly, they laughed at something that was not meant to be funny at all, unsettling me even further.

Desperate now, I began talking about the deleterious effects caused by Teenage-Romances on young imaginations. This was clearly a *non-sequitur*, and the moment I realised it, I stopped speaking, but not before sending out a brave invitation for questions.

No one spoke for what seemed like a very long time. Then, Mr Chenny broke the painful silence by gently pointing out that apart from one student—a plump giggly girl who sat opposite me—no one read anything in English outside their syllabus, and—though he left this unsaid, it had become excruciatingly clear to me—thus the question of whether young imaginations were harmed through exposure to trashy Romances did not really arise here.

He then turned to the students and asked them if they had any questions.

No one had any. An awkward silence prevailed yet again. Eager for distraction, I turned to the girl opposite me, and asked her, 'What kind of romantic novels do you read?'

She gave an inadvertent giggle, and said, 'Mostly Mills and Boon. Some Barbara Cartland...'

I felt the class following our conversation. I asked, 'Do you like them?'

She giggled again, and said, 'Not much. I read them for time-pass.'

I suddenly discovered I had no further questions to ask her. The silence deepened. I pretended to find something of great interest in a tiny wedge on the table. I heard some whispered consultations in the corner. I looked up and saw a few faces strained with the effort of mentally phrasing an English sentence.

Mr Chenny asked again for questions. I waited. I looked round and saw a few more people on the verge of speech, but my gaze seemed to discourage them, and they fell back again into relaxed poses.

I felt Mr Chenny looking at me. I met his eye, and we both instinctively decided to conclude our little session.

Mr Chenny was to later attribute his students' tongue-tiedness to their lack of confidence in English. I would have received, he said, a lot of lively questions had we talked in Kannada. But the fault, I knew, was mine. I had chosen a topic of no possible interest to any undergraduate in not just Kuvempu, but any Indian university. I had completely failed to gauge their interest in it. And the resulting embarrassment was to make me wince every time I thought of it in the days to come.

14

From Shimoga I travelled to Madras and from thence to Benares. With me in the second-class compartment of the train I took from Madras were an assortment of harried-looking North Indians. The first to arrive were a youngish couple—a Mr and Mrs Agarwal—with two sons, escorted by a large party of relatives.

Mrs Agarwal held a copy of *Cine Blitz* in her hands, and had her head covered in deference to her mother-in-law. She sat rigid on her seat, conspicuously aloof from the cheery scene out on the platform where her husband, a paunchy man in a patch-laden purple denim shirt and gaberdine trousers, was loudly bantering with his mother and sisters. Her young sons were there too, looking unabashedly eager, hanging close to their grandmother in expectation of the usual cash gift. When it was finally offered to them, they showed some fake reluctance, looking up anxiously to their mother in the train, who promptly made some ineffectual noises about how unnecessary it all was and how the kids had already been pampered silly by their grandmother. Disregarding her complaints, the grandmother pushed a few rupee notes down the kids' trouser-pockets. Mrs Agarwal now shot stern prohibitory looks at her sons as, flush with money, they looked greedily at every passing vendor. Then, the train started, and it was with unmixed relief that she said her hurried goodbyes to her in-laws.

Her expression changed back to one of haughty petulance as her husband seated himself before her.

She said, in English, 'I felt so bad sitting alone like this with all the people staring at me. Why couldn't you talk to your family from here? What was the need to stand on the platform?'

Mr Agarwal said nothing—he was probably used to her sulking over his family—and bent down to pull up one of the kids' socks. I, who was sitting next to her, pretended not to have listened to what she said by readjusting my bag below the berth.

Mrs Agarwal looked out of the window for a few seconds, and then, in the same fit of displeasure, opened her copy of *Cine Blitz*. I looked down casually at the page she had opened it on, and read: *I was contentedly nibbling at Nelson's little delicacies at the Piano Bar one night when a sight disturbed my golden fried prawns. It was this couple busy doing things in a corner. Of course, I shudder to go into explicit details, so let's just say they were glued together at the lips as well...*

On the opposite berth was a middle-aged Muslim man whose name, Anwar Syed, (that I knew from the reservation chart) rang a bell somewhere in my mind. He was going to Lucknow and it seemed possible that he was the poet I had once heard in a Mushaira there, outshining the bombast-loving mediocrities present with his understated elegance of verse. My supposition was further confirmed when he produced a cassette-player and tested some *shairi* tapes on it.

The cassette-player, which was the size of an ordinary Walkman and technologically as dated as the transistor radio, nevertheless found a fervent admirer in the man sitting next to me, a Mr Lal, whose Rajput-style curved moustache gave him a misleadingly ferocious appearance, when in fact he was a gentle soft-spoken man, with an almost child-like wonder about the world.

He borrowed the cassette-player, turned it over several times in his hand, examining it from every angle. He said, '*Kya cheez hai Sahib! Science ne bhi kya kamaal ki cheezen banai hain*, What a marvel! Such marvellous things has science produced!'

Mr Agarwal, who had been watching him, said, slightly contemptuously, in English, 'This is nothing, boss. Now we are having very very advanced things like CD Walkman and Watchman.'

Mr Lal wanted to know what these things were. Mr Agarwal obliged with a long-winded explanation which didn't speak much for his knowledge of the subject. But he had a rapt listener in Mr Lal.

The young, bearded, diminutive man sitting on the corridor seat—a Mr Shukla—interjected Mr Agarwal's explanation with: 'People in India are also making things like CD players.'

'Yes, yes, I know, Mr Agarwal said, a trifle impatiently, 'I am running three electronics business. I am dealing everyday with these things.'

But Mr Shukla was not deterred. 'We are also exporting now,' he said, 'India is very big market now for electronics items.'

Mr Lal found this more interesting. Turning away from a visibly annoyed Mr Agarwal, he said, '*Bataiye Sahab, kaun kahta hai Hindustan pragati nahin kar raha*? You tell me, who says India is not progressing?'

'It's very much progressing,' said Mr Shukla, 'but people are not understanding this properly. You see, our growth rate...'

Mr Agarwal interrupted him with: 'But all this progress is nothing if we don't control the population.'

He then went on to provide the latest, most alarming

statistics on that score: India, he said, was soon going to overtake China. Even Mr Shukla, who had looked irritated as he was interrupted, had to concede the gravity of the population problem. 'It is very true,' he said, 'but what, I mean, how can one control the population?'

Mr Agarwal had the answer. He said, 'It is very easy. You do what Sanjay Gandhi did...'

He went on to recommend forced sterilization and other drastic remedies adopted by the late Prime Minister's son in the mid-seventies. It made me consider Mr Agarwal in a new light. He had invoked a name that was almost forgotten in modern-day India. He himself could not have been out of his early teens when, aided by his cronies, Sanjay Gandhi stood proxy for his mother and her government. And it seemed to me that his memory of that time had been passed on to him by elder people in his family, people, who like many others of their class and background, heartily approved of Sanjay Gandhi and his vision of a modern middle-class India, an India cleansed of its poverty—or, what amounted to the same thing, its poor, mindlessly fecundating millions.

Mr Shukla had his reservations about Mr Agarwal's suggestions. 'But who will do this?' he asked, raising his hands. 'Where is the political will for forced sterilization?'

'You see, boss,' he then added, lowering his voice and abruptly leaning forward. 'You know and I know who's behind the population growth. It's the Mohammedans, who are marrying four times and having double-digit children. Now, you tell me who will stop them.'

I feared for Mr Syed, but he was lying on the upper berth with the cassette-player pressed to his left ear, and it was unlikely he could have heard this conversation unless he was straining to catch every word.

Mr Shukla was saying, 'I totally agree with you. But as long as there is this...' he stopped in mid-flow, looking as if he was trying to remember the right words, and then continued, 'as long as there is this pseudo-secularism and appeasement of Mohammedans, the government cannot stop population growth.'

'You force them!' Mr Agarwal cried, his voice rising to a new vehemence. 'You force them to stop having children! You put them in jail if they don't listen!'

I anxiously looked up at Mr Syed, but he still gave no sign of having heard anything.

'*Aur aise sunenge? Haraamzade kewal talwar ki bhasha samajhte hain*, Would they listen otherwise? The bastards only understand the language of the sword,' Mr Agarwal raged.

Mr Lal, who had been following this conversation with keen interest, now looked slightly distressed at Mr Agarwal's views. He said, after a temporary lull, '*Bhai, mujhe nahin lagta zor-zabardasti se kuchh hoga, education zaroori hai*. I don't think force would yield anything, it is education that is important.'

Mrs Agarwal, who had not addressed a word to her husband since chiding him for leaving her alone, and who had been reading her *Cine Blitz* at the same page for quite some time now, half-listening to the voices around her, joined her husband's side with a furious outburst.

'What education?!' she cried. 'They are reading Arabic and government is giving money to their *madrasas*. No, all that is useless. It is over. The government must tell them to stop having so many children and if they don't listen they should send them to Pakistan. We don't want them in India.'

Again, I checked to see if Mr Syed was listening. He wasn't this time, but it was likely the raised voices would reach his ears sooner or later.

Mr Lal, who was probably a conservative man and unused to women interrupting an all-male conversation, and that too in such a strident fashion, was too shocked to react to Mrs Agarwal. Mr Shukla, on the contrary, looked impressed. Mr Agarwal noticed that, and beamed with pride at the fact of possessing such a well-informed and articulate wife.

The conversation went on, with Mrs Agarwal an increasingly vocal participant in it. Mr Lal fell silent and moodily stared out of the window. Then, the conductor came, and I managed to persuade him to allot me a berth in a different compartment.

Worse things, however, awaited me at Benares railway station. The train reached there at three in the morning. Since it was too unsafe to venture out at that hour, I decided to spend the two hours remaining till sunrise in the waiting room.

But every inch of available space there had already been taken up. People dozed sitting up on plastic chairs; others lay sleeping on the floor, wrapped up tightly in blankets and sheets. I dumped my bag outside the door and paced the platform for a while, listening to various announcements for delayed trains. Then, I saw some people emerge from the waiting room, and hurriedly walked over to find a newly vacated chair inside.

I tried to doze off in the manner of the people beside me, but failed. I turned instead to following the progress of three large-sized rats, who fearlessly scurried about the floor, nimbly making their way among the recumbent bodies. Once, they accidentally climbed over a sleeping-bag and started burrowing into it, mistaking its fluffiness for something edible, and woke up its occupant.

After a brief struggle inside, a startled-looking white face emerged from under the sleeping-bag.

'Jesus Christ!' he exclaimed. 'What the *fuck* was *that*?'

He woke up a few other people with his loud cry.

Bleary-eyed faces peeped out from underneath blankets, looked around crossly, and then went back under cover.

Convinced that there had been something, the man in the sleeping-bag sat up straight, examined his immediate surroundings very closely, and then reached out and woke up his companion in the sleeping bag next to him.

'Hey get up, John, get up,' he said.

John got up, as bleary-eyed as the rest had been.

'What is it?' he asked gruffly. 'What do you want?'

'I swear to God, John, there's a fucking lizard here. It was just above me, trying to get inside.'

It couldn't have helped matters to point out that it wasn't a lizard but a rat.

'What do you want me to do about it?' asked John, looking very displeased.

His friend hadn't thought of that at all. He said nothing, and looked around very carefully once again.

John said, 'Go back to sleep, and *don't* wake me up again,' and covered his head with the sleeping bag.

His friend stayed up only for a brief while after that, looking for lizards, before he gave up and wriggled back into his bag.

The announcements kept droning out from the ancient speaker on the wall. A special relish seemed to enter the announcer's voice when he spoke of delayed trains. The two Tibetan monks sitting opposite me listened intently for news of their train, and everytime it was not mentioned they slapped their hands in frustration. Meditation had failed them; they were easily the most frazzled people in the waiting room. Through the door to the adjacent toilet, when left open by a user, wafted in a stench of urine. The rats, after a brief absence, became busy again, cleverly avoiding this time the sleeping bag. They now ventured into the toilet and left wet imprints on the floor while coming back. Meanwhile, people kept arriving and departing. Two new arrivals, both oddly dressed in three-piece suits, sat next to me and began speculating about the distance in kilometres between Allahabad and Benares. One of them said it was 800 kilometres; the other claimed it was 600. Both were so absurdly, so breathtakingly, wrong, that I spoke up irritably: 'What are you talking about? It's only 130 kilometres.'

They ignored me completely and continued their speculations: Benares is such and such kilometres from Mirzapur and Mirzapur is such and such kilometres from Allahabad... and so on.

I got up and went to the cafeteria. The speaker there was announcing the imminent arrival of a train at five o' clock. It was five-twenty now, and the train had already arrived, indeed was about to leave in a few minutes. I ordered toast, cutlets and coffee from a crusty sleep-denied waiter. The cutlets, when they came half an hour later, were soggy, as if reheated from yesterday, the coffee was weak, and the bread, untoasted and hard. But the butter looked as if it actually weighed the ten grams promised on the menu, and I was grateful for it, more grateful than I would have been at any other time. I even thanked the waiter for it. Absurd, even silly, it may have seemed in retrospect, but when all seemed lost and hopeless—as it did that long night at Benares railway station—one learned to appreciate small things like that.

Later in the morning I met Ramu whom I had known for several years now. He was the coordinator for a year-long undergraduate programme run by the University of Wisconsin in Benares. The job was tougher than it looked; it could require a bewildering variety of skills. For most undergraduates, it was their first time out of America; and India was known to overwhelm and undermine, both physically and psychologically, even much older people. For many of these young students, it remained an uphill struggle all through the year simply adjusting to their alien surroundings. Unfamiliar problems cropped up everywhere; almost everyone fell ill at least once, sometimes seriously. And Ramu then became more than a coordinator; he became an all-round Mr Fix-It, a facilitator, nurse, shrink, elder brother, often all at once.

But he liked his job, he liked the different challenges it threw up every day, he liked interacting with the students. And he had his music: in addition to his various roles, he was also an accomplished tabla-player and performed regularly in the many concerts held in Benares during the winter months.

It was Ramu who introduced me to Sarah. She was a vivacious, pleasant-faced woman in her early twenties, one of the many long-term tourists in Benares, spending a leisurely year in India before going up to Chicago next year to study Comparative Religion. She had visited several cities in India but none had held her as much as Benares had with its rich religious significance, its mythological past. She had been there for five months when I met her; she planned to stay four more.

But it hadn't been easy for her. There were other, newer aspects to Benares she had discovered during her stay. They had been unpleasant enough to make her often think of leaving. They had been a constant source of stress for her.

I myself had spent many months in Benares over the years, during which I had seen it transform itself from a sleepy pilgrimage town into a rapidly expanding minicity, with new residential complexes and businesses coming up almost every day.

For most natives, this did not portend a new influx of

wealth. They maintained that there always had been big money in Benares; the only difference was that it was now being spent. But some of the changes could not but be painfully palpable to the frequent visitor, and I found none more disturbing than the abrupt increase in noise-levels in the city.

There were other things too, namely the perennially choked traffic on the old city's arterial roads. And there were things which could remain hidden to the male visitor.

Sarah said, 'The difference between a man's and a woman's experience of Benares is the difference between day and night. You really can have no idea of what it is like to be a woman here.'

And I really did have no idea until Sarah gave me one. According to her, Benares, city of light, of Shiva, Raja Harishchandra, Kabir, Tulsi Das, Ravi Shankar and Bismillah Khan, was now a molester's paradise.

She said, 'I know my Indian women-friends get treated pretty badly, but the frequency and viciousness is much more if you are a white woman and have blonde hair. There has not been a day since I came here when I have gone out of my house and not been sexually harassed.'

'Sexually harassed': something about the words did not at first sound right to my ears. They seemed too much a part of one of those peculiarly American obsessions, whereby a genuine problem is gradually trivialized by over-reaction.

Sarah explained. She said, 'It is not *just* verbal harassment though it does get to you if everyday ten people on the street ask you to have sex with them, or comment on your breasts. It does get worse when people start actually grabbing your breasts or buttocks. It never stops no matter where you are. It's relentless. And no one ever intervenes. I was at Sankat Mochan mandir the other day, taking in the wonderful serenity of the place when this guy came up to me and squeezed my breasts. Ten people probably saw that but no one said anything. Some of them actually laughed.'

Some Indians she knew turned defensively patriotic when she told them about this. In response, they quoted back American statistics of rape at her.

Sarah said, 'It's true that I fear rape in America much more than I do here. But at least, it is *seen* as a problem there. You have some dignity even as a rape-victim. Here you don't have anyone even acknowledging that a problem exists and that it has to do with degrading ideas about women. I haven't met a single young white woman in Benares who has not been molested, but still people quote American statistics at you. Here you may not be actually raped, but you still have no dignity in the eyes of most men on the streets. The degradation through verbal and physical molesting is much more than what rape does to you, because it is such a common casual everyday affair. And what's worse is that after some time it makes you feel unclean and corrupt. You begin to feel you are to blame for all this.'

Some women, Sarah felt, *were* to blame for this.

She said, 'You have the kind of tourists coming to Benares who have no idea about how conservative the place is, or how conservative mainstream Indian culture still is. They come here basically to hang around the ghats, smoke dope, have some fun, and they go around in the most outrageous outfits. They wear these see-through tank-tops and halter-tops without bras, they go around in short shorts. And these young men who see them naturally get ideas. These sort of provocative clothes makes them think all western women are whores, just dying to have sex. And once they get that idea in their heads, it doesn't matter what you wear. I have never worn anything other than a salwar-kurta in Benares. I cover my head when I go out; you can't see a single inch of my skin, but I am still not left in peace.'

'I haven't met a single young white woman in Benares who has not been molested,' Sarah had said. I had thought it an exaggeration, but now as I met and talked to more people, it began to appear the truth. The stories didn't really have to be coaxed out of anyone; the humiliations were too fresh in everyone's memory. And the stories were truly appalling.

Susan, a slender, grave woman in her thirties, who, as an independent scholar, had spent many years in Benares, compared its streets to a minefield. 'Of course,' she said, 'you *know* it is a minefield out there and there are no alternatives, you just have to brace yourself and go through it every day with the mines exploding in your face one after the other.'

Unlike most women-visitors, she had been privileged to know a different Benares ten-twelve years ago.

'The verbal harassment,' she said, 'was there even then, but in a very minor sort of way. It was never as explicit as it is now. At the most people would say, "Hello dear" or something like that. Now, you are lucky if someone does nothing more than expose himself in a deserted alley and ask you to suck his dick. Men come up to me while I am sitting by myself on the ghats, start up a conversation, and then before I know it, they tell me they are sexually frustrated and could I please help them relieve their frustration. It really is incredible.'

Susan had tried to explore some of the causes behind such behaviour.

'As with all kinds of prejudice, this one too has ignorance behind it,' she said. 'These young men really have no proper exposure to the West. Look at their sources of information. Before satellite TV arrived there was video. Eight or nine young men would get together and hire a VCR and a porn film. Now, these films could make anyone think white women are just sex machines. Though they don't show pornography, satellite TV is no better. It arrives in a place like Benares without a cultural context, something that would make people understand that shorts and swimsuits are perfectly natural in a western setting. So it comes without that essential awareness and it just feeds into the kind of cheap fantasies people already have.

'So what happens in Benares is that people who have grown up in a very conservative traditional culture come face to face with the modern culture of the West through the media and lose their bearings altogether. What they don't realize is that they are getting a very distorted view of the West. Few women in the West actually dress up and walk like those bimbos on fashion shows on STAR TV, but how does anyone know that?'

It was only towards the end of her account that she focused on the element of personal tragedy in it.

'I came to this place having heard so much about it— the oldest living city in the world, the most religious city in India—and all those wonderful things *were* true. I can't say I haven't had some wonderful times here with my Indian friends, with my work. I have grown so much in these years. But now after spending my whole youth, my most active years here, after putting in so much effort into learning Hindi and Bhojpuri, and picking up small little things about the local culture which no book is going to tell you, after all that effort, I wonder if it was worth it. I mean, I've come to realize that no matter what I do I'll never feel at home here. I'll always be an alien, a tourist. And it'll only get worse. Benares has changed so much in the last five-six years, all the crass vulgar middle-class culture that you see in a place like Delhi is here now, and all you can do is feel sad. You can't really do anything about it except leave. It breaks my heart to even think that, but that's how unbearable it has become.'

Two British tourists I met later on a train were much

more vehement in their rejection of Benares. They were cousins travelling through the subcontinent on their way to Indonesia. They had spent eight weeks on the temple trail in the South before arriving in Benares. They had planned to spend a whole week there, but had fled after just two days.

'It was terrible,' Jane, the more articulate of the two said, 'there wasn't a moment's respite for us anywhere. After every ten metres, we would hear this: "Hello sexy, want to have sex?" "Hello sexy, want to have sex?" It was so unreal we first thought these guys were joking. But they weren't. And then the grabbing and shoving and pushing and elbowing. It was just *awful*.

'We had been warned about Delhi, about how awful the men there were. And they were. But I wouldn't have imagined in my wildest dreams that Benares would be like that as well.

'I suppose the shock was greater because of that, and also because we had just come up from the South where we had faced absolutely no problems at all. What's funny is that while we were there, we really had been looking forward to Benares. From all that I'd read about it, it seemed like the cultural capital of North India. And I suppose, having seen it now, it *is* in a way. But culture isn't just about the past, about old temples and musical traditions and things like that. I think it also has something to do with the present moment, with how people treat each other in daily life, civic manners, a certain basic decency towards women, older people, and if you take that criteria, Benares comes right at the bottom of all Indian cities we visited.'

How had things got so bad in Benares? Who were the men standing at streetcorners and sexually accosting every woman that came along? Where did they come from? What was their background?

Most people I spoke to had only easy answers to give. A lot of them would blame it all on television. Others blamed tourism. Some of them went on to hold western permissiveness guilty of undermining Benares' old culture.

It was Rahul, an old acquaintance, who made me look for an explanation in the changing character of Benares Hindu University (BHU). Most of the women I spoke to had singled out BHU as the most difficult place for them in Benares. One wasn't much surprised by that. Of late, BHU's only associations were with rowdyism, inter-group violence, strikes, gheraos, and delayed academic sessions. Like the other great North Indian university of the past— Allahabad—it had gone into steep decline over a period of ten-fifteen years, and it didn't seem it would ever recover.

The campus, or at least the part that wasn't built yet, was still spacious and pretty. The constriction of Benares could be forgotten once inside its walls; the wide vacant spaces and greenery were positively soothing—but not for long.

The prettiness disappeared once one came on the long road to the new and hideous Kashi Viswanath temple, with the row of students' hostels to the right. Adventurously built once upon a time, in a style best called Hindu-Saracenic, redolent of the palaces of Baroda, Junagadh, and Wankaner, the hostels now presented disturbing examples of decay.

The graffiti-laden walls, the broken balustrades, the pane-less windows, the piles of damaged furniture, and the lines of white underclothing hung out to dry in the corridors: this wasn't ordinary time-bound decay; the symptoms were of a man-made disaster. And it was disturbing because it was the work of people who had lived in them. It was their rage that had swept like a whirlwind through these buildings, hollowing them out, making them look so strangely empty and desolate.

It was difficult to believe that people still lived in them. But they did, and, what's more, these were prized places. University accommodation was limited; it wasn't easy to get a room in one of these hostels. A lot of out-of-town students had to live in rented rooms outside the campus.

Rahul said, 'A lot of them actually *want* to live outside the campus. These are the wealthy types, who are not really here to study or do anything in particular. They just live here, eat, drink and make merry, supported by the monthly cheque from their families, and they spend years in this manner. You'll find most of your "eve-teasers" in this crowd.'

They came, Rahul said, from rich established families of the region around Benares, the districts of Ghazipur, Jaunpur, Mirzapur, and Ballia in UP, and even some places in Bihar.

But there were also students who came from less established families, whose history of affluence did not go beyond ten-fifteen years. These were from the newly assertive backward castes, mostly Yadavs and Kurmis. They had money, they had political power, and their steadily increasing numbers were beginning to challenge the so far undisturbed upper-caste hold over not just BHU, but also the rest of Benares.

'That's why,' Rahul said, 'you see a lot more caste conflict in BHU now. It started out as a pan-Indian university where people came to study from far-flung places in the South and West. Then began the massive influx of upper-caste students from nearby regions. These people brought their own feudal ways to BHU, their own brand of violent politics, and changed—some people would say, destroyed—it beyond recognition. Now, you have another kind of influx, this time from the newly rich backward castes.'

How was all this linked to the harassment of women?

Rahul first attributed it to growing lumpenization among affluent castes. 'At first it was upper-caste goons and criminals who were the strongest: Bhumihars, Rajputs, even Brahmins. But that has all changed in the past few years. You have very strong Yadav and Kurmi groups now; it is actually the upper castes who are on the defensive. So you have hoodlums now from all the major castes. And the stakes are higher: for money, for political and administrative power. There is a lot more rivalry, greater frustration and a lot of idle energy. And naturally some of that idle energy and frustration gets channelled into molesting and harassing women.'

But there were older, more fundamental reasons too.

Rahul said, 'You have to understand that this region around Benares where most of these students come from is socially and economically the most backward in all of India. The old feudal order is still in place, and feudalism here is of a different order altogether. There is none of that humanity you see in other feudal societies of the past where the landlord acted as a sort of benevolent patriarch and carried a certain responsibility for the peasant's needs in exchange for his labour. Here it is simply cruel and barbaric exploitation. The landlord owes you nothing, he works you into the ground, and if he happens to take a liking for your wife or sister or daughter, there is nothing you can do to stop him from sleeping with her.

'The cruelty,' Rahul said, 'is unimaginable, and it goes right down to the bottom of the social structure. Everyone is cruel to everyone else. Rajputs to Bhumihars, Bhumihars to Yadavs, Yadavs to Harijans. The modern idea of regarding people as individuals with their inalienable rights is still centuries away here. For the man with wealth and power everything in his domain, whether land or human beings, is his property. It is very difficult for an outsider to understand this way of perceiving people as property, but that is the dominant ethos of this region. Not surprisingly, the status of women here is the lowest in India. Even in an urban setting like Benares, women don't go out unescorted, on any busy street the ratio of males to females would be something like 30:1. It is impossible for girls to go out without a chunni, and no one can even dare think of wearing trousers or jeans.

'Now most people who come to Benares come from this background and none of their in-born attitudes are seriously challenged by anything in Benares. Indeed, here they are given a new edge through their exposure to the new kind of urban consumerism and greed you see in India which is what amounts to 'modernity' in these places. So you become a modern consumer, part of the global market and so on, but your social attitudes have not progressed beyond the eighteenth century. Women are no more than chattel to you, and a foreign woman is even less than that. Unlike an Indian woman, she is not a wife or daughter or sister to anybody. And she has no caste. She is a pure and simple object of lust, a 'sex machine' as Susan puts it, something to be consumed, if not owned.

'And Benares is an instructive place in this regard. It is one of the most conservative cities in India, but it also has one of the largest foreign populations in India. So the confrontation between two sets of incompatible cultural values is rather direct here.

'The Indian response to this clash is as usual incorporative. It incorporates some aspects of the other culture, but those are really the worst aspects. So on top of a pre-existing distorted, valueless feudal structure you get distorted, valueless modernity. The two combine rather well, and on days when you get depressed about all this you wonder if their synthesis is not really the greatest achievement of contemporary Indian culture.'

15

I left Benares and went to Calcutta, a city I happen to like, but the subject is an exhausted one, and best left to foreign travel writers and film makers to exercise their sensibilities on.

From Calcutta I travelled north to Murshidabad. A recurring fever forced me to go by car this time. It was hired through the good offices of Sheikh Abdullah, who, apart from being one of the touts hanging around Grand Hotel, was also, he convinced me, Mark Tully's closest associate and friend in Calcutta. I had seen Tully just a week ago in Benares, reading Romila Thapar's book on interpreting early India, at one of the riverside hotels, and I challenged Mr Abdullah with this information. If he was so close to Tully, did he know then where he presently was?

But he knew that, and he knew enough other things about Tully to persuade me that he was indeed what he claimed to be. But once persuaded, I became complacent, and Mr Abdullah was able to palm me off with the slowest Ambassador among the row of cars lined across the road from the Grand.

But I didn't mind that much. I was in no hurry to get to Murshidabad. And the driver—named Iqbal—was a good man, honest, soft-spoken, and, more importantly, alert.

We started early in order to evade the office-hour traffic. But it took us an hour simply to get out of the city-centre, and then for miles after Dum Dum airport, Calcutta continued in ragged patches of roadside buildings. Most of these were new, speaking of new wealth, whose most visible emblem came at Barasat, where there was unexpectedly, in the middle of a row of low gloomy shacks, a glittering, glass-fronted 'Air-conditioned Market.'

A/C markets there may have been, along with a lot of other amusements for the rich I was not privileged to see, but there certainly was no good public transport around these parts. Only a few cart-rickshaws were in evidence, carrying both trussed-up pigs and human beings—even well-dressed, obviously middle-class types—their feet dangling dangerously close to the road, facing the impatient rear-end traffic, helplessly grabbing on to the wooden board as the cart lurched off the road to let a bigger vehicle pass.

I suppose it isn't an easy thing to admit, but growing up in the immense cultural vacuum of North India which gave to the country its politicians and nothing else, it was to Bengal that I looked for instruction. In this, I followed a family trend. Even before I reached reading age, the bookshelves in our house were full of Hindi and English translations from Tagore, Bankim and Sarat. My sisters spoke fluent Bengali. I never could, but it didn't stop me from being as much a devoted Bengal-phile as they were.

Thus my pleasure when, some miles out of Barasat, the roadside constructions began to fade, and the countryside I had been longing to see finally appeared. Childhood readings had first brought this landscape to life for me. Subsequent visits to Bengal had fixed it indelibly in my imagination. But the lushness and intimacy could still prove a pleasant surprise; and moving through these shimmering rice fields this morning, with Rashid Khan singing Raga Hamsadhwani from my earphones, moving through these clusters of banana and palm trees, these ancient pipal trees with their fantastically gnarled roots, the thick shaded bamboo groves, past the insular semi-circles of thatched mud-huts around clear green ponds, past the exuberant yells of young swimmers, I felt the old fascination for Bengal and its people revive within me.

Intervening towns, however, broke my mood of reverie. Everywhere, there were slushy vegetable markets that brought the traffic to a complete halt, and one saw then the tiny shops on low stilts tottering on the road's edge, the exposed gutters that ran behind them, the dusty unpaved lanes leading to tightly packed rows of houses.

Most of the houses looked as if they had been built in the last ten-twenty years, but an older variety could be glimpsed at times through half-open gateways, seemingly abandoned high-roofed double-storied affairs with Doric columns and green slatted windows, still asserting, in their decayed state, a now-forgotten idea of beauty and elegance.

This stretch was full of famous names: places resonant in history textbooks, but with no contemporary significance. Plassey, the site of the most important battle in post-Mughal India, was a series of low shacks collapsing upon each other. And a tidal wave of oil seemed to have swept through Berhampur—where the 1857 mutiny first broke out—leaving a permanent black stain on the town.

With its excess of auto-repair shops and stationary trucks (the fender of one said: 'Love God, Love is Life, One is Wife'), Berhampore had the appearance of an over-extended garage. I had been told about its reputation as a haven for smugglers operating from across the border with Bangladesh; and indeed there was a raffish quality about it that frontier towns have. That, and the all-prevalent soot and grime, had an immediately demoralizing effect on one, and I would have liked to press on. But I had been misinformed that Murshidabad, a few kilometres to the north, had no hotels, and that I could only stay at Berhampore.

I had the name of a hotel with me, and after futilely meandering through various dark lanes, we finally arrived at the Berhampore Tourist Lodge. The manager—a short, plump boy of about eighteen—had his attention fixed on a television set in the lobby. A Hindi film was on, and its curiously mechanical sounds—voices, background score, emanating as if from a disembowelled robot—reverberated loudly in the confined space and set up a continuous background roar in the rooms above.

Unable to read, I joined the manager and together we watched an interview with the Bombay starlet Mamta Kulkarni on ZEE TV.

The name had achieved national prominence after she posed topless on the cover of *Stardust*. So much so that her photo, blown-up and stuck on giant billboards across Bombay, was cited by the Bharatiya Janata Party (BJP) in their campaign against growing lewdness in Hindi films. She was then an aspiring actress; she has remained one, but that is beside the point. In the film industry where she worked, most people remain aspirers all their lives. To call them actors or actresses is to radically invert the original meanings of these words. But celebrity journalism requires celebrities to sustain itself, and since there aren't too many around, it periodically invents some. The heedless proliferation of TV channels and glossy magazines has meant the elevation of many of these non-achievers to unearned prominence. Kulkarni was only the latest in a long line.

In any event, she made better copy than most ambitious aspirers. Several media stories were done on her. I had been particularly struck by one which reported on her father's reaction to the picture. He was a middle-level police officer in Bombay, who, apparently, became the target of much ridicule among his colleagues after the picture appeared. He had angrily ordered his daughter to change her shameless ways. She had refused, and that, like every other media story, was where the story had ended—just at the point it became interesting.

I would have liked to know more. I would have liked to know, for example, how the rest of her family—Kulkarnis are conservative Maharashtrians—reacted to her picture. But the magazines I saw ignored that aspect altogether. They played up her affairs with various aspiring actors, producers, and directors. Never did they say anything about her family.

Nor, for that matter, did this interview. The interviewer was a tall, gawky, bespectacled youth, who swallowed nervously everytime he asked a question. Kulkarni seemed to sense the unsettling effect she had on him, and turned coyer and coyer.

Finally, after much pointless conversation about her forthcoming films, all of which could not have been anything more than an extended striptease for her, the topless photo was brought up.

Mamta had her reply ready. 'I don't think I have done wrong,' she began, boldly gazing into the interviewer's eye. 'Everyone liked it,' she added, a slight note of accusation creeping into her voice. 'You tell me, why has the magazine sold out?'

Indeed, if she was to be believed, her popularity had reached God-like proportions. Fans wrote in to say they would like to build a temple in her honour.

But, though pleased and flattered by the idea, she wasn't ready as yet for the temple.

Why?

'People say...' she began, her face and voice growing unexpectedly solemn, 'people say it's not auspicious to have temples to yourself when you are still alive.'

16

Murshidabad was the capital of Mughal-ruled Bengal when Calcutta was still a small riverside settlement. Its proximity to the river Bhagirathi made it an important trading centre; its silk was famous all over the world. It was the richest and most populous city in the region for well over the first half of the eighteenth century.

Then, the Mughal Nawab Siraj-ud-daula made the fatal mistake of tangling with the British. He attacked their fortifications in Calcutta, and, in an incident to be remembered later by generations of Britons, sent 146 men, women and children to their deaths in the 'Black Hole'.

The British bided their time. In 1757 came the crucial battle of Plassey between the British and Siraj-ud-daula, and, in an act of treachery to be remembered later by generations of Indians, Mir Jafar betrayed Siraj-ud-daula and effectively brought to an end more than five hundred years of Muslim rule in Bengal.

Political power shifted to Calcutta, the capital of British India; Murshidabad's decline was swift. Several Nawabs came and went, but they were no more than puppets in British hands. British commercial interests were now sovereign.

There is a print in Stuart Carey Welch's *Room for Wonder: Indian Painting during the British Period* dating back to this time. It is done in the Murshidabad style, which was a Mughal derivative, and by then was beginning to absorb European influences. It shows a corpulent Englishman, his paunch describing a wide arc, gazing out over the Bhagirathi river. He is probably a Company Bahadur, as the impossibly venal East India Company officers were then called. An Indian boy-servant stands behind him, tiny and emaciated-looking. The contrast is unignorable, and Prof. Welch, in the accompanying text, speculates about the Englishman's impressive girth: is it ghee, or too many puris, or too little exercise?

Indians certainly weren't suffering from lack of exercise or excessive puris at the time. Famine struck Bengal in 1769, and reduced Murshidabad's population by half. Civic amenities deteriorated; cholera and malaria became common. The city kept going downhill throughout the later half of the eighteenth century, and the true measure of its neglect comes from the fact that a committee for the improvement of Murshidabad was formed in the early nineteenth century only when it was realized that the city's declining population would lead to a loss of tax-revenues.

The place never recovered; it shrank in both people and possibilities. Contemporary guidebooks call it a 'small town'; and so it is. Narrow filthy lanes meander alongside the river; houses huddle together in a dense medieval mass; the bazaars are congested affairs of dingy shops and thelas selling garish trinkets. A general shabbiness pervades everything. The old city resurfaces at times in crumbling walls and gateways, but only to lend to the overall appearance of decay. There is no new wealth in this town, or at least none that is obvious.

Salim, whom I spoke to, confirmed this. There was no industry worth its name in Murshidabad, no scope for private businesses. There was only tourism, and that too on a very limited scale. People like himself started looking for jobs with the government as soon as they came of age. Or, they went to Calcutta to try their luck there.

The migration to Calcutta in search of better

opportunities was probably an old story in Murshidabad. What was remarkable about it was that overcrowded, overpolluted Calcutta, a city declared dead or dying by various experts, still signified hope in a place 200 kilometres away.

Or, was it a measure of the desperation felt by people in these decaying towns deep in the the hinterland of Bengal?

Salim wasn't able to answer my question. He himself was far from desperation. He had a more or less permanent job that had come down to him from his grandfather. He worked as a caretaker in a small riverfront palace-cum-museum constructed by one of the last Nawabs. His salary was low—just 900 rupees a month— but it was better than nothing. In any case, he wasn't married—he was still in his mid-twenties—and he lived with his extended family, most of whose members worked and could share his expenses.

We sat and talked on the roof of the palace where he worked. Below us the tourists kept arriving in bus loads from Calcutta, their excited voices echoing wildly in the large cavernous rooms. The view of the river before us— the pristinely white mosque close to the water's edge, the high-sterned boats with semi-circular jute deck-shelters, the dense unbroken vegetation on the opposite bank, the group of bathers and washers on broken ghats—could have come from any century. And only the terrible noise from the loudspeakers, hung from every available electric pole, broadcasting in three languages the glories of Murshidabad, reminded us that this was indeed the twentieth.

The palace itself was harder to place time-wise, and looked at best a timeless wedding-cake fantasy with its white stuccoed façade, elaborate cornice, fancy friezes, castellated roof and thick columns. Inside it was a portrait of its builder, dressed like a 1920's Parisian dandy, with something of the vice-laden melancholy air that Proust's photographs from this period have: the air of a man given to lonely decadent pleasures.

But only an affected decadence, a few poses, seemed to have survived the long journey from Paris to Murshidabad. The sensibility was always too hard to imitate; the attempt was never even made; it was not required at all. Kitsch alone sufficed to overawe and intimidate the locals, which was probably what mattered in the end. Behind this palace was a much older and grander one called Hazarduari. Absurdly colossal, it dwarfed everything in the vicinity, and would have almost certainly put the fear of God in the lowly peasant come to make his humble representation to the Nawab about repressive taxes.

The Nawabs' private wealth had grown even as the countryside was sucked dry of its riches. Salim, who told me about it, spoke of this personal enrichment in the midst of general impoverishment with something like distaste. He was a Muslim, and his family had been in the Nawabs' service for as long as anyone could remember, but he held no brief for them. The romance and nostalgia of great wealth and splendour wasn't his; the Muslim glories of the past stirred no responsive emotion within him.

There was a reason for that. His ancestors in the Nawabs' service had seen the wealth accumulate and, inured as they were to feudal inequities, thought nothing of it. Whereas he had been born in independent India, without the automatic regard of his ancestors for their masters, and had grown up in time to see the aristocracy in pathetic decline. He had witnessed the wealth slowly disappear, frittered away by the last Nawab's descendants, who sold off, he told me with palpable contempt, every thing of the slightest value in the palace. So that just in the way the palace had once undermined the peasant, the palace came to be undermined by its inhabitants.

Salim said, 'It was a good thing that the government

intervened and took over the two palaces. Otherwise, they would have started selling doors and windows.'

I asked him about communal trouble in Murshidabad. He said there wasn't any. A few years ago, some Bangladeshi fundamentalists from across the border had tried to stir up things. But the local Muslims had given them a firm rebuff. It was very difficult, he said, to tell Hindus and Muslims apart in Murshidabad. It was because the Muslims had been in Bengal for a very long time and were now well assimilated.

Even the demolition of Babri Masjid had had little impact in Murshidabad.

'*Bas thoda ajeeb laga kuch dinon tak*, It only felt slightly weird for some days,' he said.

And then the event was behind him.

He said, 'What is the point of dwelling on it? And, how does it affect my life whether a mosque or a temple remains in Ayodhya? There are enough mosques in Murshidabad, and I am not really concerned whether there are any in a place I am unlikely to ever visit in my life.'

Later in the evening I went to Moti Jheel, where in a palace built by Siraj-ud-daula, Robert Clive held the very first revenue collection after the battle of Plassey, and where Warren Hastings later resided.

I walked to the palace with Abdul who had instantly attached himself to me the moment I arrived. He was a stocky, elaborately courteous boy in a cheap cheesecloth shirt and dirty white pyjamas. As often happens, poverty and deprivation made him seem older than his sixteen years. Already, the future weighed heavily on his mind, and for good reason.

His father was the caretaker at the local mosque. The

salary that went with his job, Abdul claimed, had remained unchanged since Lord Curzon's time.

I found that hard to believe at first.

How much is it? I asked.

Rs 50 a month, he said.

Though inhumanly meagre, it still couldn't have been the same during Curzon's time. But I didn't press the point, irrelevant as it was.

What was more astonishing was that with this salary his father had supported in the past a family of five sons and three daughters. He had doggedly refused to take up any other kind of work; he valued his job not for the money but the regard it earned him within his community.

The elder sons now made some money of their own. Abdul was presently at school, but his own turn, he thought, would come soon.

He had as yet no idea about the kind of job he would take up. But ultimately it wasn't a matter of choice. One gratefully accepted whatever work came one's way.

Would he go to Calcutta? I asked.

A faint look of distaste crossed his face. No, he said. He had been to Calcutta, and disliked it intensely.

Too many people, too much noise, he said.

And indeed, Calcutta seemed far from this ethereally serene setting—the vast still lake covered in patches with water hyacinth, the sugarcane fields, the palace which was now as complete a ruin as can be, and the small dilapidated mosque in the centre of a weedy overgrown garden.

The mosque was where Abdul's father worked. The muezzin had just finished summoning the faithful to the evening's namaaz when I arrived, and he was probably one of the four or five elderly dignified-looking Muslim men who stood on a stone platform before the mosque, quietly watching me as I pottered about the garden with Abdul.

The white-bearded men on the platform, the setting sun behind the trees, the lengthening shadows, the cows coming home through the fields in a haze of sun-shot dust: a profound melancholy suddenly came to attach itself to this scene.

It was primarily, I thought later, the effect on me of Abdul's words, and the sense they created of a world in irreparable decay, a world more inward-looking than the one Salim lived in, and so, for that reason, doomed to vanish at some point: the mosque becoming one of the many abandoned ones scattered around Murshidabad, its guardians dying, their progeny taking up other professions, moving to other cities. Faith alone couldn't sustain it in these changing times. Another kind of effort was needed, but it was beyond the tragically depleted capabilities of men like Abdul and his father.

I remained in the garden for some time. Then, I began to feel slightly nervous about my presence there. The men on the platform had not stirred from their position, and were still watching me. Were they waiting for me to go? Was I preventing Abdul from saying his evening namaaz?

I asked Abdul if he was expected to join his elders.

He tried to assure me he wasn't. He said he was never very regular about his namaaz.

But I still wanted to leave as it was getting dark, and Iqbal, the driver, didn't really know his way around Murshidabad.

Abdul had been an enthusiastic and knowledgeable guide. I thought he performed this service for every odd tourist who strayed over to Moti Jheel. And I was digging into my pockets for some money when he asked me if I could do a favour for him in Calcutta.

Yes? I said, growing instantly wary.

Abdul mentioned his story about his father's salary, and then asked me if I could get someone in the state government to intercede on his behalf.

I thought for a moment, but it looked clearly impossible. There was no one I knew in Calcutta who could do something in this regard. There was no one in Delhi either.

I tried to plead my helplessness to Abdul. I began by saying I was only a student, but stopped when I saw the slightly incredulous look in his eyes. He was probably wondering about the car and the driver.

I changed tack and said I was simply without influence in these matters. They required the intervention of officials at the highest levels, and I knew none who could help.

I could, however, write a letter, if that could help, to the concerned authorities if he told me who and where they were.

But that couldn't help. He didn't say anything, but it was clear from his expression.

I stood before him in embarrassed silence for some time. Then, he gave a weak smile as if to say it didn't matter. I immediately held out my hand. We shook. His smile broadened.

It was when I was already inside the car that I remembered the money. I hurriedly took out the rupee notes and proffered them to Abdul through the window.

He reflexively held out a hand to accept them, but then he looked at them, and the smile instantly disappeared from his face.

I saw that and immediately knew I had blundered.

He looked hurt, reproachful. He seemed to say: but, I thought you were my friend.

With just one foolish mistake I had made cruelly apparent all the vast unbridgeable distance between us.

By then the car was already moving. I waved but he didn't wave back, and the last I saw of him was through the tinted back-window, still standing where I had left him, a slowly diminishing figure on the path meandering through the long-stalked sugarcane fields.

17

Malda—130 kilometres further to the north, and approached through a flat, meagrely cultivated plain reminiscent of Eastern UP, dotted with huts with elegant curved roofs of thatch or corrugated iron, past the Farakka Barrage ('India is not giving water to Bangladesh' was Iqbal's laconic comment as we drove over the interminable bridge)—has everything Murshidabad doesn't. Here are the employment-generating factories puffing out thick black smoke from their chimneys. Here are the multi-storied hotels with their gloomy restaurants. Here are the big cinema-houses showing the very latest films from Bombay. And, here are the broken roads, the rutted, slushy paths, the heaps of unclaimed and probably unclaimable garbage, the slummy residential colonies with their foetid drains and filth-strewn alleys, and other unmistakable signs of progress and development.

Here is, also, noise. I had arrived on a festival day: Saraswati Puja. The goddess of learning and music was to ·be honoured later in the evening, and already the loudspeakers were in place and going full blast. My room at the hotel Meghdoot overlooked national highway No.34 where every ten seconds a truck thundered past, its driver leaning on the horn. In the room next to mine, a party of businessmen from Haryana, stripped down to vest and underwear, and reeking of cheap perfume, watched an interview on ZEE TV, the volume turned to the loudest level.

I heard the interviewee say, 'I am a very good villain, I am a tremendous comedian, to top it all I am a very good actor,' and I ran down to the restaurant where they were playing Boney M:

> By the rivers of Babylon
> There we sat down
> And then we prayed
> And remembered Zion.

I requested the manager to tone down the volume, and, much to my surprise, he did. This had two effects: one, it made the restaurant a slightly more inhabitable place, and, two, it enabled me to eavesdrop on the two lovers conversing—oddly enough, in English—at the table next to mine.

The furtive couple in love was now a familiar sight on my travels. There couldn't have been too many places in these small towns where they could meet in privacy; and I saw them mostly in restaurants whose darkened interiors were undoubtedly the best possible setting for a secret rendezvous. And despite sensational stories about pre-marital sex and wife-swapping in that part of the metropolitan media these meetings were clearly the farthest extent to which India's so-called 'sexual revolution' had proceeded in the main.

Sex hadn't happened here as yet. Indeed, there was a touching pre-sexual innocence about these couples, a fumbling naïvete that came from the absence of fixed notions about romantic demeanour. They were one of the first people in their families to attempt a relationship of this sort, and nothing in their social and cultural background offered them any clues as to how to behave when in love. Hindi films could have only made one look ridiculous; books or television were no help either. And many of them could seem to be going nowhere, to be playing an elaborate and pointless game of hide-and-seek with each other.

Some excerpts:

The woman (plainly dressed, with no eyes for anyone except her lover): 'That Sudesh is so *bad*. Why are you not saying something to him?'

The man (flashily dressed, and shooting nervous-cum-proud glances at everyone else except his lover): 'What should I say? You tell me.'

Silence.

The man: 'Are you hurt?'

Silence.

The woman: 'You are always hurting me.'

The man: 'What did I say?'

Silence.

The woman: 'You know.'

Silence.

The man: 'One more Pepsi?'

The woman: 'No.'

Silence. Both stare at the plate of 'Vegitable Choumin' before them.

The woman: 'Are you feeling bad?'

The man: 'No.'

The woman: 'Why are you not saying anything?'

The man: 'Because you are always saying these things.'

The woman: 'What things?'

The man: 'You know.'

The woman: 'What do I know? I know nothing.'

And so on.

Then they left, and their place was taken by the four Haryanvi businessmen from the room next to mine. I was curious to know what kind of business had brought them to Malda, but they dropped no hints about that. They talked instead of that quintessentially Punjabi delicacy called butter chicken, which I'd never had (being a vegetarian) but of whose glories I'd heard aplenty from rapturous connoisseurs.

One of them claimed to have had it at a variety of places—Banihal in troubled Jammu and Kashmir, Ludhiana, Bombay-Pune highway, Bhagalpur, Lucknow, the eateries opposite Nirula's in Delhi's Connaught Circle—but nowhere, he claimed, had it been as good as it was in a restaurant in Ludhiana.

'*Kya saala gaand-phut taste hai*, What an arse-ripping flavour it has,' he said. '*Ek baar kha lo, behanchod, jeevan saphal ho jayega*, Just eat it once, sisterfucker, and you'll be blessed forever.'

One of them even had a little puzzle-cum-joke about butter chicken.

What is the national bird of Khalistan? He asked.

Given the topic under discussion for the last half-hour, the answer should have been obvious. But it wasn't so to his companions.

They racked their brains for a while: 'National bird? national bird? *Khalistan*?'

One of them even leaned to my side—I had a feeling he was drunk—and asked me if I knew what the national bird of Khalistan was. I ignored him completely, pretending to be totally immersed in writing in my notebook. And I *was* totally immersed. I was taking down their conversation.

They finally gave up and turned to the man who had posed the query.

So, what *is* the national bird of Khalistan? they asked.

The answer was preceded by a fit of giggling. Then, abruptly, he shouted: '*BUTTER CHICKEN*!'

There was a little pause, and then his companions burst out laughing. They laughed helplessly; they pushed their chairs back from the table to accommodate their shaking paunches; they clapped their hands and banged their fists hard on the table; later at night, they were retailing the joke to the hotel staff and still laughing.

It obviously takes very little to make some people happy.

The loudspeakers became even louder as evening approached. There were three to four of them after every fifty metres or so. The songs were from Hindi films, with the remotest possible connection to Goddess Saraswati. A persistently played song, which I disentangled from the general cacophony, went like this:

> *Mera jeevan kora kagaz*
> *Kora hee raha gaya*
> *Jo likha tha*
> *Aaansu-on ke sang baha gaya*

In English, it would go something like this:

> *My life, a blank paper*
> *Remained blank all along*
> *Whatever I had written*
> *Was washed away by tears.*

All things considered, it was an especially inappropriate song to play in honour of the goddess of learning.

I went for a walk through the residential colony behind the hotel. After almost every two houses there were small garishly illuminated puja-stalls with statues of Saraswati inside them. The statues could boast of no artistic distinction; nor were the decorations any remarkable. They were, at best, a labour of love.

And there were just too many of them. People stood indifferently before them, looking as if they were waiting for something to happen. Indeed, it looked from the groups of women in colourful silk sarees and fresh flowers in their hair rustling past as though there was something happening somewhere, as though there was probably a huge puja-stall somewhere in Malda, with the biggest statue of Saraswati, complete with the highest-wattage audio system.

It was at one of these neglected puja-stalls that I met Biplab. He had done the decorations around the statue and wanted to know what I thought of them. We got talking and it turned out that he was from Bangladesh, one of the Hindus who had fled that country during the wave of reprisals against them after the demolition of the Babri Masjid in Ayodhya.

A lot of people he knew had wanted to leave. But few were able to. He himself was lucky in having Indian relatives. He had gone to Navadwip where his grandparents on his mother's side lived. His father, who worked for Bangladesh Railways, was keen to see him settled in India. He thought there was no future for him in Bangladesh. He himself was in the process of leaving that country.

Biplab now went to school in Navadwip. Though separated from his parents, he was happy there. He had always looked up to India as his real homeland; he had grown up watching Doordarshan and Hindi films; he spoke fluent Hindi. And he had always hated Bangladesh.

His was the hatred of a recent refugee, and he minced no words.

He said, '*Wahan ka aadmi sab shala harami namakharam hai*, The people there are all ungrateful bastards.'

He went on to issue even stronger denunciations. He tried to enlist my own Hindu-nationalist feelings by referring to the wholesale destruction of temples in Bangladesh.

'*Ek bhi mandir nahin chhoda*, They didn't spare a single temple,' he said.

Not a single temple? Did he mean that no temples now exist in Bangladesh?

But he ignored my question altogether.

And how had he managed to come over to India? I asked. I didn't know people could do that very easily. Indeed, from what I had heard, there was a problem about growing infiltration from Bangladesh into West Bengal.

He said the problem concerned Muslims alone.

For some people, I said. But for the government, every person, Hindu or Muslim, without Indian citizenship was an infiltrator.

But he wasn't about to go into that. He said, '*India Hindu desh hai, ham kabhi bhi aa sakte hain*, India is a Hindu country, we can come over anytime we want to.'

I tried to counter this by pointing out that India was a constitutionally secular country.

He said nothing to that. His mood indicated that he wasn't going to argue with me, and that he hadn't given me all the details about his life only to have them challenged by me.

Instead, he began looking at me very closely. His eyes lingered over my beard; he searched for other clues. He had asked me no questions so far about myself. So now, after completing his examination, he asked me one.

He said, '*Tum kya Mussalman ho*, Are you a Muslim?'

Later, I saw *Darr* in a decrepit cinema-hall full of peanut shells, plastic bags, and a rambunctious lower-stall audience. The torn cushions had turned a uniform black with grime; one did well to sit on chairs without any stuffing at all. There were small puddles of urine on the toilet floor; the latrines were full of unflushed turds.

Darr was the biggest hit this season; its songs and posters had followed me all through my travels; I had heard a fair bit about it. Apparently, it wasn't your usual typical Bombay movie. There was a twist to it. It had the first full portrayal in Hindi films of the obsessive, homicidal lover: the scarifying 'other,' the vengeful maniac.

To this aged formula—new to Bombay, but as old as Hollywood in Hollywood—the director had added a few time-tested twists of his own. All the characters were fabulously rich; they lived in mansions that would be the envy of Beverly Hills; they vacationed in Switzerland. The female lead often got wet in the rain; her fiancé was a Naval Officer with an enviable amount of leave; together, they made an exceedingly pretty pair. And even the evil outsider sang and danced a lot.

A more realistic account would have cast the outsider as a lower-class man pining away for the upper-class convent-school-educated woman. He would have borne at least some resemblance to the boys on bicycles from Hindi-medium schools I could remember from my own schooldays, who hung around convent schools in the hope of catching a single glimpse of the girl they had lost their heart to before she disappeared into a waiting car. He would have touched a vein of repressed yearning in his predominantly lower-class audience.

But that wasn't to be. The director already had a full agenda. He had his sympathetic 'other'; he had managed to get the heaving bosoms and wriggling buttocks in; he didn't want anything more complicated.

And he couldn't have been wrong in feeling vindicated: the film was a hit. It *had* touched something somewhere in the audience. They had gone for the evil outsider in a big way, applauding his every victory, cheering when he finally stabbed his rival. Their response was disturbing at one level—and pop sociologists had attributed it to the growing 'anomie' in Indian society—but on another, perfectly understandable.

The cinema hall audience for Hindi films was now

overwhelmingly lower- or under-class. It was they who decided a film's fate. It was also they who, some middle-class analysts had it, were responsible for the growing lewdness and violence in Hindi films.

But this was to imply that Bombay films were exclusively geared to their needs; this was to credit their makers with far more intelligence than they possessed. In truth, most films were expensive gambles, hit-or-miss affairs. The gap between filmgoers and film makers was wide. The latter often had no idea of the former's expectations; they had difficulty even calculating the lowest common denominator. And it was only in retrospect, and in the light of success, that they were seen as playing up to this or that audience.

Darr was no exception. Made in the same mechanical, unstudied manner of other films, it had nevertheless managed to sway its audience.

But, one only had to imagine a typical film-goer, and its success was immediately apparent.

This filmgoer was born in a squalid town like Malda, in a poor, half-destitute family. He grew up in these oppressive circumstances, with a few hours at the cinema as his only diversion. He grew up hooked on these drugs from Bombay; these unimaginably rich and beautiful women, these swanky mansions and these dreamy slopes of Switzerland becoming gradually the stuff of his dreams. He grew up constantly exposed to this unreality. And then he was suddenly a grown-up, with the pressures of adulthood upon him. It didn't take long for him to discover that dreams are one thing and reality another, and that the world of beautiful women and swanky mansions and vacations in Switzerland is forever barred to him. And it didn't come as a shock to him. In the heart of his hearts he had always known that. And he had always slightly resented that world. So now it's clear it is not going to be his. Fine. He goes on. He has other things to do. He still goes to the movies, but his taste has changed slightly. He likes a little violence, a little destruction before the villains are called to account. He likes to see the delicate, rosy-cheeked heroine harassed a little before she unites with her baby-faced lover. He likes to see her forced to wriggle her hips and breasts by the villain. And then he hears about this new film. From the posters, it looks like it is about that world of beautiful women and swanky mansions. But then he discovers while watching the film that it is the same world only in appearance. It had never looked less than solid before; it remained undisturbed even as the hero and villain fought their battles over it. But here in this film it looks fragile; it is, in fact, threatened. And the threat comes from a villain he can deeply empathize with. Like himself, this villain could have belonged to that world, but has been relegated by circumstances to its margins. He is not good-looking and, like the filmgoer in the past or present, he too suffers from unrequited love. Uncared-for, unloved, he is now out for revenge, out to get the rich baby-faced hero who always got away with the rosy-cheeked heroine. He stands alone against their maddeningly pretty and exclusive world of swanky mansions and vacations in Switzerland, and he will shake it down to its foundations; he will turn its smug inhabitants into fearful ghosts of themselves. And he will have the filmgoer rooting for him all through the film.

It's easy to see why. He articulates the filmgoer's every latent resentment and desire. Even burdened with all his Bombay implausibilities, he manages to tap into his audience's accumulated store of sexual and economic frustrations. He is a villain, but with a cause. And the cause is not just his; it belongs—terrifying thought—to the countless deprived millions in his audience. It is primarily destructive, but so is, potentially, the suppressed rage and frustration of those millions. Its popularity is not accidental; it attests to a larger phenomenon; it attests to the violence that lies—simmering until now, but increasingly on the boil—just below the surface of everyday life in urban India.

18

I came back to Calcutta from where I took a train to Gaya in Bihar.

I reached there very early in the morning. It was still dark, and the platform was full of sleeping white-shrouded bodies. Rickshaw-drivers dozed fitfully in awkward postures on their vehicles in the wide concourse. Outside, away from the mournful pallor of the railway station's sodium lights, night hid the shabbiness of station-front hotels and restaurants—as well as the open manhole into which I, searching for a decent hotel, almost fell.

It was my first hour in Bihar—I had never been there previously in all my travels across India—and already it was exceeding all my dread-laden expectations.

As part of my preparation, I had been reading Arvind N. Das' *The Republic of Bihar*. The book purports to investigate the reasons behind Bihar's current state of disorder. Das is an accomplished scholar, and, unusually for a scholar, an engaging writer as well. He has the information; he has the necessary interpretative framework; he has the language.

But, though his skills are evident in this book, it still doesn't make for easy reading. For, the subject is too large, too overwhelming. Commentary frequently breaks down; despair takes over; the pile of adjectives grows; and the language begins to buckle under the strain of conveying the full horror and viciousness of Bihar.

The fault doesn't lie with the author. Detachment fails him as it must fail anyone who knows as much as he does about his subject. Detachment is hardly possible for even the casual visitor. The facts are too gross, the catalogue of atrocities too long. This, the land of Buddha and Mahavira, is where there is a caste of rat-eaters (facing starvation now due to the unavailability of field-mice), where medical colleges sell degrees and doctors pull out transfusion tubes from the veins of their patients when they go on strike, where private caste armies regularly massacre Harijans in droves, where murderers and rapists become legislators through large-scale 'booth-capturing,' where rich landowners own private planes and Rolls Royces, where a landless labourer owns nothing more than a scarf and has forgotten his own name.

This is the Fourth World, and words and emotions alike quickly declare their inadequacy before it. When that happens, one can only want to leave—as I did, barely an hour after I had arrived.

The open manhole turned out to be a mere prelude. The door of the common bathroom at my hotel had no bolt or handle on the inside, and after a sweaty anxious five minutes in the dark—the bathroom had no light either—trying to prise it open with my fingers, I had to holler for help. It came a good ten minutes later, and my rescuer's irritation was greater than mine. In my freshly whitewashed room, the wall-mirror too had been whitewashed along with the walls. There was wet paint on the sill of the enquiry window at the railway station, but no warning, and the sleeves of my light-grey pullover were to retain a tinge of green even after several drycleanings.

Minor things, admittedly; but they hinted at a deeper, more widespread apathy and disregard than what contemporary accounts led one to believe. Different standards of human conduct prevailed in Bihar, and the visitor could never know what to expect.

It was only the thought of eventual departure that held me back. But I still went to the railway reservation office and ensured it would come sooner than originally planned.

That done, I went back to my room and remained there for a long time, alternately reading and sleeping and trying to clean my ruined pullover in the lightless bathroom.

Late in the evening, I finally ventured out.

I went to see Uday Prakash Singh. I had been given his reference by an acquaintance in Delhi. He was enrolled as a post-graduate student at the local university, but his main occupation, I was told, lay in taking the various competitive exams for both Central and State Civil Services. He had spent several years in Gaya in that fashion. His father was a middle-level doctor in Patna; one of his brothers was a police officer.

It was a typical background for an aspirer to the Civil Services from Bihar. During my years at Allahabad and Delhi as a student, I had come to know this type particularly well. They came mostly from the major castes of Bihar: Brahmin, Rajput, Bhumihar, Yadav. They were fiercely ambitious, and their ambition was what dissolved their native sectarianism, gave them a supra-caste identity as Biharis, and made them easily the most distinctive group at the university, with their alien dialects and their own special exam vocabulary ('Pre' for Preliminary, 'Anthro' for Anthropology), and their unfortunate predilection—imposed on others through all-Bihari Mess Committees—for inedible breakfasts of flattened rice and curd.

Their tenacity was the stuff of legend among students from other regions. They were resolutely singleminded about their desire to get into the Civil Service; and, well-supported by their families, they could keep working on it for years on end despite successive failures. It was an obsession, no less, and so widespread that people made jokes about it. It was said that the first letters of the English alphabet for young middle-class children in Bihar were not A, B, and C but UPSC, the acronym for the examining body for the Civil Services.

I had known them for many years now, and Uday Prakash's room, though hard to find, had not been hard to imagine. It was a small cubicle with light-subduing dark-green walls, where the three basic items of furniture were a wooden cot, table, and chair. A coir book-stand tottered in the corner under the weight of thick General Knowledge guides and old issues of career-guidance magazines. The table was stacked with books and files of news-clippings and editorials. On the wall above it was stuck a clipping from *Employment Times* of the complete syllabus for the Civil Services exams. Two shirts and a pair of stonewashed purple denim jeans hung from a peg in the wall. A badly dented hindolium saucepan sat atop a cooking-heater in one corner. And the only light note in this grim setting of unceasing unrewarding labour was struck by a poster, its colours faded, of Nastassia Kinski on the door.

The poster showed a python entwined around a naked recumbent Nastassia. I could remember it as a much-wanted poster among male college-students sometime around the mid-eighties. Time, clearly, had stood still for Uday Prakash during the long years spent writing his various exams.

He was a short slight man in his late twenties, his face set in what I was to see later as a permanent frown. There were white streaks in his thick curly hair, and other signs of premature ageing in the crows' feet around his eyes. He wore a rumpled white khadi kurta-pyjama ensemble.

He wasn't pleased to see me at all, and I thought I could see why. He had guests with him; they weren't there when I arrived, but I could see behind him the spirals of cigarette smoke hanging motionlessly in the room.

He asked me what I wanted.

Nothing, I said. I was passing through, I had his address given me by our mutual friend in Delhi, and I thought I should drop in and say hello.

He didn't seem to think it was a good enough reason for disturbing him. But just at that moment his guests returned.

There were two of them, both carrying shoulder bags, returning as if from a shopping expedition: one was a tall stocky fellow about Uday Prakash's age; the other, a slightly younger man with a peculiarly wispy moustache.

Uday Prakash grudgingly introduced us. The older man was Pramod; the fellow with the strange moustache, Naveen. They were fellow-students of Uday Prakash at the university, and 'preparing', as the phrase went, for competitive exams. They lived in similar rooms not very far away. Both were also, I could tell from the last names, Bhumihars.

There were some rapid eye-exchanges between Uday Prakash and Pramod before the latter dipped into his shoulder bag and revealed his big purchase. It was a bottle of rum, and suddenly it was clear why Uday Prakash was so displeased to see me. I had intruded upon a drinking-session. It was something, I knew from experience, that people like Uday Prakash and his friends looked forward to for days and days; it was the one bright spot in their lives of mindnumbing drudgery; it could have all the solemnity and sacredness of a religious event for them.

I was eager to have them know that I was a teetotaller and thus posed no threat to their respective share in the bottle—if they were worrying about that. But they seemed to have already made allowances for me as they went about their business in the little room with practiced ease. Naveen produced from his bag some newspaper-wrapped *pakodis* and a packet of *daalmoth*, and quickly arranged them on one of the two low stools he pulled out from under the bed. Pramod struggled with the bottle opener. And Uday Prakash brought out the 'glasses'—two steel tumblers, two plastic cups—and rinsed them with water from a *surahi*.

And then we were all settled, Naveen and I on the bed, and Pramod and Uday Prakash on a chair and a low stool respectively.

Pramod poured out the rum. It was when he reached the fourth glass that I finally spoke out:

'*Mere liye nahin*, Not for me,' I said, '*main peeta nahin hoon*, I don't drink.'

Pramod paused to consider me, and then a wide smile spread across his face, revealing the tobacco-stained row of teeth inside his mouth.

'*Panditai chhodiye, Mishraji*, Put your Brahmanism aside, Mishraji,' he said, '*aur gilas uthaiye*, And pick up your glass.'

I mumbled weakly something about how it had nothing to do with Brahmanism.

'Come on, come on,' Pramod said, '*gilas uthaiye*, Pick up your glass.'

I felt Uday Prakash's coldly expectant eyes on me. He may have well been wishing me not to pick up the glass.

I said, more clearly this time and looking at both Uday Prakash and Pramod in the eye, that I would have liked to join them, but my stomach, which had lately been giving me trouble, did not allow me to.

Pramod, who accepted this explanation, said he hoped I would at least help myself to some *pakodis* and *daalmoth*.

I almost said yes before remembering my upset stomach and quickly excusing myself out of that one as well.

But the brief exchange broke the ice; there was also the rum; and I felt Naveen and Uday Prakash relaxing as they discussed some arcane exam-related point of International Law.

Pramod asked me about myself. Where did I come from? What was I doing in *gaya-gujra* (god-forsaken) Gaya?

I explained.

In between my reply, he leaned forward and held out an open packet of Charms cigarettes towards me.

'Fag?'

'Fag': that was a Delhi word; he couldn't have heard that in Gaya.

I shook my head, eliciting yet another crack at my 'Brahmanism' from him, after which I asked him if he had spent time in Delhi.

He had. He added, in English, 'You see, I have led a very.....*kya shabd hai*, What is the word?.......yes, a very *chequered* life.'

I asked him about the chequered life.

It turned out to be a very typical life: school and undergraduate college in Patna, three years in Delhi, 'preparing', four years in Gaya, 'preparing' a little more.

His family, he said, lived in Muzaffarpur. I asked him why he didn't live with them.

He thought for a while. I began to wonder if I had overstepped my limits. Then, he spoke, in a dreamy, over-earnest voice: '*Thoda jhagda ho gaya tha*, There was a little misunderstanding.'

He stopped, and thought for some time before resuming, in English, 'I am a very sensitive person. I don't tolerate nonsense. Where there is no respect for me, I do not go there. You see respect is very important to me...'

He droned on for a while about respect, and I began to think he was drunk. It wouldn't have been too surprising if he was. The students from Bihar were notoriously unable to hold their drink, the evidence for which was usually found in washbasins and toilet-bowls the night after their drinking binges.

There was a lull in the conversation during which Pramod told Uday Prakash that I was a journalist.

'*Achcha*, Really?' said Uday Prakash, turning towards me.

The usual questions now began. Which newspaper? How? What? Why? Where?

He said, after I had finished answering him, 'My family has very very old connection with the media...'

He stopped. I waited.

'My family was in BBC news. World Service. London. Big news. Many many years ago.'

What for?

'They burnt some Harijans, scheduled-caste people...'

I couldn't hear that at first, he was slurring so much.

What did he say?

But he was now refilling his glass and Pramod answered in his stead.

'His grandfather,' he said, 'burnt alive fourteen Harijans.'

The words, though spoken slowly, were without emotion.

'Really? When?' I felt myself saying, as outwardly calm as the rest.

It was Uday Prakash who replied, leaning back in his chair, his glass refilled, chewing on a *pakodi*. 'Long time back,' he said, 'early seventies.'

Why?

Uday Prakash seemed to consider and then dismiss this question. 'Why?' he retorted, 'They must be doing some mischief. I don't know why.'

It was astounding to think he had never asked anyone in his family why those Harijans were burnt alive. But this seemed to be the case. He mentioned the BBC coverage ('London', 'World Service') again, this time with some pride, and it was clearly what he thought worth remembering about the event. The ghastly murders themselves were as unremarkable an event in his memory as his first day at school.

The evening still held a few more horrors for me. A heated argument began among the three of them. Uday Prakash and Pramod argued that the Indian Police Services (IPS) were now more powerful than the Indian Administrative Services (IAS), and hence it was more profitable to join the former. Naveen argued the reverse.

Uday Prakash had a brother in the IPS; Pramod's cousin was a police inspector. And so they were able to argue far more forcefully than Naveen. Both furnished various examples where IAS officers had been repeatedly disregarded by their colleagues in the police services. Both spoke of the situation in Kashmir and Punjab in this regard.

And then Pramod mentioned a case where a Sub-Divisional Magistrate enquiry had indicted some policemen—his cousin among them—over the brutal beating of some peasants in custody. Immediately after the enquiry was over, the policemen had caught hold of the peasants and brought them back to the police station where they were kept for three days and repeatedly administered even more brutal beatings than before.

'*Maar maar ke bhus bhar diya*, They beat the shit out of them,' Pramod said, laughing, the tobacco teeth on display again, '*aur is baar aisa maara ki enquiry ke liye koi nishan nahin rahe*, And this time they beat them in such a way so that no signs remained for the enquiry.'

I would have left at this point if Naveen had not proposed watching a 'blue' film. I had seen the crudely-painted posters with the naked woman on them, a large sized *A* in the foreground and black paint slashed across the place where the breasts of the naked woman would have been. Almost the same posters had followed me from Bulandshahr to Trichur, Jaipur to Malda. The films they advertised were not 'blue' according to the general understanding of the term, and had as much sex and nudity in them as any regular European film. They were mostly film-festival leftovers that some enterprising distributor bought and sold duly embellished with titillating posters.

Though intrigued by their casual ubiquity wherever I went, I had never seen any of them. So when Naveen suggested seeing one, I was as quick in my assent as the rest.

I would have liked to see what kind of audience this film had attracted, but most of it was already inside the hall when we arrived. We hurriedly bought our tickets, and joined the restless, beedi-smoking crowd watching ads for Vicco Vajranti toothpaste, Limca and Nirma washing powder.

This went on for some time before a b/w documentary on Mother Teresa abruptly began: blurry, indistinct, half-bent nuns flitting across the screen accompanied on the soundtrack by organ music.

This wasn't what anyone had paid to see, and there was a lull of five-six seconds or so before screechy whistles filled the hall followed by loud catcalls. Someone in the lower stalls began to kick his chair. The protest seemed to have been immediately registered because the documentary was stopped.

The screen remained blank for a few seconds before an illegible certificate announced the much-awaited film.

The audience suddenly became very silent.

The film began. A vaguely European landscape flickered into view: the squat, featureless apartment blocks indicated Eastern Europe. A few characters appeared and disappeared; the dialogues—which were presumably in English—remained inaudible.

Excitement mounted as two-three women came into view. In a film full of lugubrious faces, at least one of them with her feisty manner looked promising.

Then, as minutes passed and when even she didn't make any move towards removing her clothes, the earlier restlessness returned.

Someone hooted; a few ribald shouts were heard; someone in the balcony let out a prolonged moan. Laughter cascaded down the invisible tiers of the hall.

Then suddenly a couple on the screen were kissing and a spontaneous hush moved across the audience.

The kissing grew frantic. The couple began to grope and writhe; clothes were tugged at. Then abruptly, the scene cut to a shot, taken from behind, of a naked woman sitting astride a supine man. In the next scene she was bobbing up and down, her face still invisible, accompanied on the soundtrack by what must have been sounds of pleasure, but which came across in their present distorted form as a low-octave rumble.

This continued for a few breathless seconds and then the screen went blank; a handwritten reel announcing *interval* was ushered in; the lights came on; and the hall exploded in loud curses and expletives.

The chair downstairs was kicked again; high-pitched whistles rent the air. Speaking for the first time since we went in, Pramod said that he had seen better blue films. Naveen seconded him. Uday Prakash said nothing, and after a few glances here and there, turned to gaze at the screen in wordless expectation.

Though full of scenes featuring women in bathing suits, which somewhat improved the crowd's mood, the second half offered even less in terms of real action. But I'd had enough, and it was some minutes after it started that I slunk out of the hall—to go, if someone had asked me, to the toilet—woke up one of the slumbering rickshaw-drivers outside, and asked him to take me back to my hotel.

19

One last journey remained, and this was to Jehanabad, about fifty kilometres to the north of Gaya, deep in the heart of Central Bihar, the region that was now, in trendy journalistic parlance, 'the killing fields of Bihar'.

I had been reading about Jehanabad for as long as I could remember. As with Punjab, news-items about it tended to form an episodic newspaper serial. Murders, massacres, rapes, shootouts, police 'encounters': the place became the site, mid-eighties onwards, of ceaselessly violent feuding—'Naxalites' vs. Police, 'Naxalites' vs. Landlords, and increasingly now, 'Naxalites' vs. 'Naxalites'.

Increased media coverage made it look new, but in fact violence was immemorially old to this land. What was new was the growing resistance to it.

Starting sometime in the early eighties, a Communist-led peasant movement had rapidly taken hold in this region where an overwhelming majority of the population is engaged in agriculture. Its popularity was immediate, for, in contrast to earlier communist-led movements with their grandiose dreams of a pan-Indian revolution, its aims were very basic: decent wages to agrarian labourers, seizure of surplus lands from big landowners and their distribution among the landless, the assurance of social dignity to the degraded castes.

And in barely a few years it had grown to a point where it posed a serious threat to the hitherto unchallenged power of the region's big landlords. To counter their influence, the worried landlords had raised their own 'private armies'. The activists had replied with 'armed squads'. The two clashed often, and along with the unprovoked police firings on agitating peasants, the sneaky murders in the night, the internecine fighting between rival Communist factions, the kidnappings, brutal tortures and beatings, gave Jehanabad its current reputation.

I took the early morning passenger train from Gaya. It comes in from Patna and then goes back the same way. I didn't know that, and my heart sank when I saw it approach. The squatting crowds on the roof, the row of people clinging to the engine's sides, some even sitting boldly in the front: even standing-space looked an impossibility on this train.

But then my fears proved unfounded when it emptied at Gaya and I was able to get a seat.

Most of the passengers appeared to be from nearby villages, clutching an assortment of bundles, baskets, sacks, lathis and milk pails. There were only a few middle-class passengers in my decrepit second-class compartment, which in any other part of the country would have been phased out a long time ago. The floor was littered with rubbish, bits of straw, peanut shells and scraps of paper; some of the wooden boards on the seats had been stolen; even the iron bars on windows were missing; and someone had kicked out the bottom half of the door to the toilet, so that from where I sat, I could see the swarm of flies hovering over the turds around the toilet-hole.

Luckily, the passing landscape kept me diverted. The open spaces and greenery were enchanting after the squalor of Gaya. The land was flat and heavily cultivated, with close-set fields of rice, wheat and sugarcane following each other for mile after mile, fields where old irrigation methods were still in use: the Persian wheels moved by bullocks endlessly circling a well, men swinging up water in a basket of sorts from a small reservoir into the fields. We passed huddled villages of thatched houses with cakes of dung plastered on their mud walls; shaded white temples with triangular saffron flags hanging high above the trees; clusters of mango and neem trees. There were few people to be seen apart from the men working in the fields, and only the rooftop travellers on ramshackle buses—the commonest sight in Bihar—and the thin ragged pedestrians on roads running parallel to the tracks reminded one that this was an over-populated region with far too many people and far too few means of livelihood.

More than half of the passengers got down at Jehanabad. I followed the crowd over a small overbridge to the unpaved concourse. There was no ticket-checker present at the gate; there had been none on the train; I had yet to see any in Bihar, and it was safe to assume that most of the people on the train were travelling without tickets.

A row of cowering open-fronted dhabas and sweet-shops with glass-encased coloured sweets faced the railway station. There was a road opposite them, but it was hardly visible now, the edges were so thoroughly corroded, the metalled portions so thickly overlaid with dust. It had rained here some time ago and the roadside dust had turned into slush which passing trucks had deeply rutted; into them had been directed the runnels of filth from the dhabas, so that there were little pools of foetid water alongside the road after every ten metres.

I asked at one of the dhabas for directions to the IPF office.

IPF (Indian People's Front) was an umbrella organization, whose biggest and most important constituent was the 'Liberation' group of the Communist Party of India (Marxist-Leninist). The other group of the CPI(M-L) was known as 'Party-Unity'. Both groups were currently locked in a bitter rivalry for political influence over the region. Complicating things further was the presence of the extremist Maoist Communist Centre (MCC) that openly advocated and followed a policy of extermination against its enemies—be they big landowners or rival Communist groups.

Whether or not the young slickly-dressed dhaba-owner knew about these different contending factions, he did know where he himself stood vis-a-vis the communists. His eyes narrowed; he peered at me suspiciously.

What did I want at the IPF office? he asked.

I didn't really think that was any of his business, but I still replied. I told him I was a journalist and wanted to talk to some people there.

Immediately his manner changed, became ingratiating. Grinning broadly, he held out his hand and said, 'Tab to badi khushi hui aapse milke, maine pahle socha aap bhi unme se hain, In that case I am very pleased to meet you, I first thought you were one of them.'

I shook his hand and waited for the directions.

But he wasn't through. He said, 'Sab saale paagal hain wahan, They are all mad over there.'

I know, I said, and asked him again for directions.

He would have liked to detain me for a bit more, but I was ready to go and ask somewhere else. He sensed my mood and told me.

It was very close to where I was, and five minutes of brisk walking brought me to it.

I had expected a bigger, more protected building, but this was no more than an extended roadside brick shed. Only the red communist flag hanging limply from a recess in the wall and the freshly painted signboard gave any sign of it being an office. The cramped front room bore all the traces of neglect: cobwebs high up on the naked-brick upper walls, a dust-covered kerosene stove and yellowing newspapers on an overhead rack of sorts. There was a single wooden cot covered with a rough-textured blanket and two straight-backed chairs of sagging wicker. The only bit of colour was supplied by a mural of an oddly skeletal-looking Charu Mazumdar, the leader and hero of one of the very first 'Naxalite' movements.

There were four students inside, all sitting close together on the wooden cot, talking to a young man wearing a khadi kurta and muffler. I briefly introduced myself as a student from JNU. The young man immediately vacated one of the straight-backed chairs and despite my protests made me sit on it. He then indicated that I should wait until he concluded his present business with the students.

They were discussing a forthcoming agitation against the private tuition racket in a local college. Evidently, college teachers had to all intent and purposes given up teaching outside their homes. They rarely came to class, and then did so only to while away the scheduled hour in irrelevant banter. Only those who could afford private tuitions from them received something close to an education. And not only that, those who couldn't afford them were victimized by the teachers.

Later, they talked about the increasing unavailability of rented accomodation for students. The rents were too high: Rs 500 or more for a room. And there was often no water or electricity. One of them asked me about the rents in Delhi. I said that Rs 500 was too low for Delhi, and that the rents there were much higher.

How much higher? one of them asked.

I told them, and an audible gasp went around the room.

Then they left, and I talked to the young man for a while. His name was Rajesh. He was very slight physically, and even the muffler he wore could not conceal his thin neck and chest. A pencil-thin moustache above a thin upper lip gave him a somewhat impish appearance: he could appear to be smiling even when he wasn't. He also had a habit of abruptly growing shy and looking away while talking.

He lived in Jehanabad now, but he was originally from Arwal, a nearby village where 21 activists were gunned down in cold blood by the police in 1986. His father was a farmer; so were his brothers.

Did they object to his political activities? I asked.

No, he said. They were all in fact committed supporters of the CPI(M-L).

He couldn't remember much about the massacre. He was too young then. But he did remember the village being full of khaki-clad policemen before and after the event.

Other people kept coming in as we talked: mostly farmers looking for someone who wasn't present that day. Two of them stayed behind to listen to our conversation, and for as long as they were there, they continued staring at me in a direct unwavering manner that made me feel a trifle awkward.

All of them were known to Rajesh. They weren't activists, but 'supporters', he said. The real activists were presently out in the villages, 'mobilizing' people for a big anti-GATT rally to be held shortly in Patna.

Then as we talked, an old, diminutive man came in, who, though dressed in the way other visitors had been—in a soiled kurta and dhoti—gave off an instantly palpable air of authority.

He demanded to know who I was. Rajesh introduced us. He was Raghubir Azad, founder member and former Vice-President, as he said, of the local Kisan Sabha, a farmer's organization which was an important affiliate member of the IPF.

He now seated himself before me, and talked for well

over three hours, disturbed by neither the stream of visitors that kept coming and going during this time nor the mixed reactions to his conversational performance among his floating audience.

He had clearly taken it upon himself to convey an accurate picture of the peasant movement to me. And though much of what he said was already known to me, and though there was no way I could let *him* know that, they were still a fruitful three hours.

He told me about the recent land-grabbing campaign organized by his group. They had sent a few men to the house of a *mahant* (priest) who owned land in excess of 200 acres. They hadn't found him there, but they had found something else: a large stock of pornographic magazines and condoms and four young unmarried women, who, the caretaker confessed, were the *mahant's* mistresses. The *mahant* himself had turned out to be a lawyer in Patna.

Physical confrontation became inevitable after a certain point in these campaigns. The other party, he said, was always armed to the teeth; and violence was less a mode of aggression than of defence for his side.

In any case, he asserted, violence was a part of Indian tradition. He mentioned the Ramayana and the Mahabharata in this regard—eliciting smiles and suppressed laughter from the assembled crowd—as instances of people taking to arms to fight against injustice and oppression.

I asked him about the gains of the peasant movement in recent years.

He said it had been primarily successful in implementing the Minimum Wages Act. This had been promulgated as early as 1948 and was periodically revised, but was never followed by any of the local landlords, who continued to extort more and more labour in exchange for less and less. The minimum wages—four kilos of rice and half a kilo of flour—were pathetically negligible by today's standards, but even those were not paid properly. He said parenthetically that he and his compatriots were always accused of extremism, of being trigger-happy 'Naxalites', when all they were trying to do was enforce the laws and rules laid down by the government.

A case in point was the seizure of surplus land. The legislation for that had been passed way back in 1961, but little had been done since then to implement it.

The reason was that the landlords were close to the powers-that-be. In Jehanabad, the district administration always sided with the big landowners. He cited a recent case in this regard where two activists of the rival 'Party-Unity' group were murdered by a Yadav landowner, who was then rewarded for his efforts by the local police.

But the biggest achievement lay in a less tangible sphere. It lay in the mind; it had to do with attitudes. Collective action had transformed the peasants: no longer were they the fearful cringing subordinates the landlords were accustomed to; no longer could a landlord dare to kidnap a labourer's wife or sister from the fields and force her to have sex with him. Indeed, the landlords now feared the peasants and their collective power. The peasants had had to shrug off a centuries-old fatalism to adjust to their new self-assertive role. But they had done that, and it was an achievement greater than any.

But, success had brought about new challenges. Raghubir grew a little melancholy discussing them. The movement, he said, had reached the end of a phase. They had mostly achieved what they had set out as their aims, and the peasants, having got what they wanted, had grown complacent.

He was eager to clarify that point. He didn't mean they had turned away from his group, but that they had grown less enthusiastic about it than before. He had just returned from a tour of nearby villages, and he had felt disappointed by the lacklustre response to the forthcoming rally in Patna. Where previously they were ready at a moment's notice to attend a demonstration, the peasants had now to be cajoled into going to Patna.

It didn't however mean that the movement was losing steam; it only meant that it had to now redefine its aims.

But it couldn't and shouldn't mean diluting its essential character. Here he grew quite vehement about the 'leaders in Delhi' striking alliances with various political parties. He didn't approve of that at all. It was far too ambitious; it didn't take into account the realities at the grassroot level where he and his people were engaged in combating the very forces his leaders were forming alliances with.

Towards the end—accompanied by more smiles and smirks from his audience—he grew loudly passionate about what he saw as the growing rural/urban divide within his own organization. His voice went up a few decibels; he could have been addressing a public meeting. He wasn't a communist, he said, because communists have European souls. He saw no point in reading Marx or Lenin because India was not Europe. In any case, even in Europe revolution didn't happen the way Marx said it would. If it were to ever happen in India, it would have to come as an indigenous response to specifically Indian circumstances. One couldn't make a revolution from a textbook. People had tried that in the past and failed.

Rajesh hadn't been one of the smiling and smirking people. Instead, he had sat there looking very grave as Raghubir spoke, It was clear he disagreed with a lot of what was being said, but he wasn't going to interrupt a senior comrade and air his disagreements before a visitor.

It was only later, after I came out and stood beside the road wondering where to go next, that he told me I wasn't to take Raghubir's pronouncements as reflecting the CPI(M-L)'s position on any issue.

I said I realized that.

He wanted to say more—probably that Raghubir was a maverick, none of whose views were to be given much weight. But he only brought up the point about reading Marx and Lenin. It was always useful, he said, to know what other people had thought and done in the past.

He paused. I stood waiting for him to say more, but that was all he said.

I was feeling very hungry as I hadn't eaten anything that day. I asked Rajesh if he would join me for lunch.

He immediately grew shy and looked away. No, no, he said, he'd already had his lunch.

When?

Before you arrived, he said.

But that was a long time ago, I said.

He said nothing to that and kept looking at his feet.

I was wondering how to take my leave when he suddenly looked up and said he would accompany me to the dhabas in front of the railway station.

We began walking in that direction. There was something unsettled about his gait; his head bent low, he looked to be stumbling even when he wasn't. Equally abruptly, he would begin to strut, straightening up his neck.

On the way, I asked him a few questions about local colleges. His replies were short, monosyllabic. He seemed preoccupied with something.

I saw the man I had approached for directions waving at me, and tried to ignore him. He had changed his clothes since the time I first saw him. He now wore yellowish trousers and a green shirt of some shiny material. But his shop was the first one from the direction we were coming and thus difficult to go past without acknowledging his presence in some way.

As I came nearer, he called out: '*Idhar aiaye*, Come here, best food in Jehanabad.'

I asked Rajesh who had drifted to a stop in front of the dhaba if there were better places than this one.

He said, still evading my eye, that they were all the same.

He then added that they were also very expensive.

How expensive? I wanted to know.

Seven or eight rupees per *thali*, he said.

Seven or eight ! It was the cheapest *thali* in India I had heard of.

But I did not tell him that. I said that it was all right, I could afford it.

We went in. He still looked uneasy sitting on the creaky wooden bench, and kept looking back and under the table, as though searching for something he had lost.

The green-shirted man came and stood above us. One or two thalis? he asked, staring at Rajesh, who looked away nervously.

Two. I said. I had expected Rajesh to protest, but he was again looking at something under the table.

The man went away and shortly returned with the food. He also plonked down two glasses of water. I looked into mine, and saw two tiny particles floating on the oleaginous surface. I asked the man if he had a Limca or a Citra.

He did. How many? he asked.

Two, I said, and for the first time since we entered the dhaba, Rajesh found his voice.

'*Nahin, nahin*, No, no,' he spoke out, turning towards the retreating man, his mouth full of food, '*mere liye Limca nahin*, No Limca for me.'

Why not?

'*Nahin, nahin*,' he repeated, shaking his head and waving his hands quite assertively.

I decided to leave it at that.

The food was barely edible, consisting as it did of watery dal, a tasteless, endlessly warmed-over, unidentifiable vegetable, lukewarm rotis and raw onions. I finished my *thali* in no time and then sat waiting for Rajesh. The food had somehow awakened his appetite and he ate a lot more than I did, constantly ordering fresh quantities of rotis and dal from the green-shirted man.

The man seemed to resent this. He came and stood above our table, watching Rajesh with palpable distaste as he ate. I wanted him to go away and so asked him to make two cups of tea. But he had no milk with him.

I then walked him to the counter and paid our bill. Rajesh joined me just as I was pocketing the change. Again he looked embarrassed about something and avoided my eye.

We walked over to the railway station where the news was that my train was two hours late. Rajesh's eyes held a muted apology as he told me that.

Would I like to go by bus? he asked me.

Yes, if that was possible.

The bus-station was an exposed stretch of soot-blackened ground where an assortment of garishly-painted vehicles stood blaring modernized folk-songs. The noise was unbearable, and I began to withdraw the moment we reached the place.

Rajesh saw my reaction and immediately grew anxious on my behalf. He still went around and asked a few criminalish young men about buses to Gaya. There weren't any for the next three hours, and it was with some relief that I heard that and decided to wait for the train.

On the way back to the railway station, I turned to Rajesh and told him I had taken up too much of his time already and that he was not to bother about my travel-arrangements any more.

He remained silent, walking alongside in his uncertain restless way, his gaze fixed firmly on the ground.

After buying my ticket, we stood on the platform for

a long time without exchanging any words before he unexpectedly spoke.

He asked, '*Dilli me kis tarah ka jivan hai*, What is life like in Delhi?'

He must have been mulling over that question for quite some time before deciding to speak it aloud. There was the hint of a suppressed yearning in it. Slightly taken by surprise, I turned to look at him and caught the expectant flickering in his eyes before he looked away again.

It took me some time to answer him. Basically, I said it wasn't any good, and that there were too many pressures of space and time; the air and water were too polluted; there was very little human dignity.

He seemed to ponder that, his arms folded around his hollow chest, his face turned towards the ground. But he didn't speak again.

I asked him if he had ever been to Delhi.

My question surprised him. '*Kya*? What?' he stammered.

I repeated my question.

He was oddly vehement in his reply, as much as he had been while turning down the Limca. '*Nahin, nahin*, No, no,' he said, shaking his head from side to side and jerking his outstretched palms.

Was my question too intrusive? Had it touched an old injury somewhere?

But there was no way of knowing.

Finally after several more minutes of an awkward brooding silence, I again said that I was taking up too much of his time, and that he should feel free to leave anytime he wished to.

It was what he was perhaps waiting for. He spoke no words but he looked as if he was ready to leave. He glanced at me and held out a limp hand for me to shake.

'*Achcha ji, main chalta hoon,* I'll leave you now,' he said in a curiously faltering voice as we shook hands; paused; and then added, still in that undermined tone, '*Phir milenge,* We'll meet again,' gave a brief, unsteady smile, turned and quickly walked away with that slightly erratic gawky gait of his.

Once past the gate, he inexplicably broke into a run; and later, whenever I remembered him, I saw him running across the slushy concourse, past the cowering row of shacks, the pools of foetid water, back to the tiny cramped room with the mural of Charu Mazumdar, where I had first seen him, a thin shy young man in a sagging wicker chair, worrying about high rents in Jehanabad.

Later on the train—outside, the melancholy spirals of smoke from cooking fires rising under a darkening sky— I met Sitaram. He was a seven-year-old boy who had placed himself on my lap in order to look out of the window. His father, a wage-labourer in a village near Gaya, sat and dozed on the floor, leaning against my seat. The boy's narrow thinly-covered shoulders shivered in the breeze; his hair had turned the colour of rust from malnutrition; there were the scars of an eczema infection on his dark-brown legs. But—and this was the miraculous part—he still, he told me, went to school. He had seen me writing in my notebook and now offered to prove his newly-acquired abilities. He wrote in a large wavering hand the first five letters of the Hindi alphabet. He then wanted me to write the next five. I complied; but the letters, as an amused Sitaram pointed out, were not in the right order; and for the rest of the way, he taught me what I thought I knew by heart and had actually long forgotten.

Acknowledgements

Several people have helped in the making of this book. Of them, it is possible to name only a few; some others are mentioned in the text. I have benefited much from the advice and encouragement of Alok Rai, Arvind Krishna Mehrotra, Meenakshi Mukherjee, Rukun Advani and Laura Desmond. Christopher and Sarah Sainty in Delhi and the Sharmas at Bharati Vihar, Mashobra have been generous hosts and companions. I owe my biggest debt, however, to my parents and John H. Bowles.

The names and circumstances of a few people in this book have been altered. The reasons would, hopefully, be obvious in the text.